THE
AEC STORY

BRIAN THACKRAY

AMBERLEY

Two 20-foot wheelbase Rangers, 670054 and 055, were shipped out to Canada in May 1933 for Canadian American Trailways of Windsor, Ontario. Intended for service on the 250-mile route between Detroit and Buffalo, they had coachwork built by Duple and seated twenty-eight passengers. Catering for extremes of heat and cold, the coaches had sunshine roofs and twin heaters. Note also the non-standard shutters on the radiator. (*Photograph: AEC L2317, Author's collection*)

First published 2012

Amberley Publishing
The Hill, Stroud
Gloucestershire, GL5 4EP

www.amberley-books.com

British Library Cataloguing in Publication Data.
A catalogue record for this book is available from the British Library.

ISBN 978 1 4456 0390 2

Typeset in 10pt on 12pt Sabon.
Typesetting and Origination by Amberley Publishing.
Printed in the UK.

Contents

Foreword

What, it may be asked, has a retired Bank Manager to do with AEC? As a young lad growing up in Nottingham, I was fascinated by buses and from an early age made regular pilgrimages to the AEC's sales and service depot in Brook Street and to the nearby Nottingham City Transport bus garage where there was a sizeable fleet of AEC Regents. I entertained hopes that on leaving school I would find employment at one or other of the two establishments. Fate deemed otherwise and I joined the staff of Lloyds Bank in Nottingham as a junior messenger.

Years later I acquired the ex-Huddersfield Corporation East Lancs-bodied AEC Regent III JVH 373, ownership of which I thoroughly enjoyed but frequent moves in the banking circle made its tenure unrealistic. Another posting took me to Lloyds Bank in Los Angeles where, one morning in my twentieth-floor office, I read in the London *Financial Times* of the merger of the Leyland Motors Corporation, which had already swallowed AEC, with British Motor Holdings, the Austin Morris conglomerate. Under the auspices of the new British Leyland Motor Corporation, AEC would disappear.

In that moment there was a fairly severe earthquake which rocked the building. Was this an omen? Certainly it sowed the seed in my mind that a society should be formed to preserve the name of AEC. And so it happened. In 1983 I organised a meeting of like-minded people, the end result of which was the formation of the AEC Society.

Brian Thackray was born into a Yorkshire haulage family and grew up with the sights and sounds of AECs. On leaving school in 1947, he was apprenticed at Southall and on completion in 1951 joined the AEC's Southall Service Department. Following two years National Service through 1954 and 1955, he returned to the family business in 1956. His abiding and lifelong interest in AEC and its products, first generated in those early days, is well seen in this his latest work.

Brian Goulding
January 2012

AEC
The Company

The Associated Equipment Company Ltd had been incorporated on 13 June 1912 as a wholly owned subsidiary of the London General Omnibus Company Ltd (the LGOC), which itself had been acquired by the Underground Electric Railways Company of London Ltd (the UERL) two months previously. The AEC had been set up to take over the bus chassis manufacturing facility at Walthamstow, first established by the Motor Omnibus Construction Company in 1905 and which, following a series of mergers and take-overs, had been developed by the LGOC to become the equal of any motor manufacturing factory in Europe. By the summer of 1912, at the time that the AEC was formed, the factory was building thirty B-type chassis each week.

The works had been hugely expanded during 1916 and 1917 to cover the needs of the War Office and in the period July to October 1918, production of the Tylor-engined Y-type had averaged 106 chassis per week. With the cessation of hostilities, production quickly fell back to pre-war levels. An agreement dating to 1912 had ensured that AEC supplied all the vehicular requirements of the LGOC but the needs of the LGOC alone were insufficient to support the factory. Outside sales were at best limited. By 1925, sales techniques and production methods had come under close scrutiny and Lord Ashfield, having had discussion with Sir Edward Manville of the Daimler Company, engaged one Lewis Ord to advise on latest manufacturing techniques and production methods.

Ord's findings were clearly radical and Lord Ashfield came to the conclusion that, quoting Board minute 1190 of 3 December 1925:

> it was probably desirable to remove the operations of the Company entirely from the premises at Walthamstow ... He further indicated that in his view there would be considerable difficulty in carrying into effect the reforms and economies which were suggested to be necessary on the present premises.

By February 1926 a suitable new factory site had been found at Southall and as related below, the initial discussion with Lord Manville led to further developments.

The Southall Factory

The Southall factory was built on a triangular green-field site, one mile to the east of Southall. The site extended to 58.89 acres and had been purchased from the Earl of

Jersey for the sum of £25,000 in February 1926. The northern boundary was parallel with the Great Western Railway's main line, and that to the south-west with the Southall to Brentford branch line. Windmill Lane marked the eastern boundary.

At this time AEC and Daimler had joined forces to form a new company, the Associated Daimler Company, which would design and market the commercial vehicle products of the AEC and Daimler companies. The new company had been formed with high hopes and expectations in June 1926 but mechanical failure in respect of the Daimler engine and fundamental differences in management style resulted in the two companies separating their interests in June 1928. The Associated Daimler Company nevertheless remained extant as a vehicle through which co-operation between the two companies could continue.

Work on the building of the new factory had been delayed by the General Strike but by the end of December 1926, much of the steel framework had been erected and the external brickwork completed. The transfer of machinery from the Walthamstow factory had started in January 1927 and in February it was reported that the Southall factory was partially functioning. The move was finally completed in June 1927. The Associated Daimler Company, with its sales and engineering departments built, completed its move in August and September.

This first phase, which comprised the building of the machine shops, the goods inwards section, the heat treatment department, the assembly sections, the AEC works offices and the canteen on the one hand together with the Associated Daimler office, the engineering department and the spares and service departments on the other, had in total cost £203,627. (Eighty years on, multiply by 100 for an approximate equivalent value today.)

From 1929 there was an almost continuous expansion of the works. The first part to be extended was the machine shop, at a cost of £57,910, and a new five-bay building, intended as the coach factory, cost £52,930. (The coach factory never materialised and the building ultimately housed the chassis finishing and pattern shops.) Other notable additions had been the building of the railcar shop in 1936 at a cost of £6,526, a new engine test house for the Experimental Dept, costing £2,060, and a new Service Station building (at the south-eastern corner of the site) at a cost of £20,803. The chassis inspection building (Skinner's Shop) was built in 1937 at a cost of £17,540 and further extended in November 1939 at an additional cost of £25,987. The wooden Labour Office close to the main entrance gate, also built in November 1939, cost £679.

During 1928 and 1929 the 16-acre sports ground was developed and on 3 May 1930 was officially opened by Lt-Col. J. T. C. Moore-Brabazon, the company's deputy chairman. Norman Hardie, the company's general manager opened the pavilion on 13 September following. It was noted that the ground, now administered by the Trustees of the AEC Athletic and Social Club, had been constructed by the AEC at a cost of £8,989.

Company Management

Albert Henry Stanley, born on 8 August 1874, was chairman and managing director of AEC from 13 June 1910 to 3 October 1929 and continued thereafter as chairman until 30 June 1933. He had arrived from America in 1907 to bring his expertise to the UERL and help preserve American banking interests in the company. Born in Derby, his family had emigrated to America when he was a child. First as an odd job man, he went to work for the Detroit Street Railway and, rising through the ranks, became its general superintendent at the age of twenty-eight. Moving on, he joined the Street Railway Department of the Public Service Corporation of New Jersey as assistant general manager, becoming superintendent of the department in the following year and finally general manager of the Corporation.

Now, at the age of thirty-two, with a sharp, aggressive business edge, he returned to England to take up the post of general manager of the UERL and a year later was elected on to the UERL board. In May 1910 he succeeded Sir George Gibb as managing director.

Talks of a pooling arrangement between the UERL and the LGOC in September and October of 1909 led ultimately to the take-over of the LGOC by the UERL in April 1912. As a result, in addition to his existing duties, Albert Stanley became managing director of the LGOC. Two months later, on the formation of the AEC he became managing director of that company also. He was knighted in 1914 in recognition of his services to London's travelling public.

In December 1916, he was invited to join David Lloyd George's government as President of the Board of Trade and sat in the Commons as MP for Ashton-under-Lyne. As a result of his appointment, he resigned all the offices he held within the Underground Group for such time as the national emergency should exist. He relinquished his government post in May 1919 and on his return to the commercial world the following month, was elected chairman and managing director of the UERL and its associated companies. He was created Baron Ashfield of Southwell in 1920. Consequent on his appointment as the first chairman of the London Passenger Transport Board, he resigned all offices previously held in the former UERL group of companies, effective from 30 June 1933. He was succeeded as chairman of the AEC by Henry Augustus Vernet, a member of the AEC Board since 1916 and deputy chairman of the UERL since 1919.

Charles William Reeve, born 11 February 1879, had joined the AEC at Walthamstow in 1915 as the works accountant, becoming company accountant in 1916 and joint manager (together with the American S. A. Wallace) in 1918. In 1924 he accepted the position of chief purchasing agent and stores superintendent to the UERL, remaining in that office until 1928, when he returned to the AEC as assistant to Lord Ashfield. He was elected to the AEC board on 3 October 1929 and appointed managing director. On the death of the then-chairman, Henry Augustus Vernet, he was elected to fill that office on 15 November 1933, at the same time retaining the office of managing director. He resigned as managing director of the company in 1944, aged sixty-five, but retained the office of chairman. The name of the Associated Equipment Company Ltd was changed to Associated Commercial Vehicles Ltd on 1 October 1948 and Reeve was again elected chairman. He retired in 1951. He was awarded the CBE in 1937 for services to the Air Ministry. On his retirement he was succeeded by Lord Brabazon, who had been deputy chairman since 1933.

Design Staff

Prominent at the AEC in the 1930s were three design engineers who had shaped the products of the company: George John Rackham, Cedric Bernard Dicksee and Charles Frank Cleaver.

George John Rackham, born 10 August 1885, had first joined the Vanguard Bus Company as a draughtsman in 1906 in the days before that company was absorbed by the LGOC. He became chief draughtsman with the LGOC in 1907, first at Cricklewood then at Walthamstow, leaving in 1910 to take up a similar post with David Brown in Huddersfield. He returned to Walthamstow in 1912 as chief draughtsman with the newly formed AEC but left in 1916 to take up the post of works manager at Heenan & Froude. His stay with Heenan & Froude was short-lived. He joined the Army and until the end of hostilities was engaged in tank design, attaining the rank of captain. He became a member of the Board of Roadless Traction in March 1919, moving with that company to America in 1922. In that year he joined G. A. Green (formerly assistant chief engineer to the LGOC) at the Yellow Coach Company in Chicago where he was appointed chief engineer, returning to England in May 1926 to take up the post of chief engineer at Leyland Motors.

He returned to AEC as chief engineer on 1 August 1928 but negotiations had been under way since March of that year. Following his return, work had proceeded at a rapid pace and by December 1928, the first of the new six-cylinder A130 engines was undergoing a 100-hour non-stop bench test. Records show that the first experimental Regent chassis had been completed by 13 February 1929 and despatched to Short Bros of Rochester on that date. As chief engineer he presided over the design and development of the whole range of Mark I, Mark II, Mark III and Mark IV chassis. Perhaps his greatest disappointment was the lack of acceptance of his side-engined Q-type chassis designed in 1932. He retired in the summer of 1950.

Cedric Bernard Dicksee, born 28 June 1888, had joined AEC in 1928 as an engine designer, having been employed as a research engineer with Specialloid Ltd (piston manufacturers) during 1926 and 1927. Before departing to America in 1919 to work for the Westinghouse Electric & Manufacturing Company, he had previously been employed by Earl's Shipbuilding & Engineering Company in Hull, the Aster Engineering Company in Wembley and the Austin Motor Company in Birmingham. His first work at Southall as an engine designer had been in the design and development of the AEC's first production oil engine, the A155. Pre-eminent in the field of oil engine research, he was author of The High-Speed Compression Ignition Engine, published by Blackie & Son Limited in 1940. He was chairman of the Automobile Division of Institution of Mechanical Engineers in 1951–1952 and retired as AEC's research engineer in 1955.

Charles Frank Cleaver, born 22 July 1886, was another former AEC employee, having first joined the LGOC at Walthamstow as a draughtsman in July 1909. He was commissioned in the Army with the rank of Lieutenant I.M.T. in September 1914 and was demobilised with the rank of Captain I.M.T. in September 1919. With

Henry Nyberg, he formed the Four Wheel Drive Lorry Company at Slough in 1921. The company was re-formed as Four Wheel Drive Motors in 1930 and a new range of AEC-powered four-wheel drive chassis was put into production. Four Wheel Drive Motors was absorbed by the AEC in April 1932; operations were transferred to Southall, following which Nyberg resigned.

Charles Cleaver became an acknowledged authority in the design of the oil-engined railcar, the first of which was built for the Great Western Railway in 1933. The first of four eight-wheel drive tractive units was built in 1933 to the requirements of the Oversea Mechanical Transport Directing Committee, but perhaps the design for which he is best remembered is the 0853 four-wheel drive Matador, which saw service in all theatres during the Second World War. He retired from the boards of ACV Sales Ltd (successor to Four Wheel Drive Motors Ltd) and of British United Traction Ltd on 1 January 1958.

Drawing Office and Production Control Procedures

Throughout the volume the reader will find references to U numbers, XU lists and programme symbols and without knowledge as to their significance, their inclusion in this narrative would appear pointless.

U numbers. From the AEC's earliest days, drawings, as first made, were identified by a U-prefixed sequential number. The drawings could feature an individual part, a sub-assembly, an arrangement of a complete unit or a full chassis arrangement. When the drawing was passed for production, the U number would be superseded by a number prefixed by a letter relative to that item. For example, engine parts were prefixed A, gearbox parts were prefixed D, rear axle parts F and so on. Individual parts carried a five-figure number, sub-assemblies a four-figure number and whole assemblies a three-figure number. Perhaps fewer than half of the U numbered drawings achieved production status. The last U numbered drawing was U279006, dated 28 April 1980.

XU lists. These detailed the parts required to convert a standard production unit to a new specification, either for experimental purposes or to suit the particular requirement of a customer.

Programme symbols. Production control was just one of the many complex disciplines involved in the process of manufacture. Raw materials would be ordered in accordance with the manufacturing programmes decided at board level following the recommendations of the sales department. The programmes were identified by programme symbols. They had first been employed in 1912; the first, ED1, referred to 150 3-ton chassis built for the Daimler company. The E-prefixed series was superseded in 1929 by a new series commencing AA, followed by AB, AC, AD to AZ, continuing with BA, BB etc. This series finished with programme ZG in June 1945. A new series starting AA was inaugurated in November 1944 in preparation for the building of the post-war series of chassis.

Progress sheets were issued to all departments on a weekly basis showing the current position of all outstanding programmes. London Transport used these same programme letters in their records to identify individual batches of chassis and the special requirements that attached to them.

Chassis codes. The 1929/1930 Rackham-designed range of chassis (in later years recognised as the Mark I) were identified as the 6 series, hence the first number in the chassis code was 6. The second number indicated the number of the engine's cylinders and the third number, which was arbitrary, identified the particular chassis type. As an example, the six-cylinder Reliance of 1929 was identified as type 660 and the first chassis of that type was 660001. More familiar was the Regent, with the chassis code 661. The four-cylinder Mercury was identified 640 and the Monarch 641. The logic of the sequence was lost with the arrival of the Ranger type 670 in 1931. The addition of the O prefix to the chassis code, 0661 for example, was adopted in June 1933 to indicate that the chassis was fitted with the oil engine. The record cards of a number of oil-engined chassis built before the adoption of the prefix were retrospectively altered to make that distinction. Similarly, the record cards of petrol-engined chassis, converted later in life to oil, often received an O prefix.

AEC allocated chassis numbers on the receipt of order and logical as this appeared, it did lead to anomalies. Chassis numbers were allocated in sequence and when a cancellation occurred, that chassis number became vacant. From time to time, the vacant numbers would be re-allocated and late-built chassis could be found with early, out of sequence chassis numbers. Some numbers remained vacant throughout.

Above left: Born in 1879, Charles Reeve had joined the AEC as works accountant in 1915 and was appointed joint manager together with S. A. Wallace in 1918. After taking the post of chief purchasing agent to the UERL in 1924 he returned to AEC in 1928 as assistant to Lord Ashfield. He was elected to the AEC board and appointed managing director in 1929 and on the death of Henry Vernet in 1933 was appointed chairman. In 1944, at the age of sixty-five, he resigned his post as managing director but continued in the office of chairman. He was elected chairman of Associated Commercial Vehicles, the newly formed parent company of AEC Ltd, Crossley and Maudslay in 1947. On relinquishing that office in 1951, he was succeeded by Lord Brabazon, though he retained his seat on the board for some time thereafter. (*Photograph: London Transport Museum 24252*)

Above right: John Rackham was born in 1885, joined the Vanguard Bus Company as a draughtsman in 1906 and became chief draughtsman at the LGOC following its absorption of Vanguard in 1907. He joined David Brown, the gear manufacturer in Huddersfield in 1910, returning to Walthamstow as chief draughtsman on the formation of AEC in 1912. After a short spell with Heenan & Froude as works manager in 1916 he joined the Army and was engaged on tank design until the end of hostilities. He joined the Board of Roadless Traction in 1919, moving to America with that company in 1922. He joined the Yellow Coach Company in 1922 where he was appointed chief engineer, returning again to England in 1926. He was appointed chief engineer to Leyland Motors in that same year but left to take up a similar post with AEC in August 1928. Selling upwards of 1,000 units in its first year, his Regent of 1929 transformed the fortunes of AEC. Ten years later the RT Regent would be another landmark. He remained with AEC until his retirement in June 1950. (*Photograph: AEC, Author's collection*)

Typical of the machine shops in the early days, the mass of open shafting today would give the health and safety inspectors apoplexy. In the foreground are capstan lathes. Most of the machines would have been transferred from the Walthamstow works in 1926 and 1927. (*Photograph: AEC M487, BCVM*)

The heat treatment department. Rather in the idiom of the driver of a forklift truck, except that he is carried on an overhead gantry mounted trolley, the operative is loading one of the furnaces with boxes of parts for carburising. Carburising, the first stage in the case hardening of steel, is a process where items are packed in sealed boxes with a carbon-rich material and heated to about 900° C. When so treated, the item acquires a high-carbon surface layer, the depth of which varies with time in the furnace. Subsequently heated and quenched, the item has a hardened surface of predetermined depth. In the foreground are the quenching tanks, each of which hold 2,500 gallons of oil or water. (*Photograph: AEC M527, BCVM*)

The assembly track was another piece of equipment transferred from Walthamstow and had first been devised for the assembly of the military Y-type chassis in 1917. When the factory was first built, the wall to the left of the photograph formed the outside factory wall on the south side. The chassis in the foreground was 662157, one of twelve built in March 1930 for the East Surrey Traction Company. (*Photograph: AEC M706, Author's collection*)

AEC show chassis were always finished to the highest standard and this example is no exception. Clearly set out to impress the customer, the ambience of the showroom would do credit to any home. (*Photograph: AEC M685, BCVM*)

2

The Principal
Mechanical Chassis Units

In describing the principal units of the Regent chassis, the reader will understand that these units, or derivatives of them, were common to most of the six-cylinder chassis in the AEC's 1930s passenger and commercial vehicle range. The four-cylinder engines are described in the appropriate Mercury, Monarch and Matador chapters. Development was constant and ongoing and the descriptions below refer to the first generation of chassis, i.e. those built in the period 1929–1935.

The six-cylinder petrol engine

The six-cylinder A131 engine was an overhead camshaft design of 100 mm bore and 130 mm stroke and was mechanically similar to the A130 that had powered the Reliance chassis. It differed from that engine in two respects. First, the flywheel and clutch were now enclosed within a bell housing, allowing for the gearbox to be carried in unit with the engine, and secondly, the crankcase bottom half had an oil filter mounted at the forward end and the oil sump was at the rear.

The crankcase was cast in aluminium alloy, was well ribbed internally and carried the crankshaft pendant fashion in seven white-metal lined main bearings. The main bearing journals were of 70 mm diameter, the crankpins 60 mm. The bearings were pressure lubricated from a gear-type oil pump mounted directly beneath the front main bearing, driven from the crankshaft through a pair of spur gears. In order to prevent high oil consumption at light engine loads, the oil pressure was regulated according to load and varied between 5 to 12 lbs/sq in at tick-over and 60 lbs/sq in at full load. The oil capacity was 4 gallons and in addition to the felt oil filter, a magnetic plate was fitted beneath the oil strainer in the sump to collect any accumulation of ferrous debris.

The timing case was carried on the forward end of the crankcase. The drive to the overhead camshaft was a two-stage arrangement employing a duplex chain and a helical gear set, so arranged that the cylinder head could be lifted without disturbing the timing chain. The upper shaft in the timing case carried the top chain sprocket and the camshaft's two-piece spring-loaded helical driving gear. This was so designed as to take up backlash between the camshaft's driving and driven gears. (These gears were cut rather deeper than normal to allow for variations in the thickness of the cylinder head gasket.) The forward end of the upper shaft also carried the fan. Within the fan hub was a spring-loaded clutch, so designed as to allow limited slippage and avoid undue stress caused by rapid changes in engine speed. Slippage would occur if a load of 15 lbs was applied at the tip of one of the fan blades. A lower shaft provided the drive for the water pump, magneto and dynamo and an eccentric, spring-loaded idler took up wear on the timing chain and maintained the correct tension.

The cylinder block was a simple, one-piece water-cooled close-grained iron casting in which the only working parts were the pistons. The cylinder block was attached to the crankcase by long studs, which passed through the top face of the crankcase and which also served, at the lower end, to secure the main bearing caps. The centre distance between cylinders 1 and 6 was 692 mm. Split skirt aluminium alloy pistons were employed, having three compression rings and one scraper above the gudgeon pin and a single scraper below. The connecting rods were of the I-section, two-bolt type, clamped at the little end to the gudgeon pin. At the big end, the white metal was cast directly into the connecting rod.

The cylinder head was a one-piece casting covering all six cylinders. The camshaft was carried in an oil trough, side by side with the valve stems, and was supported in four bearings, the rearmost of which was a ball-type thrust bearing. Valve operation was via bell-crank rockers, so arranged that camshaft lift translated directly to operation of the valves. When fitting the cylinder head, correct camshaft timing was ensured when, with the pistons 1 and 6 on top dead centre and the crankshaft locked, a timing mark on the camshaft gear was lined up with an indicator on the cylinder head.

Accessibility was considered of primary importance. The inlet and exhaust manifolds and all auxiliaries, including the sparking plugs, were carried on the nearside of the engine. Carburation was provided by a Solex 40MOVL instrument and vaporisation was assisted by a hot spot where the inlet and exhaust manifolds were in close proximity. The dynamo and magneto were driven in tandem on the nearside of the engine from the same shaft as that which drove the water pump, though the water pump was mounted on the front face of the timing case. The favoured magneto was a Simms SRM6. The heavy-duty axial starter motor was rather less accessible, being carried on the flywheel bell housing on the offside.

The A131, fitted only to the pre-production batch of Regent chassis, was of 100 mm bore and 130 mm stroke, resulting in a swept volume of 6.126 litres. Its quoted power output was 49 bhp at 1,000 rpm and 95 bhp at 2,500 rpm. The compression ratio was 5:1. Regent chassis beyond 661012, up to and including 661518, featured the A136, which was of the same 100 mm bore as the A131 but had revised oil pipes. Beyond 661518 the A152, again with 100 mm bore but with slow speed dynamo, became a regular fitment. The LGOC favoured the 100 mm bore A140, which had a Scintilla magneto. The A137 engine, substantially similar to the A136, was fitted to the Regal chassis and the 110 mm bore A141 engine was standard in the heavy commercial chassis. The A145 powered the six-wheeled Renown. These last two engines delivered 58 bhp at 1,000 rpm and 110 bhp at 2,500 rpm. As previously, the compression ratio was 5:1. In the fullness of time, the 110 mm bore 120 bhp A162 with the 'power' head became the preferred fitment in most of the petrol engined chassis.

The radiator

Without doubt the most immediately recognisable feature of the new Rackham-designed chassis was the radiator, which with only detail alteration remained the face of the AEC chassis over a period of three decades. In its construction, the radiator was typical of earlier AEC and LGOC practice. The radiator tubes and the tube plates together formed the central assembly to which the top and bottom tanks were attached. Substantial aluminium side brackets connected the top and bottom tanks, which at the same time relieved the tubes of stress. The tubes, forty-two in total, staggered in alternating rows of ten and eleven, were of 3/8ins diameter bound in continuous copper wire filament. Known as Still tubes, these were the product of Clayton Dewandre. So constructed, the radiator could be readily dismantled at overhaul and any blocked tubes cleared of sediment. The radiator was carried on a platform cast integral with the engine's front support bracket and insulated from it by a rubber cushion. It was secured at the top by a stay attached to the front cylinder head studs and at the bottom by special spring-loaded bolts. In this way, the radiator formed part of the engine assembly and was fully insulated against any chassis distortion.

The Eight-cylinder petrol engine

The building of the eight-cylinder engine came about as a direct requirement of the LGOC. Logically, from the standpoint of standardisation, the design would have been similar to that of the standard six-cylinder type, with two added cylinders. A study of its photograph suggests that both in form and cylinder spacing this was so, leaving ample room for future increase in the cylinder bore.

The eight-cylinder engine had cylinder dimensions of 87 mm bore and 130 mm stroke, resulting in a swept volume of 6.182 litres, almost identical to the 6.126 litres of the standard 100 mm bore engine. The power output is said to have been 85 bhp, which, with the additional friction losses involved, would appear about right. Rackham, never frightened to speak his mind, was unenthusiastic. His comments are found in paragraph (g) of AEC Board Minute 1878 of 7 November 1929:

> The Chief Engineer also recorded the opinion that the activities of the Design and Experimental Department should be dedicated primarily to the perfection of the present range of models rather than to the consideration of alternative or new designs.

Five engines, numbered SE1–5 were built and fitted in new chassis 662070 (T43), 663035 and 041 (LTs 35 and 41), delivered ex Southall in January 1930, and 661212 and 292 (STs 4 and 84), delivered in February and March 1930. The engines were short-lived and it is recorded that by December 1930, those in T43, ST4 and ST84 had been removed and the vehicles returned to standard. LTs 35 and 41 were similarly treated but at an unspecified date.

The clutch and gearbox

The engine and gearbox formed a single unit, most of the weight and all of the torsional stresses being taken through a banjo cross-member sandwiched between the two units. The flywheel and 16-inch diameter single-plate clutch were enclosed within the engine's bell housing. On the passenger chassis the forward end of the engine was carried on a tubular cross-member, while on the commercial chassis a forged I-section stamping was employed. In both cases the engine's front mounting was insulated from the cross-member by a rubber cushion.

The gearbox, identified as the D119 or the D122, was of the sliding mesh pattern and had ratios of 1st 4.38:1, 2nd 2.69:1, 3rd 1.59:1 and 4th 1:1. Reverse was 5.33:1. The change speed mechanism was totally enclosed, with the gear lever to the left of the driver and the whole assembly face mounted on the side of the engine's crankcase. The selector gear and striking forks were carried in a detachable cover on the side of the gearbox. Bonneted chassis had the D123 gearbox, similar internally to the D119 but having the gear lever turret mounted on the selector cover, operating the gear selectors directly. On the Regent, Regal and Renown, the engine and gearbox were both angled and tilted in the chassis frame in order to provide a straight transmission line to the underneath worm final drive, which was offset toward the nearside to the extent of just over 12 inches.

Axles, Brakes and Steering gear

The front axle was an I-section steel forging and the steering linkages allowed for a steering lock in excess of 45 degrees. The stub axles had a diameter of 2¼ inches, with the wheel hubs carried on taper roller bearings. The brake drums were of 17-inch diameter (20-inch diameter on the Majestic, Mammoth and Mammoth Major chassis) and the brake shoes, 3¼ inches wide, were interchangeable with those on the rear axle. The brakes were cam-operated via rods, shafts and levers from the chassis-mounted Clayton Dewandre vacuum servo, the final motion being transmitted via push rods, through the hollow king pins to the brake camshaft levers. The steering gear was of the cam and roller type of Marles manufacture.

The rear axle was a one-piece nickel-steel forging and the worm gear case of magnesium alloy. The standard worm gear had a ratio of 6.25:1, though an alternative of 7.33:1 could be specified. At an engine speed of 2,500 rpm, the direct-drive top gear provided road speeds of 42.4 mph and 36.2 mph respectively. Heavy-duty bevel gears were employed in the differential. Semi-floating axle shafts allowed for the removal of the hubs and brake drums for the relining of the brakes without disturbing the wheel bearings. The axle shafts, produced in 100-ton steel, were of 3-inch diameter with the wheel hubs affixed by key and taper, secured by a single large nut.

The rear brakes featured four shoes per hub. One pair was energised by the same servo unit as powered the front brakes and the second pair was operated by the hand brake. By law both systems had to remain independent. On later chassis, abutments on the foot brake levers provided for the interconnection of the hand and foot brake shoes, thus doubling the power of foot brake on the rear axle. As on the Leyland Titan, the prototype Regent featured a push on handbrake lever. Production chassis had the more usual pull on arrangement.

Developments

In response to the revised Construction and Use Regulations that became effective in January 1931, the wheelbase of the Regent was increased from 15 feet 6½ inches to 16 feet 3 inches and the 1932 models exhibited at the Commercial Motor show in November 1931 reflected the latest mechanical developments.

Circumstantial evidence suggests that for city work the braking performance of the Regent was no better than adequate. Accordingly, from July 1930, a triple servo arrangement where two supplementary slave servos provided greatly increased braking power at the front wheels was adopted. The LGOC's ST class (numbered 500 upwards) were the first to benefit from this modification but by November, deliveries to other operators were similarly specified.

Dating from March 1931, AEC had developed the D124 gearbox, with its so-called 'silent' 3rd speed gear. The first examples were fitted to Regents of the LGOC and became the standard fitment in August 1931. Externally similar to the D119, the 3rd gear set in the D124 was now in constant mesh. Engagement of that gear was effected by dog engagement of the now sliding 3rd speed layshaft gear with corresponding dogs adjacent to the fixed 2nd speed layshaft gear. The equivalent gearbox for the bonneted chassis was the D126.

The AEC-built Worm and Nut steering gear, which promised easier control, was introduced in November 1931. The Marles gear continued to be employed on the commercial vehicle chassis.

The Lockheed brake was an import from America. Satisfactory as the triple servo arrangement was, there was a recognition that hydraulic operation of the brakes offered near perfect brake balance and, as a bonus, the Lockheed-built cylinders provided automatic adjustment of the rear brakes. The cylinders for the front brakes were incorporated in the hollow king pins. The system was first offered as an alternative to the then-standard triple servo system; the earliest examples appear to have been built for Nottingham Corporation in May 1932, followed quickly by Northern General (with its subsidiary the Sunderland District Omnibus Company) in June. The system was adopted as standard from November 1933.

Above and right: Rackham's A131/A136 six-cylinder overhead camshaft petrol engine owed much to American practice and was, in all essential features, similar to the A130 which had powered the type 660 Reliance chassis. In its general layout it also had much in common with the Leyland T-type engine which Rackham had designed in 1927. The crankcase, cast in aluminium alloy, supported the generously proportioned crankshaft in seven main bearings while the cylinder block was a simple one-piece close grained iron casting in which the pistons ran directly. The cylinder head carried the camshaft and overhead valve gear and was so arranged as to allow its ready removal as a complete unit without disturbing the timing arrangements of the engine. As first designed the engine was of 100 mm bore, later variants like the A145 and A162 were of 110 mm. (*Photograph: AEC 3307*)

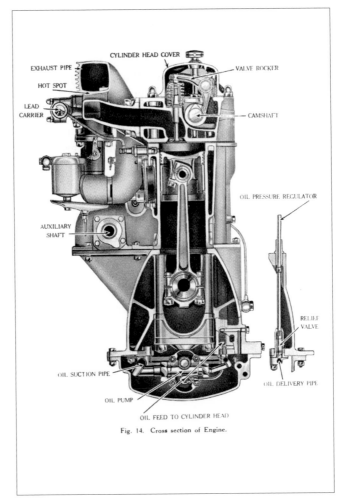

Fig. 14. Cross section of Engine.

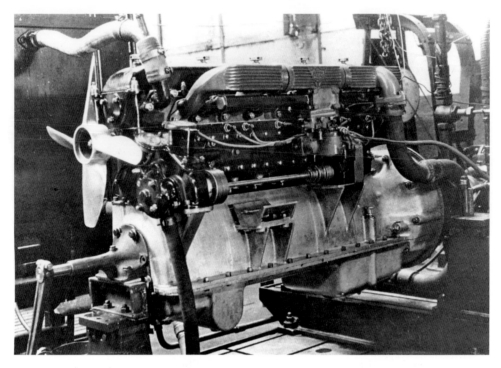

Above right: At first view, the eight-cylinder engine could be mistaken for the standard six-cylinder unit. Longer by about 10 inches, key identification points are the three-piece exhaust manifold and the five-knurled rocker cover retaining screws. Five such engines were built for the LGOC in late 1929 and early 1930. (*Photograph: Author's collection via the late Prince Marshall*)

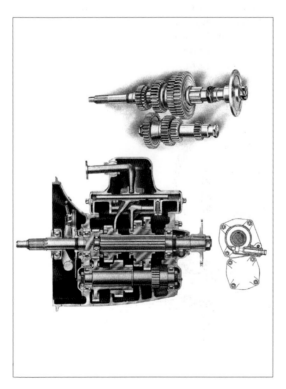

The four-speed D119 gearbox was a conventional sliding mesh design where direct drive top gear was achieved by a connection of the primary shaft with the main-shaft through a dog clutch. The primary shaft and lay-shaft gears were in constant mesh and engagement of the intermediate ratios was effected by a sliding of the respective indirect gears on the splined main-shaft and meshing with the fixed gears on the lay-shaft. Reverse gear was achieved by sliding an intermediate gear set into mesh with the first speed main-shaft gear (now in the neutral position on the main-shaft) and the first speed gear on the lay-shaft. (*Drawing: AEC. Author's collection*)

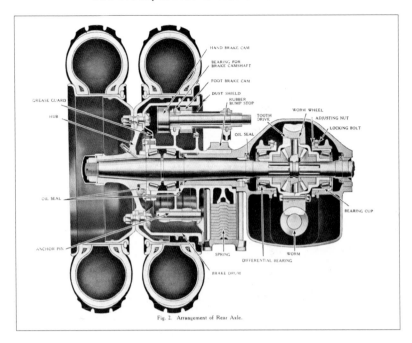

Fig. 2. Arrangement of Rear Axle.

Above and below: The underneath worm gear of the rear axle was of conventional design with a four-pinion bevel differential. The axle was a Timken-inspired semi-floating design which made possible the removal of the hubs and the brake drums as a unit without disturbing the wheel bearings. In this manner, the relining of the brake shoes was simplified but by definition, it also meant that the half-shafts were load bearing. The brake shoes, two per hub at the front axle and four per hub at the rear, had woven asbestos linings and operated in drums of 17-inch diameter. On early chassis, the footbrake and handbrake shoes in the rear hubs were independently operated. On later chassis an abutment on the footbrake camshaft lever caused both footbrake and handbrake levers to work in unison, thus doubling the braking effort on the rear axle. (*Drawings: AEC. Author's collection*)

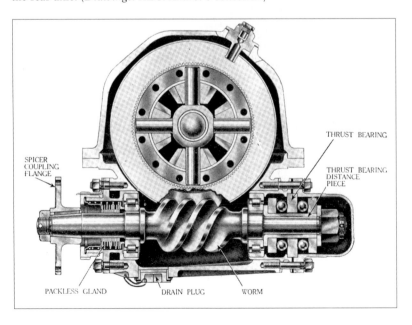

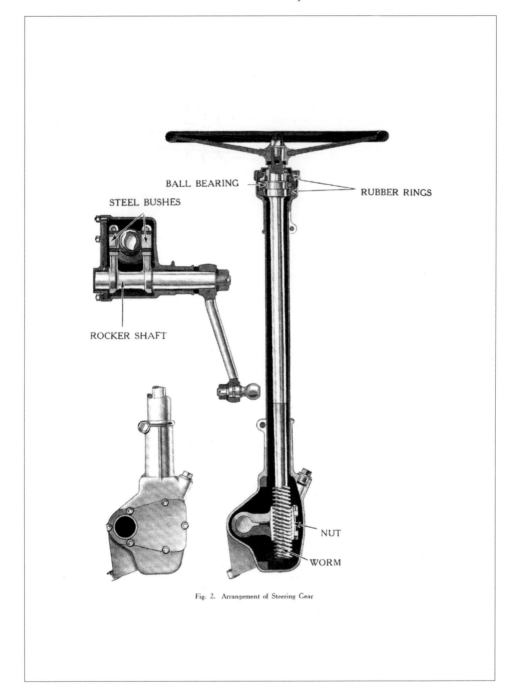

BALL BEARING ——

STEEL BUSHES

RUBBER RINGS

ROCKER SHAFT

NUT

WORM

Fig. 2. Arrangement of Steering Gear

AEC's own worm and nut steering gear was introduced for passenger chassis in November 1931. It was instantly distinguishable from the Marles type by the large bearing housing at the top of the steering column. The bearing itself was mounted in rubber in order to accommodate the angular displacement of the steering shaft. (*Drawing: AEC. Author's collection*)

3

The Regent Type 661
1929–1933

A new start

AEC, with its new factory at Southall, had clearly entertained great hopes for its alliance with Daimler, only to have them dashed by management differences and the unreliability of the sleeve-valve engine. John Rackham had already provided Leyland with a head start with the Titan and it was fortuitous, then, that for personal reasons he should want to return to London. While with the Reliance he had provided AEC with much-needed work in the short term, his primary aim was to see AEC re-established as a leading producer of double-deck passenger chassis. The LGOC believed that the three-axled motorbus best suited London's traffic, but Rackham saw the development of a two-axled double-deck chassis as being of immediate and urgent importance. Also in prospect was a new range of commercial vehicle chassis, but they would wait until the passenger chassis were up and running.

The Regent's principal dimensions

Like the Titan, the Regent chassis had an elegance of line perhaps not seen in this country before Rackham joined Leyland in 1926. As first built, the chassis had a wheelbase of 15 feet 6½ inches, an overall length of 24 feet 10½ inches and a laden frame height of 1 feet 9 inches at mid-wheelbase. From the front spring dumb irons to the end of the frame, the chassis took on an almost continuous sweep of undulating curves and changes in section. The frame had a maximum depth of 11 inches with 3-inch flanges top and bottom and a width across the frame members of 3 feet 11 5/8 inches. The height of the frame rearward of the rear spring hangers was 12 inches. The tyres were 36 inch by 8 inch singles at the front and 34 inch by 7 inch twins at the rear. The width over the front hubs was 7 feet 4½ inches and over the rear tyres 7 feet 21/8 inches. Production chassis, i.e. 661013 onward, had 38 inch by 9 inch balloon twin rear tyres which increased the width at that point to 7 feet 5 5/8 inches. The long, easy riding springs were 4 feet 2 inches long at the front and 5 feet 2 inches at the rear, shackled at their rear ends.

The Regent, as first introduced, had a dry chassis weight of 3 tons 5 cwts.

The first Pre-production chassis

While it has not proved possible to pin-point the building date of the first Regent chassis, Board Minute 1671 of 3 January 1929 gives some indication. It reads:

> Designs and Experiments
>
> The General Manager also reported the progress made in the various designs and experiments at present in hand, particularly with regard to the Regent double deck omnibus and the special design of six wheeled chassis with six cylinder engine for the London General Omnibus Company.

A pre-production batch of twelve Regent chassis had been built in the period up to July 1929, the first three in the Experimental Department, and records show that chassis 661001 was despatched to Short Bros on 13 February 1929. Registered MT 2114, it served as a demonstrator in many parts of the country before being sold to Halifax Corporation in February 1930. The unladen weight of this fifty-seat vehicle was shown as 5 tons 13 cwts. The registered laden axle weights were front axle 3 tons 16 cwts and rear axle 5 tons 3 cwts 1 qr, a total of 8 tons 19 cwts 1 qr, very close to the 9 tons legal maximum.

Chassis 002, having received its body, again built by Short Bros, was despatched to the National Omnibus Company at Colchester on 12 April 1929 and chassis 003 was shipped as a bare chassis to Agar Cross & Company, AEC's South American agents on 13 May 1929. It was returned to Southall and in June 1931 passed to L. R. Mansfield of Leytonstone, who fitted it with a van body. Finally it was sold to C. Bolton in Sydenham.

Chassis 004 was built on 8 May 1929, bodied by Shorts and despatched to Thomas Tilling on 18 June. Registered UU 9161, it was returned to AEC on 14 July 1930, from which time it was employed on staff transport duties between Walthamstow and Southall. Chassis 005, 006 and 007, all built in May 1929 and again with bodies by Short Bros, went to the National Omnibus Company while 008, UU 6610, built on 19 June 1929, went first to East Surrey on 9 July and then to Autocar on 4 October 1929.

Chassis 009 went to Wallasey Corporation on 16 July 1929 and 010 and 011 went to Birmingham. These received fifty-seat Brush bodies but remained in service for one year only. The chassis were returned to Southall and the bodies mounted on new Regent chassis. Chassis 010 then went to Clayton Dewandre in Lincoln, presumably for development work, while 011 was rebodied by Short Bros and sold to the Walthamstow Wayfarers Club.

The last of the group, 661012, was despatched to Hall Lewis on 10 June 1929, went to Glasgow on demonstration on 8 July 1929 and returned to Southall on 19 October. It went to Stockton-on-Tees and Newcastle on 21 October 1929 and returned five days later. Thence, it too joined the AEC Staff Transport fleet and, like 011, passed to the Walthamstow Wayfarers in March 1931. At some point, its engine was converted to 110 mm bore.

A Brooklands Test

A press release in Motor Transport dated 13 May 1929 revealed that extensive testing of the Regent was being carried out at Brooklands and that it was planned to run the run the vehicle for twenty-four hours in two twelve-hour sessions and to average 40 mph overall. It was noted at this point that a speed of 58 mph had already been attained. A full report appeared in the same journal on 24 June and is here reproduced in full.

ROUND BROOKLANDS WITH THE REGENT
Results of the R.A.C. Twelve-hours Trial of the New A.E.C. Double-decker

In order to demonstrate speed, petrol, oil and water consumption and reliability, one of the new A.E.C. Regent buses was recently driven round the Brooklands track for twelve hours. The trial was observed by the Royal Automobile Club, who have recently issued their report. The chassis, driven by a six-cylinder 100 x 130mm. engine, carried a 50-seated covered top deck body which was not loaded. The gear ratios were as follows: Top, 5.2 to 1; 3rd, 8.4 to 1; 2nd, 14.4 to 1 and 1st, 23 to 1, and on the front wheels 36 x 8in. tyres were fitted, and on the back twin 38 x 8¼in. The total running weight was just over 6 tons 7 cwt.
During a total (including stops) time of 12 hours 3 min. 10 sec. a distance of 507.3 miles was covered, and the average speed, excluding stops, was 43 m.p.h., which was maintained fairly constantly throughout the run. The petrol consumption was at the rate of 7.5 m.p.g., the oil 634 m.p.g., and 4 pints of water were put into the radiator.

Official Report.

As to the trial itself, we quote the words of the R.A.C. report:-

The weather was fine and warm. During the trial the vehicle was stopped on nine occasions for the purpose of replenishment, attention to the back axle, etc., the total time involved being 15 min. 29 sec. With the exception of the attention given to the back axle mentioned below, no work was done upon the bus, and engine oil and water were not replenished during the trial. At 208 miles the casing of the back axle was found to be hot, and a quantity of oil was put in. During the last 227 miles of the trial cold water, carried upon the vehicle for the purpose, was continually poured over the back axle casing. During this period oil was put into the axle on four occasions.
On dismantling and examination at the end of the trial, the teeth of the phosphor-bronze worm-wheel were found to be abraded, nearly ¼in. having disappeared. The surfaces of the teeth were not scored, nor was there any crumbling or breaking away. The steel worm on its driving side had a roughened, pitted surface, but was not scored. During one of the oil replenishments, approximately at 381 miles, it was discovered that a baffle plate and a breather tube, which were soldered on to the inner face of the filler cap, were no longer in position. They were found in the back axle casing in a crumpled condition. The condition of the soldered faces showed that the temperature within the axle had been high enough to melt the solder, but there was nothing to show whether the melting took place before or after the plate became dislodged. The removable portion of the bonnet, namely the top

and nearside flaps, were taken off for the trial. For ease of replenishment during the trial the normal tank of the bus was not used, a special tank being fitted within the body. The fuel used was a marketed brand of petrol, supplied at the track.

Shell petrol, Triple Shell oil, a Solex carburettor and Lodge plugs were used.

The press had been invited to a private showing of the Regent at Southall on 21 October 1929. This was in advance of the vehicle's official launch at Olympia. The exhibition was due to be held from 7–16 November and two of the three new passenger chassis, the Regent and Regal, and four commercial chassis, the Mercury, Monarch, Majestic and Mammoth, were to be exhibited. Though the six-wheeled Renown had been described in the technical press in August and previewed at Southall, it was not to be exhibited at Olympia as at this time it was considered to be a special chassis for the LGOC. As shown at Olympia, the Regent chassis carried a list price of £1,200.

The first 250 production chassis

Programme E214 had provided for the building of the first 250 production chassis.

The first of these, a group of five, had been built out of numerical sequence in September, in preparation for the forthcoming Olympia exhibition. Three chassis, 661033, 034 and 035, were despatched to Short Bros, two on 3 October and one on the 4th. One appeared on the AEC stand, one on the Short stand and the third did duty in the demonstration park. These became demonstrators MY 2542, MY 2126 and OF 8368 respectively. OF 8368 went to Birmingham Corporation and as a demonstrator was numbered 96 in that fleet. After purchase by Birmingham, it became number 368.

Mystery surrounds the early life of 661036. Having been built on 24 September 1929, it appears likely to have been the show chassis exhibited at Charing Cross, its presence there timed to coincide with the Olympia exhibition. It was rebuilt on 8 February 1932 and passed to Western Welsh in Cardiff in May 1932. Chassis 661037, built on 28 September for the Anglo American Oil Company, was shown on the Fry Bros stand. It had first gone to the LGOC on 4 November for the fitting of a lorry-type cab, thence to Fry Bros' works at Greenwich for the mounting of a 1,500-gallon triple-compartment spirit tank.

Mainstream production commenced in October 1929 and the first ten were built and despatched to Brush for Birmingham Corporation. These, 661013 to 022, were followed by 661045 to 054 and 065 to 072, a total of twenty-eight. Nottingham took twenty, 661023 to 032 and 055 to 64, with English Electric bodywork and Halifax had 661038 to 040, 125, 126 and 130, with bodies by Short Bros, six in total. Newcastle took three, 661041 to 044, with Hall Lewis bodies and a single chassis, 661073, built in October and with bodywork by Davidson, went to Sheffield Corporation in May 1930. Importantly, 661074, having been built on 3 October 1929, went to the LGOC at Chiswick on the 7th of that month and was followed by 661148 on 27 November. These became ST 1 and ST 2.

Chester Corporation took 661075 to 080, with bodywork by Shorts, and 081 was shipped to AEC Australia two days before Christmas. City of Oxford Motor Services took 661107–124, built in November 1929 and delivered in January 1930, with bodywork by Hall Lewis, and Eastern National had 661127, 128, 134 and 135, with Short Bros bodywork. Independent operators Lewis of Watford and Southern General in Truro took five and four respectively. Somewhat out of date order were twenty-five for Glasgow Corporation, 661082–106, with bodywork by Cowieson, built in January, March and April 1930. As of 31 December 1929, 148 Regent chassis had been built.

Such was the varied pattern in the first weeks of production and it was clear that the Regent had already gained a wide acceptance. With the exception of Glasgow Corporation, which did not return to AEC until 1937, all of the municipal undertakings were to figure prominently in future orders.

The year 1930 opened with forty-two chassis for East Surrey and eighteen for Autocar, interspersed with ten more for Newcastle, after which the first of the LGOC's first order of 299 were put into production. By April, AEC was able to announce that orders for 1,180 new-type passenger vehicles had been received since the November 1929 Commercial Show. Moreover, this number did not include orders for the six-wheeled Renown. Nottingham had come back with a further requirement of twenty chassis, Tilling ordered 125 for its London operation and Birmingham Corporation wanted a further seventy-five. Oxford wanted twenty-four, Exeter six and Walsall eight. Such was the continuing hunger, not least that of the LGOC, whose orders for the Regent alone now totalled 836, that in the closing months of 1930, AEC had to install extra production capacity to meet the demand. Board Minute 2053 of 2 October 1930 reads:

> The Managing Director also reported that in order to meet the needs of the London General Omnibus Company Ltd and Green Line Coaches Ltd, it has become necessary to increase the production capacity of the factory by from 10 to 15 chassis per week during the next six months: that accordingly the working of overtime will be recommenced, that between 200 and 300 more men will be employed and that additions to the existing plant and machinery will consequently be necessary.

The A155 oil engine

AEC had been engaged in experimental work on the high-speed compression ignition oil engine since the early months of 1928. The latest engine was a six-cylinder unit of 110 mm bore and 142 mm stroke in which the 'Acro' chamber was incorporated in the cylinder head. It is examined more fully in a later chapter; suffice to say that its power output was 95 bhp at 2,000 rpm and had an operating range from 300 rpm to 3,000 rpm. The economics of the oil engine were convincing. Not only was there the difference in basic fuel cost, fuel oil at 4d per gallon compared with petrol at one shilling (in present day parlance 1.66 pence and 5 pence per gallon respectively), but there were in addition significant savings to be had in terms of specific fuel consumption. The opening paragraph of an article in the AEC Gazette of December 1930 reads:

> If any indication was needed as to the intense interest now being taken in the use of crude oil for motor transport, it would have been found at the demonstrations held on 30th October

when the Press and a large number of Operators came down to Southall and saw the results of A.E.C.'s experimenting with a power unit designed to run on this form of fuel.

Three demonstration vehicles had been available on that day, though which three of the four available were actually on the road is not recorded. The Short-bodied AEC demonstrator 661131, MY 2102, had been built in November 1929 and originally powered by petrol engine A136/64. It now carried oil engine A155/1. Three brand-new LGOC Regents, 661960, 962 and 964 (ST 462, 464, and 466), had oil engines A155/2, A155/6 and A155/5 respectively. Following the demonstration and with seating reduced to forty-four to allow for the extra weight of the engine, the three STs were allocated to Harrow Weald. At one year old, i.e. the first overhaul, the oil engines were removed and transferred to LT-class buses. The STs were re-equipped with A140 petrol engines and the seating capacity was restored to forty-nine. The demonstrator MY 2102 ultimately went to Northern General, its A155 engine being replaced by one of the later A164s in May 1933.

It was still too early to see the A155 as anything other than experimental but progress had certainly reached the point where it was desirable to place a number out in the field. In March 1931, Glasgow, Walsall and Halifax Corporations took delivery of A155-powered Regents 6611106, 1107 and 1108. Birmingham took 6611127, also in March. The Eastern and Western National Companies had one each, 6611146 and 1147, in April. Stockton had 6611157 in April and Leicester 6611156 in May. In June Lowestoft had 6611548, while in the same month Wallasey took two, 6611549 and 1550. Portsmouth had 6611583 in September. A round dozen in total.

The reliability of the A155 was clearly patchy. Halifax's A155/43 appears to have lasted until April 1933, when it was changed for A164/71, while Leicester's A155/44 failed early in life. This was replaced by A155/56, which in turn was replaced by A161/66 in June 1932. A155/44 was rebuilt in time to be fitted to the Lowestoft Regent in June 1931 and was in turn replaced by A164/47 in February 1933. Walsall's A155/41 was changed for petrol A152/394 and Western National's A155/14 was changed for petrol engine A136/89 in April 1932, taken from one of their own earlier Regents. Eastern National had A155/20 rebuilt and the two Wallasey Regents had A155s 33 and 40 changed for 61 and 62. Portsmouth's 6611583, initially fitted with A155/63, received A161/17.

The LGOC's last new STs

The LGOC had taken the last 191 short wheelbase petrol-engined Regents into its dedicated London fleet by May 1931, bringing the ST class total at that time to 836. A further thirty chassis with Short Bros bodywork were allocated to East Surrey and were ultimately numbered ST 1040–1069. Tilling had added a further sixty-two to its London fleet and fifty-two went to service its Brighton operation. Birmingham Corporation took another sixty, but AEC lost out thereafter to Morris Commercial, Daimler and Leyland.

By the summer of 1930, the single servo formerly adopted for the Regent's braking system had been replaced by a triple servo arrangement, some of the first examples being found on the LGOC's ST-class chassis. Though still operated through a rod linkage, braking effort to the front wheels was provided by two independent slave servos mounted on the cross-member immediately rearward of the gearbox. With the front wheel brakes now separated, balance was more readily achieved. The rear brakes were operated as before through the master servo.

The sixty Birmingham chassis, as well as the thirty destined for East Surrey, are noted as having Westinghouse brakes. Though the Westinghouse Brake & Saxby Signal Company were pioneers of the automotive compressed air brake, the company was at that time also producing a vacuum servo system. These last mentioned Regents were so equipped.

Relaxed Regulations

On 13 March 1931, the Ministry of Transport issued new and relaxed limits of length and weight for public service vehicles which would allow a general increase in seating capacity of the double-decker from forty-nine or fifty to as many as sixty. The Public Service Vehicles (Conditions of Fitness) Provisional Regulations 1931 required that the four-wheeled double-decked vehicle did not exceed 26 feet in length nor the laden axle weights exceed 6 2/3 tons. The sum of those axle weights was not to exceed 10 tons. The Metropolitan Short Stage Carriage regulations issued in April 1932 allowed that those same limits be applied in the London Metropolitan area.

A longer Regent

The changes precipitated the development of the long, 16-foot 3-inch wheelbase Regent chassis. The overall chassis length was increased from 24 feet 10½ inches to 25 feet 8 inches and in this guise it was identified as the type 661/4. While for flat London operation the 100 mm bore, 100 bhp A140 engine remained favourite, the 110 mm bore, 120 bhp A162 engine with the 'power head' now became the standard fitment. With this engine, the 5¾:1 rear axle was frequently specified. The D124 four-speed crash gearbox with constant mesh 3rd gear had been introduced in the midsummer of 1931 in succession to the all sliding mesh D119. The gear ratios remained as before. The original F129 semi-floating rear axle had given way to the F145 at the end of 1931 and a worm and nut steering gear, replacing that manufactured by Marles, had been introduced at about the same time. Servo-assisted Lockheed hydraulic brakes, more complex and more expensive than the triple servo system but having excellent self-compensating properties, could be specified from November 1931. They became standard from November 1933.

The first examples of the 16-foot, 3-inch long wheelbase chassis had been built in May 1931. Chassis 6611158 and 1159 were built as demonstrators and 6611160, built in July 1931 with A162 engine, was rebuilt to the 1932 standard and went to Dundee in April 1932. It is recorded that the first production batch was 6611731–1750, twenty chassis built in November and December 1931 for Hull Corporation with A140 engines and D124 gearboxes. Recent information, however, supports the belief that these chassis were in fact of 15-foot 6½-inch wheelbase and the chassis frame code, Y155A, certainly lends credence to this. Chassis 6611801–1804 with A162 engines were built for Charles Pickup in November 1931 and February 1932 and these thus appear to have been the first production 16-foot 3-inch wheelbase chassis built.

Through the first six months of 1932, Tilling had added forty-five short wheelbase chassis, 6611759–1797 and 1886–1891, to its Brighton fleet. These had A140 engines, D124 gearboxes and triple servo brakes and the LGOC took twenty-three similar chassis, 6612021–2043, for its newly formed London General Country Services based at Reigate in July. South Wales Transport, established AEC users in an earlier era, now added fifty long wheelbase Regents to its fleet, 6611868–1879, 1898–1905 and 1991–2020, all with A162 engines. New user Mansfield purchased thirty-four similar long wheelbase A162-powered chassis, 6611947–1980, on which were mounted bodies by both Short Bros and Weymann. These had Lockheed brakes with Dewandre G120 series 7202 servos. Other new Regent users included Northern General, which took eight, Sunderland District ten, Bournemouth Corporation six and Morecambe & Heysham also six.

The Wilson Gearbox

Back in 1929, AEC had purchased three Wilson epicyclic preselective gearboxes for evaluation. The results had clearly not been sufficiently encouraging to take up the exclusive option that they had secured and it was left to Daimler to profit from this lack of vision. Daimler's success had come in combining the Wilson gearbox with the fluid flywheel, a coupling devised by the German engineer Dr Fottinger and developed in this country by Harold Sinclair. Daimler had tried the fluid flywheel in conjunction with the spur gearbox and found it useless but by sheer good luck had found it to be the perfect partner to the Wilson gearbox. Daimler lost no time in patenting the combination of these two units and the rest, as they say, is history.

In December 1930 the LGOC had acquired three Daimler CH6 chassis and these, as DST 1–3, were placed in service in February 1931. The least endearing feature of these vehicles was the sleeve valve engine but the combination of the fluid flywheel and preselective gearbox held promise. In March 1931 Regent chassis 6611391, ST 746, had been built with the new transmission and this was followed in April by two three-axled Renowns, 663440 and 449, similarly equipped. A further twenty Renowns, again with preselective gearboxes, were built in July.

Though the Associated Daimler Company as a joint AEC/Daimler selling organisation was dormant, an agreement made in June 1928 provided for the free interchange of technical information between AEC and Daimler. A new joint agreement, dated 5 November 1931, between AEC, Daimler and the Associated Daimler Company provided for the exclusive supply of Daimler Fluid Flywheel Transmission sets to AEC for a period of three years, subject to the purchase by AEC or its Associated Companies of 100 units in the first year of the agreement and a quantity equal to 20 per cent of passenger vehicle production in the second year.

Into production

Long wheelbase Regent demonstrator 6611800, with Wilson gearbox, fluid flywheel and A162 engine, was built in December 1931. Registered MV 1518, it was ultimately taken into the Lancaster fleet in December 1932. In March 1932, E. Brickwood Ltd, operating as the Red Line Omnibus Co., became the first operator outside the LGOC to adopt this form of transmission with 6611810, also A162-powered. Slowly, other companies followed suit. City of Oxford Motor Services purchased six, 6611862–1867, with the A140 engine in June and Leeds Corporation took twelve in August 1932, 6611935–1946. Huddersfield Corporation, with a purchase of six chassis, had three with preselective gearboxes and three with the D124. Newcastle took delivery of three in September in 1932. These, numbered 6611932–1934, had the A162 engine and preselective gearbox in the shorter 15-foot, 6½-inch wheelbase frame.

The Tilling STLs

Tilling had taken delivery of the first of eighty long-wheelbase Regent chassis in October 1932. The chassis, 6612164–2243, had been built to Tilling's own specification with the A140 engines linered down to 95 mm bore, giving a capacity of 5,529 cc. Electric starters were deemed superfluous. The gearbox was the standard D124 and the brakes were Lockheed hydraulic. The Tilling-designed fifty-six-seat bodies were constructed in Tilling's own workshops. Owned by the LGOC and operated by Tilling on the LGOC's behalf, the vehicles were numbered STL 51 to 130 in the LGOC's fleet.

The LGOC's STL class

STLs 1 to 50, with the new square sixty-seat Chiswick-built body, began entering service in January 1933. This group again featured the A140 engine and D124 gearbox but STLs 1–10 and 41–50 were notable for the fact that they were fitted with the first of the then-experimental fully floating rear axles, the F156. Like the Tilling chassis, the brakes were servo-assisted Lockheed hydraulic. The last of this group, chassis 6612120, STL 50, was fitted with the Wilson-designed and Daimler-built preselective gearbox but without fluid flywheel. The record card shows it to have been fitted with a conventional plate clutch.

In advance of the formation of the London Passenger Transport Board, the LGOC's last intake comprised 100 Regent chassis, the delivery of which commenced in May 1933. These were numbered 6612298 to 2397, STLs 153 to 252. The F156 rear axle had now been adopted as standard, as had the hydraulic brakes, but experiment was still the order of the day. The A140 engine now featured coil ignition. Half of the intake, STLs 203 to 252, like STL 50, were fitted with the Daimler/Wilson preselective gearbox, again without fluid flywheel. Some appear to have been fitted with the plate clutch and others not.

Experience was to show that without the fluid flywheel as a cushion, the take-up of the drive in the preselective gearbox was harsh and that wear on the 1st gear brake bands was excessive. Early problems with the fluid flywheel centred on the leakage of oil past the coupling flange gland, a problem not wholly cured until the development of the bellows gland, but the combination of fluid flywheel and Wilson pattern gearbox provided the long-awaited transmission system for high-density city operation.

Provincial oil-engined chassis

Equally interesting were the oil-engined chassis built through the second half of 1933. Bury Corporation had taken delivery of ten, 06612153–2162, in September 1933 with the A165C engine, Daimler preselective gearbox and fluid flywheel. Baillie Bros had chassis 06612163 built at the same time but with the D124 crash gearbox. A larger group covering fifty-eight consecutively numbered chassis was built in the period November 1933 to February 1934. These, 06612401–2458, were all of 16-foot, 3-inch wheelbase and had been built to the same mechanical specification: A165J engine governed to 2,300 rpm, D124 gearbox, F156 rear axle and hydraulic brakes. Chassis 06612401–2404, with bodywork by Northern Counties, went to Cardiff Corporation. Rhondda Tramways had 06612405–2434, a total of thirty, with Weymann bodywork and Devon General had twenty-four, 06612435–2458, with bodywork by Short Bros. Also built in the same period were the twelve 'Godstone' STLs. Numbered 06612271–2282, these had a similar specification save that the engine was more conservatively governed to 2,000 rpm. The front entrance, low height forty-eight-seat bodies were built by Weymann.

The additional weight of the 8.8-litre A165 had of course to be balanced against seating capacity. Rhondda's Weymann-bodied examples weighed 6 tons 8 cwts 0 qrs 2 lbs and those of the Devon General with Short bodies 6 tons 7 cwts. The seating capacity in both cases had been reduced to fifty-two in order to keep within the 10-ton limit, whereas the petrol-engined types would usually seat fifty-six.

The development of the Regent chassis was ongoing. We leave the story in December 1933 when the first fifty or so petrol-engined, preselective Regent chassis from a batch of 200, STLs 253 to 452, were being built for the newly constituted London Passenger Transport Board.

Production totals

From the time of the Regent's introduction until the end of 1933 the overall annual totals built, but not necessarily delivered, were: 1929, 148; 1930, 1,051; 1931, 570; 1932, 365; and 1933, 389. Those built for the LGOC and its associate companies (East Surrey, Thomas Tilling and the London General Country Services) in the same periods numbered 28, 822, 264, 83 and 251.

LGOC licensing problems

If the LGOC had always appeared all-powerful, there were occasions when it fell foul of authority. File MEPO2 2170, lodged at the Public Record Office at Kew, is revealing. From a Public Carriage Office report dated 24 January 1931, we learn that the laden axle weights of the LGOC's ST 1 (661074) when first licensed were:

Front Axle Weight: 3 tons 11 cwts 2 qrs
Rear Axle Weight: 5 tons 8 cwts 0 qrs

Unladen Weight: 5 tons 11 cwt 2 qrs

The sum of the front and rear axle weights were thus just below the required 9 tons total. In similar vein, the laden weights for ST 182 (661390) as supplied to the Police on licensing were:

Front Axle Weight: 3 tons 10 cwts 1 qr
Rear Axle Weight: 5 tons 7 cwts 1 qr
Unladen Weight: 5 tons 10 cwts 0 qrs

When check weighed, presumably in January 1931, the actual weights of this vehicle were found to be:

Unladen Weight: 6 tons 12 cwts 0 qrs 7 lbs
Laden Weight: 9 tons 16 cwts 1qr 13 lbs

This was more than one ton in excess of the weights previously disclosed. In answer to questions from the Public Carriage Office, the LGOC in its defence said that the company had taken advantage of the concession afforded by the Heavy Motor Car (Amendment) Order 1930, dated 29 April 1930 and effective from 1 June, to strengthen up this type of vehicle generally. Subsequent correspondence between the Public Carriage Office and the Ministry of Transport indicated that the Public Carriage Office had no objection to an increase in weight to 10 tons laden. The case against the LGOC was seemingly dropped but it could well be argued that the LGOC had anticipated the change in regulation and thus, by its action, had hastened the adoption of the higher weights in London.

LGOCs maintenance

Under file MT33/136, in a report dated 18 January 1935, we learn that the LGOCs Short-bodied Regent ex-demonstrator UU 6610, 661008, on loan to East Surrey, had been inspected at Grays on 17 January 1935. Though the vehicle had been overhauled in September 1934, the body was found to be in a dangerous condition. The lower deck floor was rotten, the platform unsafe, and the staircase was adrift, loose and broken at the bottom bracket. In addition, the upper deck floor was unsafe and the roof was leaking.

Another report in the MT33/136 file, dated 15 February 1935, only one month later, reveals that the lack of maintenance at Country Service Garages had resulted in Chiswick taking over the supervision of the Country Service vehicles. Fleet History LT7, published jointly by the PSV Circle and the Omnibus Society, shows that the original body, No. 10954, carried by UU 6610 was replaced by body No. 15551 in 1935. The vehicle went on loan to Coventry Corporation from December 1942 to November 1945 and was scrapped in October 1948.

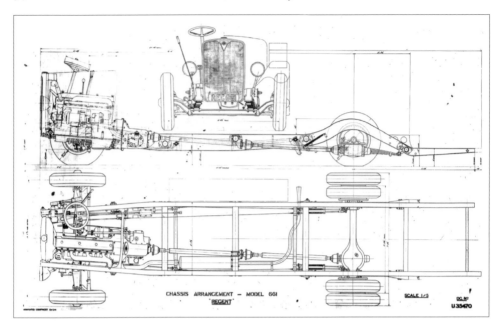

Drawing U35470 is a rare drawing of the Regent chassis in its pre-production form. (*Drawing: AEC, Author's collection*)

The location of this photograph is on the northern side of the experimental department building and to the left is the sports ground. The chassis is again the prototype Regent, 661001. Notable is the push on handbrake, an echo of Yellow Coach and Leyland practice. Not immediately apparent is the difference in tyre sizes. Those at the front are 36 inches by 8 inches and the rears 34 inches by 7 inches. (*Photograph: AEC, Alan Townsin collection*)

Seen outside the main office at Southall is 661001, MT 2114, with a fifty-seat Short Bros body. In appearance, the body had much in common with that designed by Rackham for the Leyland Titan but there was a fundamental difference. In the original low height design, which had come from the Fifth Avenue Coach Company in Chicago and for which Leyland had acquired the patent rights, the top deck gangway was positioned to the offside of the body and the gangway floor lowered by a full step height. This offset gangway facility was denied to AEC and in order to provide clearance over the normal centre gangway yet retain the illusion of low height, the camel roof was evolved. In many photographs, and from street level, this feature is well disguised. (*Photograph: AEC, Alan Townsin collection*)

Though the pre-production prototypes had been in the hands of operators since the summer of 1929, it was not until November at the Commercial Motor Transport exhibition at Olympia that the Regent had its first official showing. Among the exhibits was Regent 661035, again with a body built by Short Bros to the individual requirements of Birmingham Corporation, similarly styled to a batch of ten bodies built by Brush and mounted on chassis 661013–022. Registered OF 8368, this show exhibit became a demonstrator numbered 96 in the Birmingham fleet. Such was the success of these vehicles that during 1930 and 1931 Birmingham went on to build a fleet of 167 similar vehicles. Thereafter, AEC lost out principally to Daimler with the COG5. (*Photograph: AEC, Author's collection*)

Among the exhibits at Olympia was this Regent tanker, 661037, for the
Anglo-American Oil Company registered UW 5745. The three-compartment,
1,500-gallon spirit tank had been manufactured by Fry Bros of Greenwich
and the cab constructed by the LGOC. Its unladen weight was 5 tons 16 cwts
2 qrs. Two further similar vehicles in the same striking green and red livery
were commissioned in 1930. (*Photograph: AEC, Author's collection*)

Though the London General Omnibus Company had placed Short-bodied
661008 in service with East Surrey in July 1929, it was not until November
1929 that 661074, the first of the General's ST class, was placed in service. ST
73, GC 3989, chassis No. 661281, with forty-nine-seat Chiswick-built body
was placed in service in March 1930. It was allocated to Hanwell garage and
is seen here when new at Oxford Circus working route 184 between Southall
and London Bridge. (*Photograph: Transport for London, 21834*)

Three Regents, 6611806, 1807 and 1808, were the first to be purchased by Devon General. With the recently introduced 110 mm bore high-power A162 petrol engine and D124 four-speed gearbox, they were among the earliest of the 16-foot 3-inch wheelbase chassis to be built. Their somewhat upright but nevertheless distinctive bodies, built by Brush in April 1932, seated fifty-two. (*Photograph: AEC 0616, Author's collection*)

Sold right into Leyland's heartland was Regent 06612160, EN 5639. One of ten sold to Bury Corporation in September 1933, the chassis was notable for having the 8.8 litre A165 oil engine, a Daimler-built preselective gearbox and the recently introduced fully floating rear axle. Again on the 16-foot 3-inch wheelbase chassis, the unusual yet attractive dual entrance, dual staircase body was built by Charles Roe and seated forty-eight. (*Photograph: AEC 0903, Alan Townsin collection*)

4

The Regal Type 662
1929–1934

Specification

In its specification, the Regal chassis closely followed that of the Regent. The engine, the 100 mm bore, 95 hp, six-cylinder A137, differed from the A136 of the Regent only in respect of its 6½-inch dynamo. The gearbox, until the middle of 1931, was predominantly of the type D119 though the D122 with 'Poldi' gears featured strongly among the first 300 chassis. The rear axle was the semi-floating type F129 or F131, both of which had the underneath worm drive, usually with a ratio of 6¼:1, though alternatives of 6½:1 and 5 1/5:1 were available. As with the Regent, the underneath worm gear was markedly offset to the nearside. The front axle was the L118 and movement of both front and rear axles was damped by Luvax shock absorbers. The brakes, with drums of 17-inch diameter and operating on both front and rear axles, were energised by a single Dewandre vacuum servo. Tyre equipment was 38 inches by 8¼ inches on 22-inch ten-stud rims. The bare chassis weight was given as 3 tons 6 cwts.

The Regal had a wheelbase of 17 feet and overhang could be tailored to suit body lengths of 26 feet or 27 feet, 26 feet being the generally accepted maximum in the United Kingdom when the Regal was first introduced. The chassis frame, itself a work of art with its gently flowing curves and changes in section, had a laden height, both at mid-wheelbase and rearward of the rear spring rear spring hangers, of 1 foot 9½ inches. For a more extensive description of the engine, the reader is directed to Chapter 2.

Into production

It had been an open secret for more than a year that AEC was developing a whole new range of passenger and commercial vehicle chassis but it was not until the Commercial Motor Show at Olympia in November 1929 that the official launch of the Regal was made. Regent 661002 had been in service with the National Omnibus Company since April 1929 and Renown 663001 went into service with the LGOC in August. Regal chassis 662001 and 002, which had been built in the experimental department and with bodywork by Mumford, went into service with Plymouth Corporation in September and October 1929. The balance of the order, ten chassis numbered 662003–012, was built in October 1929 and entered service in the following November, December and January.

On the AEC stand at the 1929 Commercial Motor Show were two Regals: 662013 was a bare chassis and 662014, which had been bodied by the LGOC, was shown in the livery of Timpson's of Catford. The bare show chassis was later mounted with a half-length Strachan-built saloon body and became the AEC's dual-purpose development and demonstration vehicle. (Ultimately rebuilt, it was re-numbered 6621388 and, with Metcalfe body, passed to Davies of Ynysybwl in July 1932.) On the Harrington stand was 662015, with an elegant twenty-one-seat body built for the London, Midland & Scottish Railway Company, and the Elkington Carriage Company had built a horsebox body on 662016 for The Hon. Dorothy Paget of Leeds Castle in Kent. On the Duple stand was 662017, with a twenty-eight-seat body for Elliott Bros of Bournemouth. Chassis 662018 went to Agar Cross & Co. for exhibition at the XII Salon del Automoviles in Buenos Aires.

Regal 662019, built on 3 October 1929, was AEC's demonstrator MY 2421, being sold to J. Cormie of Dysart in August 1930, and chassis 020, demonstrator MY2276 with Strachan body, went to the Watford Omnibus Company in December 1930. Following the absorption of the Watford Omnibus Company by the LGOC, 662020 became T371 in the LGOC fleet. Chassis 021 went to the Royal Arsenal Co-op and 022 to the Folkestone Harbour Garage. Another of AEC's development chassis was 662023. First built in October 1929, it was rebuilt in November 1930 and re-numbered 662803. In this form it went to Green Line Coaches Ltd., the LGOC's subsidiary, in substitution for 662716, which up to that time had been identified as T220. Chassis 662716 was transferred to East Surrey and the rebuilt 662803 became the new T220. Brown Bros of Sapcote took 662024 and R. Cockburn of Edinburgh had 662025. Chassis 662026 was sold via the Dublin depot to J. Dwyer of Rocksavage and 027, with bodywork by Short Bros, became No. 1 in the fleet of Chester Corporation.

By the end of December 1929, no fewer than 146 Regal chassis had been constructed and sixty-five were in the hands of the operators. From this total, fifty, 662028–077, had been built for the LGOC and nine, 662078–086, built for Chester Corporation brought that undertaking's total to ten. Yeoman of Hereford had 662087. The first five of an order for thirty chassis, 662088, 133, 162, 164 and 166 had been built for the London coach operators Blue Belle Motors and four chassis, 662089–091 and 136, part of an order for eighteen, had been built for Elliott Bros of Bournemouth. A single chassis, 662092, went to J. R. Street of Hertford and the Royal Arsenal Co-op had five, 662093, 134, 135, 137 and 200. Chassis 662094–097 went, in sequential order, to Enterprize of Clacton, H. P. Britten of Forest Gate, Don Everall of Wolverhampton and Bilaktebolaget Urania of Stockholm. E. Paul of Forest Hill had three, 662098, 099 and 100.

Continuing with the December 1929 build, Airedale Motors of Bradford took 662101. Chassis 662102 is thought to have been held back as a development chassis but ultimately went to Arlington Motors in June 1931 with bodywork by Maltz of Ealing. Chassis 662159–161, 163, 165, 167 and 168 went to Autocar and 662169–184 and 186–188 went to join 662014 at Timpson's. Chassis 662185 went to Waugh Bros in Brighton. Aston Motor Services of Watford took 662199 and Eastern Motorways of Norwich had 662201. Scottish Motor Traction took delivery of the Strachan-bodied demonstrator 662202, MY 3479, in September 1930. Bevan &

Barker of Mansfield had 662217, Bush and Twiddy, coachbuilders and bus operators of Norwich, had 662227 and Jacobs of South Woodford took 662228, 229 and 230. These chassis then, built in the period to 31 December 1929, set the pattern for the future.

Chassis development

Regal 662038, the LGOC's T43, having been built on 9 December 1929, was the first of five chassis to be built with an experimental eight-cylinder engine, similar in all respects to the standard six-cylinder unit save that it had two extra cylinders. The other chassis were Renowns 663035 and 041, built in January 1930, and Regents 661212 and 292, built in February and March 1930. The engines, with dimensions of 87 mm by 130 mm bore and stroke and a swept volume of 6.182 litres, reputedly produced 85 bhp. Gavin Martin, in his book London Buses 1929–1939, reports that T43 retained the eight-cylinder engine until the time of its first chassis overhaul in December 1930.

Development of the Regal continued and the 110 mm bore, 110 hp A145 engine became available in April 1930. Though the Dewandre vacuum servo had been the standard fitting, Westinghouse vacuum servos had featured strongly on chassis built for the Green Line, East Surrey and Autocar fleets, also on chassis built for the independent coaching company Keith & Boyle. From August 1930, Dewandre triple servo brakes (G10 series 881) replaced the earlier pattern single servo arrangement (G6 series 840). The D124 gearbox, with its constant mesh 3rd gear replaced the D119 in August 1931. From November 1931 the more powerful 120 bhp A162 engine with the power head became available, a worm and nut steering gear replaced the Marles type and the wheelbase was increased to 17 feet 6 inches.

Production in 1930 and 1931

In 1930, 653 Regal chassis were built. Of the London players, the LGOC had taken 248, primarily for its Green Line services, East Surrey had sixteen, Autocar seventeen and Tilling fourteen. In the provinces, Western Welsh had taken twenty and Rhondda Tramways six. The Southern and Western National companies had each taken eight and East Midland, which would feature strongly in future years, had taken ten. Ayr and District had twelve. Among the many independents, Timpsons had taken forty-four, Blue Belle and its subsidiary Queen Line had taken thirty-five and Salisbury of Blackpool ten.

With only the last remnants of the LGOC's Green Line order to complete, Regal production in 1931 fell to 394 chassis. East Surrey took a further eighteen chassis and Autocar added another six. During the year, the Belfast Omnibus Company added sixteen to the single chassis taken in September 1930 (one of them oil-engined, detailed below) and the Eastern, Southern and Western National fleets together had added thirteen. Ayr and District had increased its total to twenty-four. Keith & Boyle, having taken ten chassis in 1930, added a further ten in time for the 1931 coaching season. East Midland had added twenty to its fleet and the Scottish Motor Traction

Company had taken eleven. In Yorkshire, Huddersfield Corporation and Hull Corporation had each taken ten and Halifax Corporation had nine, three bodied by Hoyal and six by English Electric. Late in 1931, Scottish Motor Traction had ordered a further sixty chassis for its growing fleet, of which twenty had been built before the year's end.

The A155 engine

Following the press demonstration of the A155 oil engine in October 1930 and its official launch at the Commercial show at Olympia in November, both Scottish Motor Traction and the Belfast Omnibus Company had been persuaded to take one on board. The SMT had A155/8 in Regal 662839, built on 16 February 1931, and Belfast had A155/45 in 662808, built on the 20th of that month. East Surrey's Regal 662124 (PG7503), new in March 1930, had its A137 engine exchanged for A155/20 on 13 March 1931. Engine A155/8 in the Scottish Motor Traction vehicle 662839 was replaced by A161/20 on 11 October 1931. Legend has it that three Green Line Regals, 662712 (T216), 662770 (T274) and 662801 (T305), had their A145 petrol engines exchanged for A155s in 1931. It is recorded that T305 had received A155/23 on 18 May 1931, later replaced by A155/8 (from the Scottish Motor Traction's 662839), and at some point T274 did receive A164/52. In truth, the writer has failed to find any Southall record of an oil engine having been fitted to T216.

Production in 1932, 1933 and beyond

Only 244 Regal chassis were built in 1932, forty of which were the balance of the Scottish Motor Traction order. The Belfast Omnibus Company took another fifteen and Huddersfield Corporation had ten. Thomas Tilling took delivery of twelve in July, August and September. Cumberland Motor Services had eight and Leeds Corporation took delivery of six with Weymann bodies in August. In the private sector, ten had been built for Blue Belle Motors in October, though not delivered until the following April and May, and the first nine of an order for twenty-seven had been built for Timpson's in September and December, again for delivery in 1933.

By 1933 the economic depression was starting to bite and only 104 of the standard six-cylinder Regals were built. Orders primarily came in single units from the smaller independents. Deliveries into the Welsh valleys were an exception. South Wales Transport took ten Weymann-bodied examples registered WN 5401–5410, Bassett of Gorseinon and Gough of Mountain Ash took three each and Enterprize of Gorseinon had five, these last eleven all being bodied by Short Bros.

In 1934, building of the Regal came to a halt in July when just eighty-nine chassis had been built and it was largely to the municipal undertakings that deliveries had been made. Western Welsh had eight, with Weymann bodies, Halifax Corporation had four, bodied by Park Royal, and Northern General six with bodies by Short Bros. Scottish Motor Traction and Huddersfield Corporation each had twelve and Sheffield

Corporation took six, unusually with bodywork by Roberts of Wakefield. In the coaching sector, United Service Transport took ten with Harrington bodies.

Production totals for the type 662 Regal in the years 1929, 1930, 1931, 1932, 1933 and 1934 were 146, 654, 394, 244, 104 and 89 respectively, a total of 1,631.

Mechanical variety

While orders had become increasingly difficult to secure through 1932, 1933 and 1934, there had been no shortage of variety in specification. The Midland Bus Company of Airdrie had put three Regals, 6621160, 1161 and 1162, into service in March 1932 with the A161 oil engine, D124 gearbox and triple servo brakes. Burnley and Colne, with A162-powered 6621244 and 1245, had the distinction of being the first, in July 1932, to have the Daimler pre-selective 'fluid' transmission. Lockheed hydraulic brakes were also a feature of these two vehicles. In August 1932, Huddersfield Corporation, within a batch of ten chassis, 6621365 to 1374, had six with the A162 petrol engine and one with the A164 oil engine coupled to the D124 gearbox, and two with the A162 and one with the A164 oil engine coupled to the Daimler gearbox. All ten had triple servo brakes.

In the same month, Leeds Corporation took delivery of chassis 6621381–1386, also with the Daimler transmission and powered by the A152, 100 mm bore petrol engine. In March 1933, Scottish Motor Traction took six, 6621476–1481, with the A165 oil engine, Daimler gearbox and Lockheed brakes. Orange Bros of Bedlington, with 6621524, was one of the first companies in June 1933 to take delivery of a Regal with the fully floating axle, the F156. In this instance, the engine was the A162, the gearbox the D124 and the brakes triple servo.

London Transport had been the front runners in the adoption of the Daimler-built Wilson pre-selective gearbox and such was its success in the STL-type Regents that arrangements were made whereby AEC would build the gearbox and the fluid flywheel under licence from Daimler. The first Regals to feature the AEC-built gearbox, identified as the D132, was a batch of twelve, 06621594–1605, built for Scottish Motor Traction in March 1934. Note also that the prefix O had, since about June 1933, been adopted to identify chassis fitted with the oil engine. By 1933, the oil engine in its A164/A165 form had become well established, but the petrol engine still held the high ground. Of the 104 chassis built in 1933, sixty-six had the petrol engine (mainly the A162) and thirty-eight had oil engines (five A164 and thirty-three A165).

Caution was the key note when it came to the transmission; ninety-four featured the D124 crash box and ten only opted for the Daimler pre-selector. The year 1934 told a different story. Only forty featured the A162 petrol engine and forty-eight the A164 oiler, while in respect of the transmission, fifty-five had the D124 and thirty-three the pre-selective type. These also split, with ten Daimler-built D128 gearboxes and twenty-three of the AEC-built D132s.

The 7.7 litre engine

Successful as the A165 had become, its bulk had always demanded compromise in its installation. The smaller 106 mm x 146 mm A171 (developed in tandem with the Q type's A170) was the first oil engine specifically designed to be interchangeable with the six-cylinder petrol engine and chassis 06621588, built on 15 September 1934 and shown at the Scottish show, was the first Regal to be so equipped. This chassis had engine A171/3 and the demonstration chassis 06621619 had A171/46. Chassis 06621619 was itself interesting, having been first built as a Regal 4, chassis no. 642058.

In service

Little has been recorded in respect of the performance of the early Regals but there is little doubt that those fitted with the 110 mm bore petrol engines, particularly those with the with the power head, were brisk performers. The operators of the long-distance express services clearly demanded reliability and annual mileages of 150,000 were not unusual. It is recorded that petrol-engined Regals operated by Majestic Express Motors, working the daily service between London and Manchester, returned a fuel consumption of between 6 and 7 mpg. Midland Bus Services, with the A161 oil-engined Regal, on its inaugural run from London to Glasgow covered the 410 miles on 34 gallons of fuel, an average of 12.06 mpg. The scheduled journey time was 16 hours 23 minutes.

When introduced, the Regal chassis had a list price of £1,100, exactly the same as that of the Reliance, which it had replaced. In November 1931 the list price was reduced to £1,050. Notwithstanding the improvements in the chassis specification, the fully floating rear axle and the hydraulic brakes, the data sheet of September 1934 shows the price of the petrol-engined chassis remaining at £1,050. Fitted with the A165 oil engine the price increased to £1,350 and the addition of fluid transmission incurred a further penalty of £100. Without naming the respective manufacturers, this same data sheet quoted net prices of £500 for a bus body and £650 for a coach.

Left: This photograph of the prototype Regal chassis, similar in all essentials to the Regent, well illustrates its salient features. Two chassis, 662001 and 002, had been built in the experimental department and the record cards show that the engines were A137s (numbered 14 and 15 respectively), the gearboxes four-speed D119s, the front axles were identified as L118s and the rear axles F129s. The chassis had four-wheel brakes operated through a single Dewandre vacuum servo. The steering gear was by Marles and the tyres by Dunlop. (*Photograph: AEC, Author's collection*)

Below: Regal VG 2284, chassis 662201, was purchased by Harrison & Ives of Norwich in April 1930. Its mechanical specification was similar to the prototype with the A137 engine but had the alternative D122 four-speed crash gearbox. The attractive body with fashionable curtains at the windows was built by United Automobile Services of Lowestoft. (*Photograph: AEC L215, Author's collection*)

The Belfast Omnibus Company had been formed in 1927 and by 1928 had built up a fleet of more than 100 AEC type 416 and 426 buses. After a brief flirtation with Daimler (CF6), Guy (fourteen-seat OND) and a single Dennis Lancet, the company returned to AEC in 1931. The BOC was absorbed into the Northern Ireland Road Transport Board in October 1935, by which time it had added thirty-two Regals to its fleet together with eight Regents and a single Q-type. AZ 6779, chassis 662695, with body built in the BOC's own workshop, is shown in June 1931, resplendent in the early summer sunshine. (*Photograph: BOC 16.6.1931, Author's collection*)

With its white upper panels, red lower panels lined and lettered in gold, David MacBrayne took delivery of this Park Royal-bodied Regal US 2246 in August 1933. The chassis, 6621534, built in June 1933, had, in addition to the other features introduced in 1931, hydraulic brakes and the F156 fully floating rear axle. The rather higher and forward projecting bonnet hides the optional 130 hp A165 oil engine. Based in Glasgow, its daily return journey was to Ardrishaig on the shore of Loch Fyne, some 88 miles distant. The route took it along the shores of Loch Lomond to Tarbet, thence by Clen Croe and Glen Kinglas to Inverary and onward to Lochgilphead and Ardrishaig. In an unusual arrangement, the vehicle carried a locked Royal Mail post box by which means letters from the remote areas could be posted and be with the Post Office in Glasgow each night. (*Photograph: AEC 0867. Alan Townsin collection*)

5

The Renown Types 663 And 664

Origins

At the time that John Rackham returned to AEC in August 1928, the LGOC was in desperate need of a replacement for its obsolescent S and NS-type buses. The company already had a dozen six-wheeled, Associated Daimler-built LS-types in operation and experience with these led the management to believe that the high-capacity three-axled vehicle was the correct way forward. Rackham was openly sceptical of six-wheelers. In a paper read before the Institution of Automobile Engineers in December 1927, he had said:

> At the present moment the six-wheeled bus is dead in America and the author quite anticipates that it will be dead here within a year or so, except possibly for a few very large double-deckers.

He was convinced that its theoretical advantages would soon be overturned by the practicality of the less complex four-wheeler. Nevertheless, the LGOC saw passenger transport in London as a special case and experience with the 30-foot LS suggested that an overall length of about 27 feet was probably the best compromise for double-deck operation in crowded city conditions.

The first reference to the Renown at AEC board level is found under Minute 1671 of 3 January 1929 when the General Manager, George Rushton, reported on progress in respect of:

> the special design of six wheeled chassis with six cylinder engine for the London General Omnibus Company.

Following its construction in AEC's experimental department, the prototype Renown chassis, 663001, was delivered to Chiswick works on 24 June 1929. As LT1 it entered service on 6 August 1929 on route 16A, running between Cricklewood and Victoria. At the board meeting on 3 October 1929, C. W. Reeve was able to report on the performance of the Renown under operating conditions, following which, at the same meeting, approval was given for the construction of 200 similar chassis.

Specification

As first built, the Renown chassis was powered by AEC's A140 six-cylinder overhead camshaft engine, an engine similar in most respects to the A136 fitted to the Type 661 Regent and to which, for a description, the reader is referred. The cylinder dimensions of 100 mm x 130 mm were the same as the A136 but featured a Scintilla magneto and an 8-inch dynamo. The power output of the 100 mm bore engine was generally reckoned to be 95 bhp at 2,500 rpm.

Like the Regent, the engine clutch and gearbox formed a single unit. Chassis 001 had the then-standard D119 gearbox but chassis 002–051 were fitted with the D122, which is noted as having 'Poldi' gears. To date, the significance of the term 'Poldi' remains obscure but the use of these gears appears to have been a short-term expedient.

Thus far, the specification of the Renown closely followed that of the Regent but the arrangement of the rear axles calls for more detailed examination. The suspension comprised a pair of inverted semi-elliptic leaf springs 5 feet 2 inches long, trunnion-mounted at mid point and carried on substantial brackets, one each side of the chassis frame. These were in turn braced by 4-inch diameter cross tube. The axles were attached to the springs at their outer ends and a torque blade mounted between the axles allowed a limited amount of interaction between the axles but prevented any rotation of them. It also ensured that there was no excessive angularity of the short inter-axle propeller shaft.

The axles, identified as the F133 and F134, were of the semi-floating type with the axle pots offset to the nearside by some 14½ inches. The worm and wheel of the underneath worm gear were on 7-inch centres and the worm gear on the front bogie axle incorporated a third differential. This negated any mismatch of tyres on the two axles. The axle ratio on chassis 001 and 002 was 8¼:1, on subsequent chassis it was 8 1/3:1 which on top gear provided a road speed close to 33mph at 2,500 engine rpm.

The brake drums, on both front and rear axles, were of 17-inch diameter and the brake shoes 3 inches wide with ¾-inch-thick linings. The brake shoes were interchangeable, having two shoes per hub at the front axle and four at the rear. The footbrake was servo assisted and operated one pair of shoes at each wheel hub. The handbrake worked independently and operated the second pair of shoes. Photographic evidence shows that as first built, the prototype Renown chassis was without brakes on the front axle. The chassis record card indicates that the omission was later rectified.

The type 663 Renown had a wheelbase of 16 feet 6 inches, measured from the centreline of the front axle to the mid point of the rear bogie, and an overall length of 26 feet 9 3/8 inches. The chassis had a maximum frame depth of 11 inches and a laden frame height at mid-wheelbase of 1 foot 9 inches. The employment of single wheels on the rear axles allowed for a frame width of 5 feet at the rear bogie, which in turn provided for wide spring centres and an improved resistance to body roll. The width of the chassis over the wheel-hubs was 7 feet 4½ inches (at both at front and rear) and over the front mudguards 7 feet 5½ inches. The wheel track at the front axle measured 6 feet 5 5/8 inches and at the rear 6 feet 2¾ inches. The wheel and tyre equipment was single 36 inch x 8 inch on all axles.

The LGOC's LT class bus

The short wheelbase type 663 Renown had been designed to fill the needs of the LGOC. The double-deck bodywork for LTs 1–150 (661001–050 and 052–151) was constructed by the LGOC itself, LT1 having seats for fifty-four passengers and the remainder seating sixty, all with open staircases. Thereafter, enclosed staircase bodies for LTs 151–511 (661152–512) were built, seemingly in random order by Park Royal, Short, and Strachan as well as the LGOC itself. Most seated fifty-six, but some only fifty-four. LTs 512–949 (663513–950) had standard LGOC bodies, mainly fifty-six-seaters. LT741 was an exception, which carried the prototype sixty-seat Bluebird body. This became the standard body for LTs 950–999 and 1204–1426 (663951, 955–1003 and 1004–1226).

Private hire coaches LTC1–24 (6631227–1250) were built in July and August 1937. Powered by A145 petrol engines, they were fitted with elegant twenty-eight and thirty-seat bodies by Weymann. The first entered service in November 1937.

There were four non-LGOC deliveries. Chassis 663051 went to Northampton Corporation. With a fifty-four-seat body by Grose, it was registered VV119. Chassis 663952, 953 and 954 were built as demonstrators. Brush-bodied 663952 was sold to Birmingham Corporation, chassis 953 with Cowieson body went to Glasgow and 954, having served as a show chassis, was dismantled and parts returned to Stores in November 1933.

Though the building of the Renown chassis for the LT-class bus had finished by September 1932, it had been the subject of almost constant development right through until the wartime years of 1939 to 1945. Two chassis, 663035 and 041, had been built in January 1930, initially powered by the experimental AEC eight-cylinder 87 mm bore x 130 mm stroke overhead camshaft engine. Any theoretical advantage that the eight-cylinder engine may have had in respect of smooth running appears to have been negated by its mechanical complication and inferior power output. At one year old, the engines were replaced by the standard six-cylinder type.

Engine and gearbox variations

In September 1930, chassis 663137 had its engine converted from 100 mm bore to 110 mm. Its engine A140/332 received a new identity, A145/55, and from November 1930 and chassis 663152, the 110 mm bore A145 became the standard fitment. As a consequence of this, the axle ratio was changed from 8 1/3:1 to 6¾:1.

The development of the oil engine was high on the list of priorities, both at AEC and the LGOC. In consequence, as soon as AEC had developed what appeared to be a viable engine, nine of the LT-class vehicles were so powered. The selected chassis were 663192–200 (LTs 191–199), the first of which was built on 12 December 1930. The engine, a six-cylinder Acro pattern indirect injection type, was identified as the type A155. With cylinder dimensions of 110 mm x 142 mm and a swept volume of 8.1 litres, it had a power output of 95 bhp at 2,000 rpm.

The D119 gearbox had given way to the D124 at chassis 663402 in February 1931. This gearbox was externally similar to the D119 but featured a constant mesh 3rd gear, which provided a much easier gear-change on this much used ratio. Experiment continued and in April 1931, chassis 663440 and 449 (LTs 439 and 448) were built having the Daimler-built Wilson preselective gearbox and fluid flywheel. Chassis 663550–553, 567–572 and 584–593 (LTs 549–552, 566–571 and 583–592) followed in July 1931, similarly equipped.

Ricardo developments

Further oil engine development led to the A161. This shared much with the A155 but had a new 115 mm bore cylinder block and cylinder heads developed by Ricardo of Shoreham. With the capacity increased to 8.85 litres, the power output was now 140 bhp at 2,500 rpm. Chassis 663591 (LT590) was the first to be so equipped. Originally built on 23 July 1931 with an A145 engine, it had been one of the twenty chassis fitted with the Wilson gearbox and fluid flywheel. Delivered to the LGOC on 11 August 1931, it was returned to the AEC's experimental department, where it received engine A161/8. It was retained by the experimental department for six months and eventually re-delivered to the LGOC on 26 February 1932.

Chassis 663644, LT643, had been built on 21 August 1931. This, like 663591, had had its standard A145 engine removed and replaced by engine A161/6. It was delivered to the LGOC on 24 August and on being fitted with a standard fifty-six-seat body, it was despatched to Manchester to be inspected by Municipal Transport Chiefs at their annual convention. A further twenty-one similar chassis, 663751–769, 949 and 950 (LTs 750–768, 948 and 949), were built with A161 engines and D124 gearboxes in the period September 1931 to January 1932.

The building of the LT-class chassis continued apace and by May 1932 more than 1,100 had been built. The last petrol-engined LTs were numbered 1325–1354 (chassis numbers 6631125–1154). These had hydraulic brakes, Wilson gearboxes and fluid flywheels.

LTs 1355–1374, built between 23 June and 17 August 1932, had the same combination of hydraulic brakes and fluid transmission but were powered by the new A165 oil engine. Of 115 mm bore and 8.8 litre capacity, it was similar in most respects to the A161 but had many detail modifications, including hardened cylinder liners. Now slightly de-rated, its power output was 135 bhp at 2,200 rpm and was readily identified by the new combined Bosch fuel injection pump and governor.

With the A165 engine came a change in axle ratio from 6¾:1 to 5¾:1. LTs 1375–1416 (6631175–1216) featured the same A165 engine but had the standard D124 crash gearbox and triple servo brakes. They were built in the period 23 May to 5 September 1932. LTs 1417–1426 (6631217–1226) were otherwise similar but powered by the Gardner 6LW engine. These were built between 13 and 22 September 1932.

October 1933 saw the start of a programme where, at overhaul, selected LTs were converted from A145 petrol to A165 oil. The petrol engines removed from these chassis were overhauled and despatched to AEC for fitting in new STL Regent chassis (STLs 253–341, 353–552 and 559–608). New A165 oil engines were supplied by AEC in exchange. In this manner, by October 1934 169 of the 1931 pattern LTs and 170 Bluebirds had been so treated. A further twenty-four LTs were converted to A165 in 1937. Here again, petrol engines supplied by Chiswick for fitment in new type-663 LTC coach chassis were exchanged for A165s supplied from Southall. The conversion programme continued and during 1939 and 1940, AEC supplied Chiswick with a further 550 8.8 litre engines. These were supplied in two batches (400 and 150) and were of the direct injection pattern A180 with Leyland pattern 'pot' type pistons. Finally, 500 sets of direct injection cylinder heads and parts were supplied in order that the A165 engines could be converted to 'pot' type A180.

The long wheelbase type 664 Renown

Whereas the type 663 had been built almost exclusively for the LGOC, deliveries of the 30 feet long, 18-foot 7-inch wheelbase type 664 had a more diverse pattern. The 100 mm bore A140 petrol engine, standard when the first Renown chassis were built, quickly gave way to the 110 mm bore A145. This was in turn ousted by the A162 with the high power head. The A165 8.8 litre oil engine became the usual fitment from the early months of 1933 and the A171 '7.7' with the Ricardo head from January 1935. The direct injection A173 arrived in 1938 and the A180 direct injection 8.8 in 1939. Exceptionally, the Gardner 5LW powered a batch of forty Renowns for the China General Omnibus Company in 1939.

Transmission systems were less diverse. The D119 crash (or in LGOC parlance, 'clash') gearbox was replaced in April 1931 by the D124 with the constant mesh 'silent' 3rd gear. The D122 with 'Poldi' gears featured briefly. The drive from engine to gearbox was taken through a conventional single plate clutch. The Daimler-built Wilson gearbox, identified as the D128, with the fluid flywheel came into general use from 1933. The AEC-built preselective gearbox, the D132, became available in 1934.

Triple servo Dewandre brakes had been the standard fitment until the summer months of 1932; thereafter, a Lockheed hydraulic system in conjunction with a single Dewandre servo was adopted. It was claimed that the hydraulic brakes were always in balance, a feat which was less easy to achieve with the servo assisted mechanical linkages.

As detailed below, the first deliveries of the type 664 Renown had been to Warrington Corporation, but of the 346 type 664s built, the LGOC had taken 200. They were chassis 664003–052, 664063–112 and 664114–213 and like the 663 chassis, were numbered in the LT series to become LT1001–1050, LT1052–1101 and LT1102–1201. Chassis 664003 had been built on 18 September 1930 and with A145 engine and D119 gearbox, its specification closely followed that of the then-current type 663. The rear axles had a ratio of 6¾:1, the tyres were 38 inches x 7 inches in single formation all round. Chassis from 664063 were fitted with the D124 gearbox and chassis 664163–213 had the 100 mm bore A140 engine. All had been built by September 1931 and all carried single deck, front entrance thirty-five-seat bodies. They were employed primarily on suburban services.

Non-LGOC deliveries

The two Warrington deliveries, 664001 and 002, carried dual-staircase, fifty-nine-seat bodies by Massey Bros of Wigan. Built on 21 January 1930, these vehicles had A140 engines, D122 gearboxes, 36 inch x 8 inch Dunlop tyres and a final drive ratio of 8 1/3:1. Different in detail were Liverpool Corporation's 664053 and 054, built on 3 June 1930. These had 110 mm bore A145 engines, D119 gearboxes, 38 inch x 9 inch Dunlop tyres and 6¾:1 axles. They carried single deck bodywork constructed in the Corporation's own transport department.

Chassis 664055, built on 6 June 1930, was sold to Pickfords in September. It received a pantechnicon body and was registered GN9172. Originally powered by the then standard A145 petrol engine, it received an A165 oil engine in October 1932. Copenhagen Tramways had 664056, with single deck body, and Imperial Motors of Abercynon had 057, 058 and 059, also single decked. Chassis 664060 was AEC's demonstrator MV468, with single deck thirty-five-seat body by Beadle of Dartford. Built on 25 October 1930, it was sold to an East Ham operator in March 1932.

Very much in the commercial vehicle field, the Anglo American Oil Company took delivery of three special Renown chassis, 664061, 062 and 113, on 9 September 1931. Registered GN1419, GN1420 and GT523, these had 110 mm bore A144 petrol engines, D119 gearboxes and a final drive ratio of 8 1/3:1. The front tyres were 38 inch x 9 inch high-pressure and the rears were 44 inch x 12 inch balloon-type. The cabs had been constructed by Weymann and the 2,500-gallon tanks by the Steel Barrel Company.

Another of AEC's demonstrators was MV2906, 664214. Representing latest AEC practice, it had been built on 17 September 1931, powered by the newly introduced 110 mm bore A162 engine. The D124 gearbox replaced the D119 and a worm and nut steering gear was employed in place of the previously employed Marles. The brakes were of the triple servo pattern and the axles had a ratio of 6¾:1. It carried a sixty-five-seat body by the Cammell Carriage Company and was ultimately sold in June 1933 to White's Motors (Thomas White & Company) of Cardiff. White's had already taken delivery of 664215 with a similar specification in December 1931. Registered KG340, 664215, it carried a sixty-seat Short body.

Eastern National took 664216–219 with sixty-six-seat Short Bros bodies to serve their Chelmsford operation in May 1932 and single decked 664220 went to Gellygaer Urban District Council in June 1932, registered TG3523. The chassis had been built on 25 April 1932 and featured the A164 oil engine coupled to the D124 gearbox. With a thirty-eight-seat, single decked rear entrance and front exit body, it was the first oil-engined Renown to work in Wales.

Edward Hillman of Romford had taken 664221, with A162 engine, D124 gearbox and single deck thirty-one-seat coach body by Harrington in September 1932. It was the first chassis of this type to have Lockheed brakes. It became LT1429 in the London Transport private hire fleet in 1935. The Ebor Bus Company of Mansfield took 664222 and 223 with sixty-six-seat bodywork by Strachan and the London General Country Services had 664224 and 225 with A140 engines, D124 gearboxes, 5¾:1 axles and Westinghouse brakes, believed to be vacuum servo.

South Wales deliveries

Chassis 664226 had been built on 23 August 1932. As AEC's demonstrator MV3711, with single decked thirty-eight-seat body by Park Royal, it had been despatched to South Wales Transport in October 1932 for trial on Swansea's Townhill route and was purchased by that company in June 1933. Having the Daimler-built fluid flywheel and Wilson preselective gearbox, it was the first long wheelbase Renown to be so fitted, though short wheelbase London Transport Renowns had had the Wilson gearbox since May. Its A162 petrol engine was replaced by an A165 oiler in September 1933 and the axle ratio changed from 8 1/3:1 to 5¾:1.

In March, June and July 1933, Thomas White of Cardiff took delivery of three oil-engined chassis, 664227, 228 and 229. With sixty-seat bodies by Short Bros, they were registered KG2176, KG2699 and KG2700. The engines were the recently introduced A165 and, like the South Wales demonstrator, chassis 664227 and 229 had the Wilson gearbox and fluid flywheel. The rear axle ratio of 6¾:1 was to become the norm for the Southern Welsh operators. Close neighbours the Western Welsh Omnibus Company had taken delivery of four Renowns, 664230–233, in April 1933 to a less adventurous specification. With A162 petrol engines and D124 crash gearboxes, they had fifty-six-seat bodies by Weymann and were registered KG2201 to KG2204. They passed to Thomas White when only fifteen months old, in June 1934.

A single chassis, 664234, with an A162 petrol engine and D124 gearbox was shipped to AEC Australia in March 1933.

In the southern counties of Wales, the combination of A165 oil engine, fluid flywheel, preselective gearbox and Lockheed brakes was to become a near mandatory specification. Bassett & Sons of Gorseinon took delivery of 664235, 236 and 237 with sixty-three-seat bodies by Short Bros in June 1933. Following the experience gained with the single decked Renown demonstrator MV3711, South Wales Transport ordered five preselective chassis for the Townhill route. These, 664238 to 242, were built in July 1933 and with forty-seat single deck bodies by Brush, they entered service in August 1933 registered WN5811 to WN5815.

Chassis 0664243 had been built on 3 October 1933 with the A165 engine but coupled to the D124 gearbox. Despatched to Short Bros on 7 October 1933, it appeared on that company's stand at the Commercial Motor Show at Olympia the following month. Carrying a fifty-three-seat front entrance double deck coach body, it was shown in the colours of White's Motors of Cardiff but was eventually sold to Westcliffe Motor Services in July 1934.

An additional requirement by South Wales Transport for eight high-capacity double-deckers resulted in the building of chassis 0664244–251 in February 1934. With a very similar mechanical specification to chassis 664238–242 and with double deck sixty-four-seat bodies by Weymann, these were put to work on the Swansea–Llanelly service in March and April 1934. They were registered WN6230 to WN6237 but not in strict numerical order.

Beyond South Wales

Renown 0664252, with the A165 engine and preselective gearbox, was built for Doncaster Corporation on 4 May 1934. Its double deck sixty-seat body was built by Charles Roe of Leeds and as DT5337 it entered service the following August.

Two quite different chassis had been built on 25 January 1935. Chassis 0664253 had been built for export to Johannesburg, with A165 engine and the AEC-built D132 preselective gearbox. Unusual at this time was the fitment of triple servo brakes. The engine was governed to 2,400 rpm and, perhaps indicating arduous operating conditions, the thermostat set to open at 195 degrees F. This vehicle became No. 1 in the Johannesburg Municipal Transport fleet. The second chassis, 0664254, had been built as a demonstrator for Cumberland Motor Services. The engine was the recently introduced A171 indirect injection 7.7, with the governor also set to 2,400 rpm, and the gearbox was again the preselective D132. The rear axles had an unusually low ratio of 9.3:1. The single decked thirty-nine-seat body was built by Weymann and the vehicle was registered CMF843. It passed to Valliant, then of Acton, on 14 December 1938, with the engine governed to a more conservative 2,000 rpm and the axle ratios changed to 5¾:1.

February 1935 saw the building of four chassis for Doncaster Corporation. With A171 engines, preselective gearboxes and Lockheed brakes, they were numbered 0664255–258. Charles Roe built the sixty-seat bodies and as DT6100–6103, they entered service in May and June 1935. A similarly specified chassis, 664259, was built for Baillie Bros of Dumbarton in December 1935. This received a sixty-three-seat body by Pickering and was registered SN7175.

Chassis 664260 was built on 10 February 1936 for Bracewell of Colne. Much in the same idiom as the Hillman coach, it had the A162 petrol engine. Believed unique on a passenger vehicle, it was fitted with an auxiliary gearbox, which had been designed for military use on the six-wheeled 3-ton Marshal. Built in unit with the normal D124 four-speed unit and identified as the D127, the auxiliary gearbox provided a step down ratio of 1.6:1. It was intended for use only in extreme conditions, in conjunction with the first gear in the main gearbox. The thirty-nine-seat front entrance body was built by Duple and, registered ATE690, the vehicle entered service in March 1936.

Operated by Schoyens Bilcentraler in Oslo were six chassis, 0664262–267, built with the A165 engine and D132 preselective gearbox between April 1936 and March 1937.

A single chassis, 0664268, with the A171 Comet III engine and D136 crash gearbox was built in July 1937 for the British-owned China General Omnibus Company in Shanghai.

After a break in production for more than a year, Leicester Corporation took delivery of nine Renowns, 664269–277, the first of which had been built on 19 October 1938. They were notable for the fitment of the A173 direct injection 7.7 engine, D132 preselective gearbox, F180 and 181 fully floating rear axles and the late 1930s long pattern radiator. With sixty-four-seat double deck bodies by Northern Counties, they entered service in February and March 1939, registered CBC913–921.

Quickly following, the China General Omnibus Company took delivery of forty chassis powered by the 5LW Gardner driving through the D124 gearbox and F180 and F181 rear axles. These were in two groups, 664G278–303 and 317–330.

In 1939, South Wales purchased a further thirteen single deck, thirty-nine-seat Brush-bodied Renowns for use on the Townhill service. These, 0664304–316, were registered CCY951–957 and CWN395–400. They were powered by the A180c engine and had the AEC-built D132 preselective gearbox. The last Renowns built were 664331–346, a batch of sixteen built for Leicester Corporation between September and November 1939. With the direct injection A173 engine, they were similar in specification to those delivered in 1938 but carried Metro-Cammell bodies. They went into service in May and June 1940, registered DBC221–236 in random order.

The Six-wheeler in retrospect

The middle and late 1920s had seen something of a revolution in the motor vehicle industry with the introduction by Guy and Karrier of the three-axled chassis and the London Public Omnibus Company in particular had given the LGOC a wake-up call when it put the first of its Guy FCX on the London streets in September 1927.

From about 1930, sales of both Guy and Karrier motorbuses faded. Even Leyland, which with AEC had dominated much of the passenger vehicle market in the 1930s, produced only a very few of the six-wheeled TT1 and TT2 Titanics. The TS6T and TS7T Tigers were equally rare. Had it not been for the insistence of the LGOC in 1929 that the sixty-seat bus was its required vehicle, the Renown story may well have been very different.

The short wheelbase Renown certainly filled the LGOC's requirement for a high-capacity double-decker but its advantage evaporated with the change in regulation and the arrival of the sixty-seat STL Regent in the early months of 1933. Its 200 long wheelbase single-deck Renowns were specialist vehicles for use on routes which precluded the use of the double-decker and where the 30-foot overall length provided a greater seating capacity than could be obtained with the single-deck four-wheeler.

The concentration of the long wheelbase Renown among the South Wales operators is interesting. South Wales Transport was the major operator of the type, having taken delivery of nineteen single-deckers for work on the Townhill route and eight double-deckers for the Swansea–Llanelly service in the period 1932–1939. It remains open to question which of the Renown's features was the primary attraction. On balance, it would appear that it was the additional seating capacity afforded by the 30-foot-long body (forty seats in respect of the single-decker and sixty-four in the double-decker) rather than the theoretical advantage of the two driven axles. All were fitted with the preselective gearbox, which reduced the possibility of a missed gear on the 1 in 5 Townhill gradient, and the 8.8 litre oil engine made for an easy ascent. Traction does not appear to have been a significant problem as this route was also worked by single-decked four-wheeled buses. The long wheelbase double-deckers, with their ability to seat up to sixty-four passengers, proved well suited to the Swansea–Llanelly service, where passenger loadings were high, a service that was run in conjunction with Bassett's of Gorseinon.

Footnote

Following the separation of AEC and Daimler, there had clearly been an element of disquiet at Chiswick. Rackham's well-voiced dislike of the six-wheeler raised serious doubts. It has even been suggested that the Chiswick chassis had been designed as a hedge in case AEC failed to survive the trauma of separation. In the event, three four-wheeled Chiswick CB-type chassis and four six-wheeled CCs were built during the eighteen-month period between July 1930 and December 1931. By 1931, the new AECs had proved themselves and much of the steam behind the Chiswick project evaporated.

The engine for the Chiswick CB and CC chassis was of advanced design, with six cylinders of 100 mm bore and 130 mm stroke, identical in dimension to the AEC's A136 and A140 and said to have been built by Meadows. The cylinder block and crankcase was a one-piece construction with wet cylinder liners and with the crankshaft carried in seven main bearings. The inclined overhead valves were operated via push rods and rockers from a mid-mounted camshaft and the combustion chamber was wedge-shaped. It is perhaps significant that by the end of 1933, all the Chiswick chassis had received AEC engines.

By 1939, in suburban London and in many provincial cities, the six-wheeler, in trolleybus rather than motorbus guise, had proved itself a capable alternative to the tram as a mass mover of people.

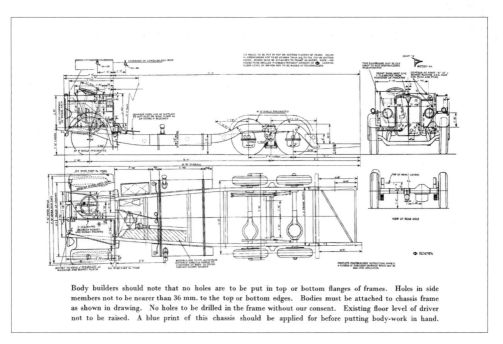

Body builders should note that no holes are to be put in top or bottom flanges of frames. Holes in side members not to be nearer than 36 mm. to the top or bottom edges. Bodies must be attached to chassis frame as shown in drawing. No holes to be drilled in the frame without our consent. Existing floor level of driver not to be raised. A blue print of this chassis should be applied for before putting body-work in hand.

By 1929, interest in the three-axled chassis generally was on the wane but having proved to its own satisfaction the economics of the type with the ADC's Type 802 'London Six', the London General Omnibus Company had plans to construct its own chassis at Chiswick. It was against this background that the Renown chassis was designed and built, primarily with the requirements of the LGOC in mind. Shown is the short 16-foot 6-inch wheelbase Type 663 Renown. (*Drawing: AEC, Author's collection*)

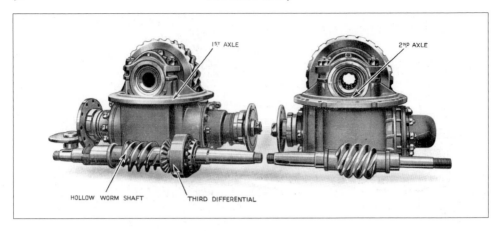

The third differential eliminated the build up of stresses between the two axles which would naturally occur where, either due to wear or deflation, there was a miss-match in the effective rolling radius of the tyres. In construction, the differential unit was carried on the drive shaft, which passed through the hollow worm on the leading axle, and the bevel gears within the differential meshed with those on the leading axle worm and the output shaft to the second worm shaft. (*Photograph: AEC, Author's collection*)

Details published in the AEC Gazette in September 1929 indicate that three Renown chassis, one of 16-foot 6-inch wheelbase and two of 18 feet 7 inches, had been built prospectively for service with the LGOC. In the short term, of the three, it was only the short wheelbase chassis which was taken up by the LGOC. Fitted with a Chiswick-built, fifty-four-seat open staircase body, as LT1, the vehicle was placed in experimental service working route 16A between Cricklewood and Victoria Station in August 1929. (*Photograph: London Transport Museum U5776*)

LTs numbered 2–50 all had open staircase bodies and square dash panel cabs, much the same as LT1 save that the seating capacity had been increased from fifty-four to sixty. The curved dash panel was introduced on LT51 and the enclosed staircase fifty-six-seat body followed on LT151. LT 511 had been built in June 1931 with engine A145A/1079, a D124 gearbox and triple servo brakes. By September 1934 it had been converted to A165 and is seen here in September 1934 standing over at Victoria. (*Photograph: G. H. F. Atkins via Alan Townsin*)

Featured in the Renown brochure dated October 1931, by a process of elimination the chassis illustrated has been identified as one of three, 664058, 059 or 060. All three had been built on 20 October 1930 and all shared the same specification: A145 engine, D119 gearbox, F133 and F134 rear axles and triple servo brakes. Crucial in their identification were the 36 inch by 8 inch India tyres. Chassis 664058 and 059 with Berw bodywork went to Abercynon and 060 became AEC's Beadle-bodied demonstration coach MV468. Note the driver's seat hung on the bulkhead panel. Useful, uncomfortable and still in common use twenty years later. (*Photograph: AEC 3509, Author's collection*)

KF2097 was one of two Renowns supplied to Liverpool Corporation in June 1930. The imposing bodies were constructed in the Corporation's own workshops. The chassis numbers of these two vehicles were 664053 and 054 and the engines A145/20 and 21. KF2097 is seen in St John's Lane, near the Old Haymarket. (*Photograph: AEC, Author's collection*)

The Anglo American Oil Company was at the forefront in the use of extravagant, eye-catching vehicles to publicise their product. With three Regent tankers already on the road, Anglo placed these three Renowns in service in October 1931. The cabs, built by Weymann, were to AEC's standard design and the unusual five-compartment, 2,500-gallon spirit tanks were produced by the Steel Barrel Company. The chassis, to near-standard specification, had modifications listed under XU558 dated 19.3.31. The chassis were 664061, 062 and 113 and the engines A144/3, A144/2 and A144/1 respectively. The silencers were mounted just below the radiator. The tyres, of Dunlop manufacture, were high-pressure 38 inch by 9 inch at the front and 44 inch by 12 inch at the rear. (*Photograph: AEC, Author's collection*)

AEC's demonstrator MV3711, 664226, was the first of the Renowns to work Swansea's testing 1½-mile Town Hill route. Petrol-engined (A162) and fitted with Daimler-built fluid transmission, its performance was sufficiently encouraging for South Wales Transport to order five similar vehicles but powered by the A165 oil engine. The demonstrator, MV3711, was purchased by South Wales in June 1933 and fitted with an A165 engine in September 1933. With front entrance thirty-eight-seat Park Royal body, it is seen here at Town Hill when new. (*Photograph: Author's collection*)

Short Bros had built the double-deck body on Renown 0664243 in October 1933 in time for the Commercial Motor Show at Olympia in November. The fifty-three-seat low height coach was finished in the colours of White's Motors but was ultimately sold to Westcliff Motor Services in July 1934. It is seen here on 28 May 1934, posed on the AEC's sports field with the Cierva Autogiro. Among the assembled company, fourth and fifth from the left, are Charles Reeve, recently appointed to the office of Chairman of the AEC, and Juan de la Cierva, the Autogyro's inventor. (*Photograph: AEC L1587, Author's collection*)

6

The Mercury Type 640 and Monarch Type 641

THE TYPE 640 MERCURY

The type 640 Mercury was the smallest of the new Rackham-designed range of commercial chassis and was exhibited at the Commercial Show at Olympia in November 1929. With a payload of only 3½ tons and a platform space no longer than 14 feet, it was never likely to be employed on long-distance operations but it quickly became an established favourite with the fuel companies for the local distribution of motor spirit and lubricants. By November 1931 its payload rating had been increased to 4 tons, now the same as the mechanically similar forward-control Monarch. In November 1933 the chassis was shown as having a gross load capacity of 5 tons (i.e. body plus payload), which still equated to about 4 tons nett. The dry chassis weight in its original petrol-engined form was 2 tons 19 cwts and ready for the road, 3 tons 6 cwts. The oil-engined chassis (introduced in 1933) was 7 cwts heavier. Literature produced in October 1935 gave it a rating of 10 tons gross. When first introduced, the Mercury had a list price of £775 on 34 inch x 7 inch pneumatics and £710 on 920 mm x 120 mm solids. Its last listed price, in January 1935, was £700 if fitted with the petrol engine and £850 if oil-engined.

The A139 and A163 petrol engines

The overhead camshaft four-cylinder A139 engine was similar in all its principal features to the larger six-cylinder A136 and A137 engines of the Regent and Regal. The drive to the camshaft was via duplex chain from the front of the crankshaft and a pair of 2:1 helical gears, so arranged that the cylinder head could be removed without disturbing the timing chain. The teeth on the camshaft gears were cut somewhat deeper than standard to allow for variation in head gasket thickness and backlash was taken up in the smaller, split, spring-loaded helical gear.

The cast iron cylinder block was totally free of encumbrance and could be replaced with the minimum of effort. The die-cast, aluminium pistons were of the split skirt type. The crankcase was cast in aluminium alloy and the five bearing crankshaft was pressure lubricated. The main bearings were of 70 mm diameter and crankpins of 60 mm diameter. The oil pressure was controlled through an interlinking of the oil pressure relief valve and the throttle linkage, 80 lbs/square inch being obtained at full load and 5 lbs/square inch at idle. In this manner, the oiling of plugs at tick-over was avoided.

Of 112 mm bore and 130 mm stroke, the A139 was rated at 31.1 hp. It had a swept volume of 5.12 litres and a power output of 38 bhp at 1,000 rpm and 65 bhp at 2,000 rpm. No extravagant claims were made for the A139 in respect of the upper limit of its rotational speed, unlike the six-cylinder engine, which was said to have a range from 300 to 3,000 rpm. The later 'high-power' A163 engine (still of 112 mm bore but producing 80 bhp at 2,400 rpm) featured two additional balance cams on the camshaft working against spring-loaded plungers. These went some way to smooth out the harmonic vibrations inherent in the four-cylinder engine and so equipped, the four-cylinder engine enjoyed the same 300 to 3,000 rpm range of its six-cylinder stable-mate.

The carburettor, dynamo and magneto were all grouped on the nearside of the engine, with the dynamo and magneto driven in tandem from the rear of the timing case. The water pump shared the same drive and was face mounted on the front of the timing case and the fan was driven from the timing chain top sprocket shaft. Electric starting for the A139 engine was not deemed necessary. The elegant and distinctive radiator was carried on the engine's front mounting and braced at the top by a bracket attached to the cylinder head. In this manner, it was totally isolated from any chassis-induced stresses.

Chassis details

The Mercury chassis was of 14-foot wheelbase, had an overall length (exclusive of the starting handle) of 20 feet 1½ inches and a maximum width, over the front mudguards, of 7 feet. A chassis of 10-foot wheelbase for tipper and tractor unit applications became available from late 1933. The frame itself had a depth of 8 inches, a flange of 3 inches and material thickness of 5/16 inches. The clutch and gearbox, J138 and D119 respectively, were of the same type as fitted to the Regent and Regal, save that in respect of the gearbox, the selector mechanism was re-arranged so that the gear lever operated the gear selectors directly. The gear ratios were: 1st, 4.37:1; 2nd, 2.69:1; 3rd, 1.594:1; and 4th, 1:1; which with a rear axle ratio of 6¼:1 provided road speeds of 7.5, 12.1, 20.5 and 32.5 mph at 2,000 rpm. Reverse was 5.33:1. The later D125 gearbox provided the same gear ratios but had a constant mesh, 'silent' third gear.

The rear axle, identified as the F135, was of the semi-floating type with an overhead worm gear carried centrally in the axle casing. The standard axle ratio was 6¼:1 but alternatives of 5 1/5, 7¼, 8¼, 9 1/3, and 10 2/3:1 were available. The rear brake drums were of 17-inch diameter and each housed two pairs of brake shoes 3¼ inches wide side by side. The footbrake was servo assisted and operated one pair of shoes and the handbrake operated the second pair. Front wheel brakes were optional, again with 17-inch diameter drums and 3¼-inch-wide shoes. November 1933 data shows that the rear brake levers were interlinked, such that operation of the footbrake worked all four shoes in the rear drums. The steering gear was of the Marles type and the ten-stud, 20-inch disc wheels carried 34 inch x 7 inch tyres, twins at the rear.

The A166 and A168 oil engines

In February 1933, the four-cylinder A166 oil engine was launched as an alternative to the A139. In November of that year it was adopted as the standard power unit in the Mercury chassis, though the petrol engine continued to be available. The A166 drew heavily on the lessons learned in the development of the six-cylinder A161, A164 and A165 oil engines. Slightly more bulky than the A139 petrol engine, it had a cylinder bore of 108 mm, a stroke of 146 mm and a swept volume of 5.35 litres. Its power output was 75 bhp at 2,000 rpm. The larger 120 mm bore variant, the A168, became available from December 1933. The power output was increased to 85 bhp at the same 2,000 rpm.

Inevitably, the oil engine was heavier than its petrol counterpart; consequently, weight saving had been high on the agenda in the design the new engine. To this end, the crankcase was cast in electron. It was heavily ribbed internally and the walls were extended well below the crankshaft centreline. The crankshaft was heavily counter-balanced to reduce dynamic loadings and was carried in five main bearings of 85 mm diameter. The crankpins were of 72 mm diameter and the connecting rods were of the four-bolt pattern. All the bearings were of the steel-backed, babbit-lined type, though in the fullness of time lead-bronze bearings would be adopted. The main bearing bolts were carried up through the crankcase to form the studs by which the cylinder block was secured.

The cylinder block was a monobloc cast-iron casting with the outer cylinders on 502 mm centres. It was fitted with renewable hardened cylinder liners, which were easily replaced when overhaul became due. The flat-topped pistons, each with four rings above the gudgeon pin and one below, were of heat-treated 'Y' alloy. The gudgeon pins were fully floating and the pistons were especially long to prevent tipping, which in turn reduced ring wear.

The cylinder head was cast in high tensile aluminium alloy and incorporated the spherical combustion chambers developed in association with Ricardo's of Shoreham. The valve gear was of similar arrangement to the four-cylinder petrol engine, the valves being operated through 90-degree rockers from the overhead camshaft. The fuel-injection equipment was manufactured by the Anglo-German company CAV-Bosch Ltd of Acton.

Production

The prototype chassis, 640001, had been built in the Experimental department and was exhibited at Olympia in November 1929. First employed as a demonstrator, it was transferred to the AEC works transport fleet in September 1930. Of the first batch of thirty production chassis, National Benzole took 640002 and 003 for work at its Willesden depot and somewhat exceptionally, Timpson's of Catford had 640004–013. These carried twenty-two-seat canvas-topped coach bodies by Harrington. Thomas Ridley of Bury St Edmunds had 640014 and Redline Motor Spirit at Battersea took 015 and 016. Beveridge & Skinner of Kirkaldy had 640017, Copeman of Norwich had 018 and chassis 019 went to AEC Australia. Agar Cross took 640020, noted as having ACLO plates and a 9 1/3:1 axle ratio. The American Oil Company took 640021–030 and Baxter & Sons of Billingsgate had 640031, with a boarded tilt body by the Eason Carriage Company.

These chassis virtually set the pattern for future deliveries. Ultimately, the Anglo American Oil Company took fifty-one chassis, National Benzole fifty-two and Timpson's, having taken ten out of the first batch, followed up with a further twelve. Redline Motor Spirit eventually had eight, Shell-Mex nine and the Texas Oil Company and the Glico Petroleum Company had one each. The Co-operative Wholesale Society had thirty spread across twelve depots. Acton had seven and Watford five, while Birmingham, Guildford and Slough had three each. Manchester and Reading each had two and Ashford, Grays, Kilbernie, Salford and Slough each had one. The London Midland & Scottish Railway had six powered by the A166 oil engine and Fred Edlin of Leicester had three 10-foot wheelbase articulated combinations fitted with the large-bore A168 oil engine. Production had started in April 1930 and continued through to May 1937. Some 274 were built.

THE TYPE 641 MONARCH

The types 640 and 641 shared an identical mechanical specification, but unlike the type 640, the 4-ton type 641 was of forward control layout. Introduced at the same time as the Mercury, it had a wheelbase of 12 feet and an overall length of 18 feet 9½ inches, which allowed for a body not exceeding 14 feet in length. A longer chassis of 14-foot wheelbase became available in 1931, the first example being recorded in May of that year. Chassis up to 641125 were all fitted with the A139 petrol engine; thereafter, the incidence of the oil engine and the high-power A163 petrol engine became ever more frequent. Axle ratios were limited to 7¼, 8¼, and 9 1/3:1. As first built, the standard tyre equipment was 38 inches by 7 inches but examples of 40 inches x 8 inches and 36 inches x 8 inches were noted on later chassis. Following the introduction of the type 647 Monarch in November 1933, the type 641 was identified as the side type Mercury. As first built, it had a list price of £850 on 38 inch x 7 inch pneumatics and £780 on 940 mm x 140 mm solids. From November 1933, both the type 640 and 641 shared the same price, £700 with the petrol engine and £850 with the oil engine.

Production

The prototype chassis, 641001, had been built in the experimental department and in October 1929 had received a fixed-sided body built by the LGOC. First employed on demonstration duties, it was transferred to the spares stores in September 1930. Production of the Monarch commenced in March 1930 and continued through to January 1937, the last built being 0641301. Mercury chassis 640026, originally supplied to the Anglo American Oil Company, was rebuilt as a forward control chassis and became 0641302.

As with the type 640, the first production batch comprised thirty chassis. Of these, the Co-operative Wholesale Society in Stockport took 641002, 003 and 025, Shell-Mex had 004–008 and 026–030. The Danish Bacon Company had 641009–013, 016 and 022. The remainder were all single deliveries. Chassis 641014 went to the Shrewsbury and Wem Brewery, 015 to the Anglo Dutch Oil Company and 017 to Isler & Co. of Southwark. Chassis 641018, 019, 020 and 021 went to W. G. Gamblin of Salisbury, the Cement Marketing Company, Miskelly & Nevin in Belfast and J. & H. Robinson of Deptford respectively. Birmingham Garages took 641023, The Medway Milling Company in Maidstone had 024 and E. J. Scivier of Botley in Hampshire 031.

Thereafter, production continued steadily and by the end of 1930, seventy chassis had been built. Many, of course, were single deliveries but the Co-operative Wholesale Society had added three to its fleet, the Danish Bacon Company had added four and Miskelly & Nevin two. The London North Eastern Railway opened its account with six, 641040–045, and the Improved Wood Paving Company of London EC took chassis 050 and 051.

In 1931 forty-five were built, with the Co-op adding a further six and the LNER two. Of the fifty-one built in 1932, the Co-op featured again with four and the LNER with six. Two of the 1932-built chassis were fitted with the newly introduced A166 oil engine and of the thirty-three type 641s built in 1933, twenty-six were so equipped. Forty-one were built in 1934, twenty-three with the type A166 and one with the 120 mm bore A168. Chassis 641216–220 marked a new development. These were five petrol-engined Tower wagons built on the 12-foot wheelbase chassis for Birmingham Corporation. The towers were built by the Eagle Engineering Company of Warwick. In order to ensure smooth progress when the men were working aloft, these chassis were fitted with fluid flywheels and pre-selective gearboxes.

The year 1935 saw the building of thirty chassis, thirteen with the A166 oil engine and five with the A168. London Transport took eight petrol-engined chassis, 641245–252, identical to those supplied to Birmingham Corporation. H. A. Newport of Cambridge had four with the A166 and the Gas, Light & Coke Company took four for work in Australia, powered by the A168.

In 1936, of the twenty-nine chassis built, ten were finished as Tower wagons. London Transport took delivery of eight, again with the petrol engine, fluid flywheel and pre-selective gearbox, and St Helens Corporation and Capetown Tramways each had one to the same London Transport specification. Six 14-foot wheelbase petrol-engined chassis were built for London Transport for use as pole carriers and Johannesburg Municipality had eight 12 foot, 1-inch wheelbase chassis for tipper work. One had the A166 oil engine and seven the high-power A163. All eight had the four-speed D136 crash gearbox, basically the same as the D124 but with a cast iron case. Finally, in January 1937, Express Dairies took a petrol-engined 12-foot wheelbase chassis and Charles Hurst, AEC's Irish agent, had a similar chassis with the A166 oiler.

The last numbered chassis, 0641302, with direct-injection 120 mm bore engine A186/121, had been converted from 640026, originally supplied to the Anglo American Oil Company in April 1930. Engine A186/121 had itself been converted from A168/914.

Road test

A road test of the Monarch, undertaken by Modern Transport, dated 9 August 1930 made interesting reading. The vehicle, thought to be 641001, clearly proclaiming its type and origin, was fitted with a fixed-sided body and carried a test load of 4 tons. It had four-wheel brakes and a non-standard final drive ratio of 6¾:1. The bare chassis weight was 2 tons 18 cwts but there was no indication of either the vehicle's unladen weight or its gross weight as tested. The test started from the Airport Hotel on Purley Way, near Croydon, and the Monarch, now well run in, had covered some 10,000 miles.

In acceleration tests, 0 to 30 mph through the gears took 20 seconds and 10 to 30 mph, on top gear only, took 14 3/5 seconds. The 1 in 5 gradient of Succombs Hill at Warlingham proved to be beyond its capability but the 1 in 6 Bug Hill was climbed without difficulty. The ascent of Titsey Hill, with a maximum gradient of 1 in 6, was completed in 4 minutes 34 seconds, mainly on 1st gear at 13 mph, but as the gradient eased, 2nd gear was engaged at 15 mph, 3rd at 22 mph and the climb was completed on 3rd gear at 27 mph. The brakes were smooth and powerful, 30 mph to zero being achieved in 4 seconds without any tendency to skid or to wheel lock. A speed of 50 mph was well within the capabilities of the Monarch, and on slightly falling ground 60 mph was achieved. Nimble, and with a turning circle of 46 feet, the testers were well impressed.

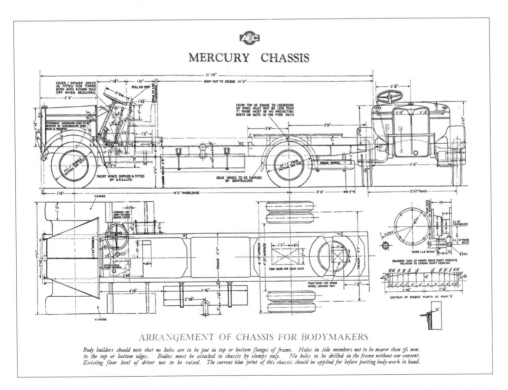

Arrangement drawing of the Mercury chassis taken from AEC sales brochure No. 98, dated March 1931. (*Drawing: AEC, Author's collection*)

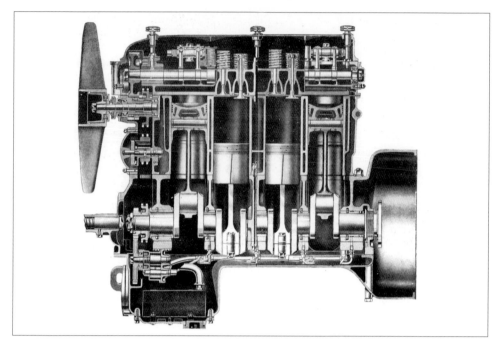

Though the four-cylinder oil engine had been available from the early months of 1933, the four-cylinder 112 mm bore A139 petrol engine and the similarly sized but more powerful A163, seen here, remained a popular fitment through to the end of the Mercury's production in May 1937. (*Drawing: AEC, Author's collection*)

As first built, the Mercury had a wheelbase of 14 feet, an overall length of 21 feet 4½ inches and an overall width of 7 feet. This allowed for a platform area of 14 feet by 7 feet. Chassis of shorter wheelbase could be specified to suit individual applications. (*Photograph: AEC, Author's collection*)

Billingsgate fish merchants Baxter & Son purchased Mercury 640031, GJ 9596, in April 1930. The boarded tilt body was built by the Eason Carriage Company. Behind, in stark contrast, stands the LNER's horse-drawn, steel-tyred lurry, noted as having a tare weight of 1 ton 8 cwt 2 qrs and a load capacity of 5 tons. (*Photograph: Author's collection*)

Anglo American. Redline, Texas Oil, Shell Mex and the National Benzole Company all found the Mercury well suited for the local delivery of fuel and oil. GO 9605 was one of fifty-two Mercurys supplied to the National Benzole Company between April 1930 and March 1935 and is seen here in attendance of Sir Alan Cobham's ex-Imperial Airways Handley Page W10-2 *City of Pretoria*. Clearly dedicated to this particular duty and immaculately presented, the Dunlop 'Trakgrip' tyres on the rear axle allow for off road travel. (*Photograph: AEC L921, via BCVM, Leyland*)

Altogether more modern in appearance than its predecessor, AVX 361, 640233, was the second of Green's Mercurys. As first introduced, the Mercury had a payload rating of 3½ tons. By 1934, the weights had been re-evaluated. Complete and ready for the road, the chassis had a weight of 3 tons 12 cwts and a gross weight of 9 tons 12 cwts. Green's Mercury would have had a tare weight in the order of 4 tons 15 cwts and a useful payload approaching 5 tons. (*Photograph: Author's collection*)

GJ 4448 was one of ten similar vehicles, 641004–008 and 026–030, supplied to Shell Mex Ltd in May and June 1930. The cab, described as being of AEC's fully enclosed pattern, was built by Bonallack and the body by Carriemore. Unusual to modern eyes, the widely spaced headlamps regularly featured on AEC commercial vehicles in the early 1930s. (*Photograph: AEC, Author's collection*)

A long-established papermakers in the Midlothian town of Penicuick, Alex Cowan & Sons Ltd took delivery of Monarch SY 4914, 641165, in March 1933. With the cab built by Weymann and the body by Bayley's, it had a licensing weight of 4 tons 3 cwts 2 qrs 11 lbs. While the Dunlop tyres were a regular fitment, the front wheel brakes, fitted here, were optional. Its engine, A139/392, was changed for 7.7 litre A173/8101 in January 1947. (*Photograph: AEC, Author's collection*)

A. E. Gash of Bitterne was one of the earliest operators to take delivery of an oil-engined Monarch. With engine A166/77, chassis 641168 had been built on 22 August 1933 and like Cowans's 641165 above, featured front wheel brakes. As yet unregistered, it is seen outside the works of Osborne & Hasell, which company had apparently constructed the cab and body. (*Photograph: AEC L1410, Author's collection*)

7

The Majestic Type 666 and Mammoth Type 667

Introduced at Olympia in November 1929, the Majestic and Mammoth chassis were the heaviest of the load carriers in AEC's new range of chassis. The normal control (or bonneted) Majestic was rated as having a carrying capacity of 6 tons while the forward control Mammoth was deemed capable of carrying 7–8 tons. The two chassis were generously specified and mechanically identical, save that the Majestic had eighteen leaves in the front springs and seventeen somewhat thicker leaves at the rear while the Mammoth had twenty leaves at the front and eighteen at the rear. Further, the standard tyre equipment for the Majestic was 40 inches x 8 inches while those on the Mammoth were 42 inches x 9 inches. Both chassis were seen as suitable for drawing a 5-ton trailer. The Majestic chassis carried a list price of £1,060 and the Mammoth £1,160. The driver's cab was an additional £60. In November 1930, the Majestic with the A155 oil engine was priced at £1,360.

The regulation detailing the maximum permissible gross weight for a heavy motor car had been set at 12 tons in 1904, and indeed was to remain so for the four-wheeler until 1955, though local authorities had the ability to impose lesser weights if deemed necessary. The relevant Heavy Motor Car Order 1904, Article V. (2.) reads:

> The registered axle-weight of an axle of a heavy motor car shall not exceed eight tons, and the sum of the registered axle weights of all the axles of a heavy motor car shall not exceed twelve tons.

> (Additional regulations were drawn up in 1927 and 1930 to cover the emerging three and four-axled vehicle types.)

It was not until the late 1920s, with the arrival of the giant pneumatic tyre, that motor vehicles began to approach the legal limits of speed and gross weight. With the pneumatic tyre also came the growth in the road transport industry and the establishment of the long-distance haulier, much to the distress of the railway companies. Within the industry were the few who knew the law in respect of permitted gross weight and the many who did not. Most were prepared to load the vehicle according to their own arbitrary limits. The commercial reality was then, and so remains, the higher the payload, the greater the reward.

It was against this background that AEC's two heavyweight chassis were introduced. The Majestic, if laden to its rated six-ton capacity, remained acceptably within the

British legal limit but the 7–8 ton Mammoth was well in excess of it. Nevertheless, with their generous specification and high performance, both found a ready market.

THE TYPE 666 MAJESTIC

Specification

The Majestic chassis had a wheelbase of 16 feet 7 inches, an overall length of 24 feet 10¼ inches and a clear body-space of 16 feet 6 inches. The wheel-track measurement was 6 feet 3 inches at the front and 5 feet 8½ inches at the rear and the overall chassis width, over the front mudguards, was 7 feet 5 inches. The width over the rear tyres was 7 feet 4 inches. The frame had a width of 3 feet and had a laden height of 3 feet 0 5/8 inches. The side-members were of 5/16ins thick nickel steel, 10 inches deep with 3½-inch flanges. The front springs were 4 feet long and the rears 5 feet.

The six-cylinder A141 petrol engine was of 110 mm bore and 130 mm stroke, giving a capacity of 7.412 litres. With an RAC rating of 45 hp it produced 56 bhp at 1,000 rpm and 110 bhp at 2,500 rpm on a compression ratio of 5 to 1. The later A162, with the same cylinder dimensions but with the high-power head, produced 120 bhp at 2,400 rpm. The general features of the engine are as described for the Regent in Chapter 2, to which the reader is referred. The radiator was the longer, high-capacity N134.

The J138 clutch and D123 gearbox were standard units, the gearbox having the following ratios: 1st, 4.37:1; 2nd, 2.69:1; 3rd, 1.59:1; and 4th, direct. Reverse was 5.33:1. By 1931 the D123 gearbox had given way to the four-speed 'silent third' D126 but having the same ratios. At 2,500 engine rpm, on 40 inch x 8 inch tyres and with an 8.1:1 axle ratio, the road speeds in the various gears were: 1st, 7.62 mph; 2nd, 12.5 mph; 3rd, 21.0 mph; and 4th, 33.87 mph. Reverse was 6.25 mph.

The rear axle was a heavy-duty double-reduction type with fully floating hubs, identified as the F137. The reduction gear was carried in a separate steel case, and on early chassis, this was a two-piece construction. Later types had a one-piece case. The primary reduction was via spiral bevel gearing and the secondary through double helical gears. The differential gears were of the bevel type and the half shafts of 100-ton steel were of 2¼ins dia. The standard axle ratio was 8.1:1 with alternatives of 7, 9 1/3 and 10.6:1, the ratio variations being effected through the spiral-bevel gears.

A single vacuum servo operated the brakes on both front and rear axles. The front drums were of 17-inch diameter and those at the rear 20 inches. The brake shoes were 3¼ inches wide with 7/16-inch thick linings. From 1931 the lining thickness was increased to ¾ inch. The footbrake and handbrake operated independently with separate brake shoes side by side in the rear drums. On late chassis, through an interlinking of the footbrake and handbrake levers, operation of the footbrake caused both the footbrake and the handbrake cams to be operated in tandem. When lining wear caused the cam angularity to approach 45 degrees, rubbing plates interposed between the cam and the brake shoe restored the situation. The front brakes were operated through rods and levers and finally via push rods, which operated through the hollow king-pins. This arrangement ensured that the brakes were unaffected by steering angularity.

Servo-assisted hydraulic brakes were adopted in 1933. Greatly increased braking power was claimed but this of course would depend on the relative sizes of the servo and the master cylinder. The claim of full compensation could however be well justified. A single vacuum servo operated the master cylinder from whence fluid under pressure was transmitted to the brake operating cylinders. The cylinders for the rear brakes were standard Lockheed pattern and were self-adjusting. The front brake cylinders were of AEC manufacture and were incorporated in the hollow king-pins. The handbrake on both the Majestic and the early Mammoth chassis was of the simple ratchet and pawl type. Later Mammoth chassis had the multi-pull variety.

The steering gear was of Marles manufacture and a steering lock of 45° provided a turning circle of 65 feet.

The Majestic was first shown as having a dry chassis weight of 3 tons 12 cwts, though with the passage of time, this inevitably increased. With cab and lightweight flat platform body, it would have had a licensed weight in the order of 4 tons 19 cwts. Adding 6 cwts for fuel, oil, water, batteries and spare wheel, the weight, ready for the road, would be about 5 tons 5 cwts, which allowed a payload of 6 tons 15 cwts. A 1,500-gallon spirit tanker would have had a licensed weight of around 6 tons and an insulated milk tanker perhaps as much as 7 tons.

Production details

The prototype Majestic had been built in the experimental department and was fitted with a cab and body built by the LGOC in September 1929. It was exhibited at Olympia in the livery of the Cement Marketing Company in November and delivered to that Company on 30 December 1929. The first production batch of forty-nine chassis was built in the period April 1930 to February 1931 and successive orders resulted in a total of 147 chassis being built, the last in June 1936.

Deliveries of the first forty or so chassis through 1930 had tended very much toward single units and of these, Oswald Tillotson, AEC's Yorkshire distributor, had secured orders for nine. From that time, multiple deliveries became more common. Truman, Hanbury & Buxton, having taken delivery of a single chassis in 1930, followed up with a further five in 1931. These particular vehicles were much modified in 1934 and 1935, when both the front and rear axles were moved rearward, the front by about 3 feet and the rear by 1 foot, much in the manner of the then-current Leyland Rhino. This was done in order to bring the axle loadings closer to the required 4 tons front, 8 tons rear when working at the legal limit.

As agent for the individual societies, the Co-operative Wholesale Society had taken its first Majestic in May 1931 and in due time twenty-one were to pass through its hands. Of these, Stratford Co-op had seven, Cricklade in Wiltshire five and Manchester four. Claydon in Suffolk had two and Ipswich, Uttoxeter and Clapham each had one. Thomas Glover and R. A. Main together had ten. Thus far, all had been petrol-engined, either A141 or A162. Pickfords became the second largest user of the type, having taken delivery of eighteen during 1932 and 1933. The first ten had been powered by the then-new A164 oil engine and the remainder by the A165. Slightly cautious, Vaux brewery in Sunderland had two with the A162 and one with the A165.

Exports

On the export side, Agar Cross in Montevideo took a single petrol-engined chassis with a 10 1/3:1 axle in 1930. AEC's Canadian offshoot had a single left-hand drive chassis, 666033, with the A141 engine in 1931. It returned to Southall in 1937 and was found a new home with a Mr Fitzpatrick in Ireland. Astro Romano SA in Bucharest had a similar left-hand drive chassis, 666142, but with the high-power A162 engine. Three were despatched to Australia, again, all A162-powered. The Marquis de Sales, AEC's agent in Madrid, took eight, three with the A141 petrol engine and five with the A165 oiler. Two A165-engined, left-hand drive chassis, 0666141 and 144, built to XU1168, were supplied to Hermes for the Societe Anonyme d' Industrie, de Commerce et des Transportes in Athens. The last three chassis in this series, 0666145, 146 and 147, were unique. Also with left-hand steering, they were powered by the A171 7.7 litre oil engine. Apart from the Mark 1 rear axle, they had more in common with the Mark II Matador. Equipped for trailer work, they were exported to Egypt for work in the Sukari gold mines in June 1936.

Road test (Oil-engined chassis)

Probably on account of the ease of access afforded by the bonneted layout, Majestic chassis 666011 and 666028 were employed extensively in the development of the six-cylinder A155, A161, A164 and A165 oil engines.

The experimental department's Majestic had acted as host chassis for much of the development work on the A155 oil engine. It was natural then that the first road test of what was described as 'Britain's First Really High Speed Oil Engine' should have been made with this vehicle. AEC had, since 1928, been engaged in the development of the oil engine, the intention being that it would ultimately replace the petrol engine. It was not claimed that AEC had reached perfection with this engine, but it did mark the point where significant progress had been made and where selected operators could evaluate the engine in everyday service. One of the requirements set for the oil engine was that it should have the same speed range as the petrol engine, i.e. 300 rpm to 3,000 rpm.

The road test was conducted by The Commercial Motor in November 1930 and comprised a 30-mile outward journey on the A40 to a point beyond High Wycombe and return to Southall. Prior to the test, the chassis had covered some 5,000 miles with the experimental department and with the exception of the engine, the chassis was to the standard specification. The tyres were Dunlop 40 inch x 8 inch and the rear axle ratio was 9.33 to 1. The six-cylinder A155 engine was of 110 mm bore and 142 mm stroke and developed 95 bhp at 2,500 rpm and the chassis was loaded to 11 tons 3 cwts 3 qrs (11 tons 7 cwts 2 qrs with driver and two observers).

On the road, the maximum speed was found to be 39.15mph (corrected), at which speed the engine was turning close to 2,900 rpm, and the minimum speed on the ascent of the new Dashwood Hill was 18 mph in 3rd gear. This represents 2,150 rpm. The fuel used was gas oil with a specific gravity of 0.885 and it was said that any other fuel oil of a similar specific gravity would be suitable. Three sets of fuel consumption figures were taken:

1. High Wycombe towards Oxford, including the ascent of the new Dashwood Hill, 8.87 miles including 1.3 miles on 3rd gear, 1.45 gallons or 6.1 mpg at an average of 22.2 mph.
2. Turning about, 8.87 miles return to High Wycombe on top gear throughout, restricting the speed to 25 mph, 0.65 gallons or 13.6 mpg at an average of 19.7 mph.
3. High Wycombe to the AEC works, 21.22 miles, 2.45 gallons or 8.66 mpg at an average of 21.9 mph.

Overall, fuel had been consumed at a rate of 9.45 mpg at an average speed of 21.26 mph.

Acceleration from rest to 26.1 mph (corrected speed) using 2nd, 3rd and top gears took 36 seconds and braking from the same speed to standstill, using both foot brake and hand brake together, occupied 45 feet.

Road test (petrol-engined chassis)

A petrol-engined example of the Majestic was road tested by Motor Transport in October 1931. It was carried on standard 40 inch x 8 inch tyres and had an axle ratio of 8.1 to 1. With 50 gallons of petrol on board, the chassis was laden to a gross weight of 11 tons 17 cwts and the two drivers would bring the all-up weight to 12 tons. Leaving Southall, the 56-mile test route went to Watford by way of Harrow-on-the-Hill, Wealdstone and Bushey, thence to Kings Langley, Berkhamsted, Chesham and Rickmansworth, returning again to Southall via Watford. Of the vehicle, it was said:

> It was found to be easy to maintain a steady speed on the level of between 30 and 35 m.p.h. At this rate of travel the engine was reasonably quiet and free from vibration, the suspension was excellent and the steering as light and accurate as one could desire.

In the face of a strong head wind and in driving rain, a maximum speed of 43 mph was recorded on Watford by-pass and it was later discovered that a gradient of 1 in 8 could be surmounted on 2nd gear without undue stress. Scotts Hill between Rickmansworth and Croxley Green, with a maximum gradient of 1 in 7, was also climbed on 2nd gear, but had the gradient not eased, a change into the lowest ratio would have been necessary. On returning to Southall, it was found that 9½ gallons of petrol were required to refill the tank, which reflected a fuel consumption of 5.9 mpg. The running time for the test had been 2 hours 50 mins and the average speed was 19.76 mph. Braking and acceleration tests were carried out in dry, level conditions within the factory boundary. The foot brake brought the vehicle to rest from 20 mph in 52 feet and the hand brake in 100 feet 9 inches. Using both foot brake and hand brake together brought the vehicle to rest in 32 feet 6 inches. Acceleration from 0 to 30 mph through the gears took 41 seconds. Tractive resistance was measured at 25 lbs/ton.

The name Majestic was dropped in November 1933 and the Type 666 became known as the bonneted Mammoth.

THE TYPE 667 MAMMOTH

Of the 7–8 ton Mammoth, it was written in the AEC Gazette of November 1929:

> This vehicle has been designed as a high-speed goods-carrying vehicle of large overload capacity in accordance with the most modern and advanced engineering practice.

By 1930 the wind of change was blowing. The Road Traffic Act, with all its ramifications, had received Royal assent in August 1930 and enforcement was becoming more rigorous. By January 1931, AEC no longer described the Mammoth as a 7–8 tonner but simply as a heavy-duty goods vehicle. There is no doubt that had there been an increase in the permitted gross weight of the four-wheeler in the 1930 Road Traffic Act, the Mammoth would have been the leader in its class. As it was, many spent their lives working on the wrong side of the law.

Specification

The Mammoth, as first built, was powered by the six-cylinder overhead camshaft A143 petrol engine of 110 mm bore and 130 mm stroke. It delivered 110 bhp at 2,500 rpm. The chassis was offered with two alternative lengths of wheelbase, 16 feet 7 inches being the standard with an alternative of 13 feet 6 inches for tipper applications. The long wheelbase chassis had an overall length of 24 feet 11 inches and a platform area of 20 feet by 7 feet 6 inches. The front track measured 6 feet 3 inches and the rear track 5 feet 8 5/8 inches. The width (on 42 inch by 9 inch tyres) over the front wheel-hubs was 7 feet 5 inches and over the rear tyres 7 feet 6 inches. It had a bare chassis weight of 4 tons. The oil engine, first in its A155 form, had been available from about August 1930 and the 'dual high' D125 auxiliary gearbox with ratios of 1.58:1 and 1:1, produced for the Mammoth Major in 1931, was quickly adopted as standard.

Despite its high unladen weight, the popularity of the Mammoth as a trailer model continued undiminished through 1932 and into 1933. By 1933, now with the A165 engine and the auxiliary gearbox fitted as standard, (which together had added 12 cwts) the chassis weight ready for the road had grown to 4 tons 19 cwts. The chassis was described as having a gross load capacity, i.e. cab, body and payload, of 7 tons 1 cwt and this allowed for a legal carrying capacity in the order of 5 tons 16 cwts. Used in conjunction with a trailer, the permitted gross weight was 22 tons, which in turn provided a payload of about 13 tons.

Road test (petrol-engined chassis)

The Mammoth prototype was tested by the Commercial Motor in March 1930 and, ready for the road, had an unladen weight of 5 tons 5 cwts. Carrying an 8-ton payload, it turned the scales at 13 tons 5 cwts. The vehicle was already well run in having covered some 10,200 miles and impressed by the vehicle's sparkling performance, the Commercial Motor road test staff described the Mammoth as 'A Large-capacity Goods Vehicle with a Coach-type Performance'. Despite its laden weight of 13¼ tons, its 110 bhp petrol engine was sufficient to propel it to 30 mph in 40 seconds and a speed of 45 mph was attained in comfort. (It should be remembered that the legal maximum was 20 mph.) The axle ratio was 9 1/3:1 and at 45 mph the engine was turning at 3,320 rpm. Hill climbing was equally effortless and a restart on a gradient of 1 in 7 was possible on 2nd gear. Under undulating conditions, the fuel consumption averaged 6¼ mpg at an average speed of 23.5 mph. Braking from 30 mph to rest required 80 feet.

If further proof of its ability was needed, an illustration in the AEC Gazette of March 1930 shows the Mammoth demonstrator MY2127, 667001, outside Odhams Press in London's Long Acre, unloading 9 tons of newsprint, brought in from the paper mills in Kent.

Production

The Mammoth prototype, 667001, had been built in the experimental department and despatched, first to the LGOC on 10 September 1929, thence to Medley, Brooker & Smith on 4 October, for the mounting of cab and body. Registered MY2127, it served as a demonstrator until seconded to AEC's North Road service depot as a towing lorry.

Production of the Mammoth chassis started in May 1930 and by the end of the year 136 had been built. Ninety-eight were built in 1931 and a further ninety-three in 1932. In 1933 the number fell to forty-five and in 1934 to only ten. Two were built in 1935. The highest chassis number recorded was 667386, converted from 666127 in July 1936 at AEC's North Road depot. Chassis 667383 is recorded as not having been built. The number of Mammoth chassis actually built was therefore 384.

Tillotson's featured strongly in the sale of the Mammoth, no fewer than 115 being shown as having passed through that agency. Of the larger fleets, Bouts Bros of Bow are recorded as having taken eleven Mammoths for their intensive night trunk operations. It was said that these vehicles each covered in the order of 60,000 miles in a year, which in 1932 was a quite prodigious mileage. Fairclough had eleven and

L. Terry ten. Hall & Co., the sand and gravel producers of Redhill. had nine tippers on the shorter 13-foot, 6-inch wheelbase chassis. Ryburn United Transport of Bradford had eight. Bowaters took delivery of sixteen in 1933, of which eight worked between Northfleet in Kent and the newspaper offices in London. The remaining eight worked between the then-new paper mill at Ellesmere Port and Manchester.

The articulated Mammoth

Three 10-foot, 6-inch wheelbase chassis were built to XU482 for operation with the Carrimore single-axled semi-trailer. Chassis 667140 was the first with petrol engine A141/165, built for H. Sutton of Yarmouth in December 1930. Pickfords had 0667258, built in April 1932, powered by oil engine A164/25, and Jewson & Sons of Norwich had 0667378 with engine A165/1023, built in September 1934. Together with its trailer, Sutton's Mammoth had a licensed weight of 8 tons 2 cwts and was, in 1930, extravagantly described as a 12-tonner.

Conversions

The fact that it was not legally possible for the Mammoth to carry its rated 7–8 ton payload was sufficient incentive for some operators to have it rebuilt as a six or eight-wheeled Mammoth Major. The additional trailing axle, springs and associated gear added just 30 cwts to the chassis weight and the un-braked second steering axle added a further 15 cwts. With legal gross weights of 19 and 22 tons for the three and four-axled machines, genuine payloads of 11½ and 13½ tons could be achieved.

Six chassis, 667007, 024, 130, 251, 264 and 281, are known to have been rebuilt as Mammoth Major 6s. Four other chassis, 0667298, 317, 359 and 360, all owned by Fairclough, were rebuilt as Mammoth Major 8s in the early months of 1935.

In April 1934 AEC announced a new and lighter trailing axle conversion for the Mammoth. Six hundredweights lighter than the standard two-spring bogie, it employed the same driving and trailing axles but featured a four-spring balance beam suspension, similar to that which became standard on the six and eight-wheeled Mark II chassis in 1935. Two Mammoth chassis, 0667217 and 667234, were so converted.

Three chassis, 0667379, 381 and 382, were built new in October 1934 with the A165 engine and the same lightweight bogie and were designated 0667/17. Chassis 0667384 was different again, built as an eight-wheeler and powered by the A171 7.7 litre oil engine.

In Conclusion

Until 1933, regulation of the road haulage industry itself had been minimal. Having put the necessary bodies in place for the regulation of the passenger vehicle industry in 1930, Government now turned its attention to the road haulage sector. The Road and Rail

Traffic Act, which came into effect on 1 January 1934, brought in new controls and the traffic commissioners had the authority to impose sanctions where there had been a failure to comply with the statutory conditions regarding speed, weight or hours of duty.

Added to this, from 1 January 1934 there were to be increased rates of road fund duty on the goods-carrying motor vehicle. Taxation was based on the unladen weight of the vehicle. The new scale started at £50 for vehicles of up to 4 tons unladen, increasing by £20 for each additional ton or part of a ton. The effect of these increased sums on overall operating cost were only marginal, but taken in isolation were sufficient to send waves of panic throughout the transport industry. Moreover, the 12-ton limit of gross weight for a four-wheeled vehicle was to remain in force. By the end of 1933, then, there were new and urgent pressures to reduce the unladen weight of the vehicle, not so much for the reduction of the tax burden but to maximise the vehicle's carrying capacity. It was these factors which led to the introduction of the lighter Mark II range of goods chassis in 1935.

On a personal note

Our own Mammoth, 667288, VN3990, was collected from Oswald Tillotson's Bradford works on August Bank Holiday Monday 1932. With a Tillotson cab and body, it had cost £1,000, an astronomical amount of money at that time but still heavily discounted. Monty, the writer's father, a keen twenty-seven-year-old, had persuaded his father to buy the new AEC as a replacement for a disappointing second-hand 5AD Saurer. Monty's grandfather's reaction to the new acquisition was 'What's tha want a great ugly thing like that for?' With a 20-foot body and a tare weight approaching 5½ tons, a vehicle of that size would rarely have been seen in Malton. Ugliness, one has to say, like beauty, was in the eye of the beholder.

The vehicle was barely a month old when the Salter Report with its recommended increases in road fund duty was published. The first thoughts were that the Mammoth would have to go back. Young Monty persuaded his father against such an action and promised that the vehicle would never be in debt. Human endeavour and long, often very long, hours of work ensured that the promise was kept.

The Mammoth had its first overhaul at 105,000 miles in 1936 and the second at 270,000 miles in 1940, when its petrol engine was replaced by a 7.7 litre A173. At this time an auxiliary gearbox was also fitted. The vacuum servo brakes were replaced by a Westinghouse compressed air system with American pattern diaphragm brake chambers in 1946 and the vehicle had its last major overhaul in 1956. By this time its licensed taxation weight had gone up to 5 tons 18 cwts. It was finally retired at the end of 1962 with a claimed mileage exceeding 1 million.

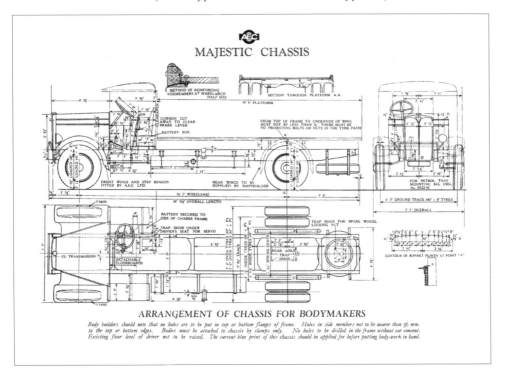

Arrangement drawing of the Majestic chassis taken from the AEC sales brochure No. 97 dated January 1931. (*Drawing AEC: Author's collection*)

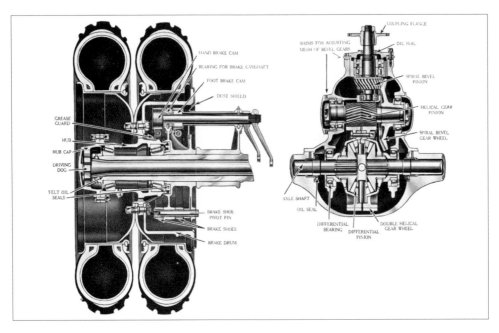

A distinguishing feature of the Majestic and Mammoth chassis, and indeed the later Matador and Mammoth Majors, was the robust proportion of its double reduction rear axle. Weighing in the order of 5 cwts, the final drive assembly was virtually indestructible. (*Illustrations: AEC, Author's collection*)

GJ 8505, 666005, was the first of six similar vehicles built for Truman, Hanbury and Buxton in April 1930. With a wheelbase of only 14 feet 7 inches, the shorter of the two options, weight distribution was always going to be a problem. In order to overcome the difficulty, late in 1934 five of the vehicles, 666005, 042, 043, 045 and 075, had the rear axles moved rearward and the front axles repositioned underneath the driver's cab, much as would be with a conventional forward control lorry. Fashionable at that time, Leyland had a similar arrangement with the Rhino. (*Photograph: AEC, Author's collection*)

C. C. Wakefield & Company had gained an enviable reputation in motor racing and aviation circles in the 1920s and 1930s with its castor oil-based lubricants and well knew the value of publicity. This smart Majestic was one of two similar vehicles, 666092 and 096, supplied in 1932 for work from its water-front oil blending factory at Hayes, only a few miles distant from Southall. (*Photograph: AEC 5203, Author's collection*)

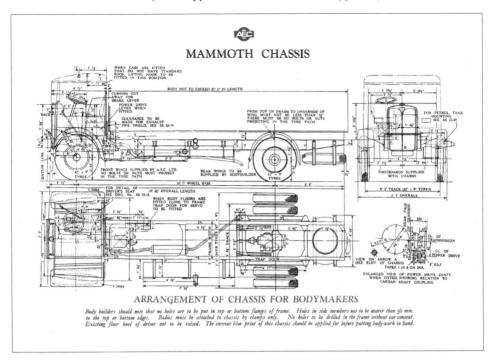

Arrangement drawing of the Mammoth chassis taken from the AEC sales brochure No. 96, dated January 1931. (*Drawing AEC, Author's collection*)

Heralding a new era in road transport, AEC was happy to promote the Mammoth as a high-speed goods-carrying vehicle of large overload capacity. JD 674 was 667052, one of three Mammoths operated by Samuel Rogers of Stratford, E15, and is seen here laden with 9 tons of newsprint. The AEC's standard cab was, in this instance, manufactured by Medley, Brooker & Smith. (*Photograph: AEC, Author's collection*)

Mammoth JG 2036, chassis 667186, had been built on 20 June 1931 for C. & G. Yeoman of Canterbury. Supplied by Stanhay Ltd of Ashford, it is seen here smartly lettered and ready for work. The cab and body were built by Weymann and the engine is noted as being A141/249. (*Photograph: AEC L586, Author's collection*)

With Tillotson cab and body, the Thackray Mammoth VN 3990, 667288, had been bought new in August 1932 at a cost of £1000. Painted in Post Office Red, lettered in Gold leaf and with a polished aluminium front panel, it stood out among lesser types. It had a licensing weight of 4tons 19cwts and is seen here on King George Dock in Hull, perhaps a year old, laden to its legal capacity with 7 tons of wheat. Behind, the Eagle trailer carries a further 4 tons. (*Photograph: Author's collection*)

8

The FWD R6T and AEC Type 850

Four Wheel Drive Motors Ltd

Seemingly lacking the necessary backing from its American parent company for its future development, the Four Wheel Drive Lorry Company Ltd entered into an agreement with the AEC on 15 October 1929 for the supply of major mechanical components. Following closely on this event, a new company, Four Wheel Drive Motors Ltd, was formed to take over the business of the Four Wheel Drive Lorry Company Ltd as a going concern. The new company was incorporated on 31 October 1929 with the Underground Electric Railways Company of London Ltd (the UERL) subscribing 51 per cent of the share capital.

Sir Ernest Clark, a board member of the London General Omnibus Company Ltd (the LGOC) since 1926, was appointed the company chairman and Charles Reeve, the recently appointed managing director of AEC, was appointed the company secretary pro tem. Henry Nyberg and Charles Cleaver, directors of the Four Wheel Drive Lorry Company Ltd, having subscribed the remaining 49 per cent of the share capital, became directors of Four Wheel Drive Motors Ltd. It was required that the Four Wheel Drive Lorry Company Ltd was wound up within 2 months of 31 October 1929. In May 1930 Reeve was appointed chairman in succession to Sir Ernest Clark.

Origins

The FWD R6T, variously identified as the R.6.T, the R/6/T, the Hardy-AEC tractor and latterly as the AEC Type 850, was the last in a line of vehicles, the origins of which could be traced back to the 3-ton American FWD Model B of 1912, built by the Four Wheel Drive Auto Company of Clintonville, Wisconsin.

The Four Wheel Drive Lorry Company Ltd had been formed in 1921 by Henry Nyberg and Charles Cleaver for the purpose of overhauling ex-military FWD chassis from the 1914–1918 conflict and adapting them for civilian applications. Henry Nyberg had come from America to run what was effectively the English branch of the American company. Charles Cleaver had been an LGOC and AEC designer at Walthamstow in pre-First World War days and had been closely associated with military transport during the war. The company established its offices at 44 Kingsway, London WC2 and the works and service departments were located in Buckingham Avenue on the Slough trading estate.

From the military FWD chassis were developed all manner of specialist four-wheel-drive and half-tracked vehicles, clearly constructed to individual customer requirements. An associated company, Hardy Rail Motors, formed in 1924, marketed a range of rail-borne vehicles and shunting locomotives, built by the Four Wheel Drive Lorry Company, which employed the same FWD mechanicals.

In May 1927, the War Office issued Specification No. 30 for the subsidy-type 'Medium' rigid framed six-wheeled lorry. Special attention was drawn to the design of the suspension for the two rear axles, which had been devised by a Lt-Col. H. Niblett. Though patented by the War Office, the design was made available to all British manufacturers in a clear attempt to promote the more rapid development of the six-wheeled subsidy chassis.

In 1927 the Four Wheel Drive Lorry Company built the R.46, a long wheelbase 6-ton, six-wheel-drive chassis. With its four-cylinder T-head Wisconsin derived engine, transfer gearbox and front wheel drive, the chassis had much in common with FWD's latest half-track design, save that the tracked bogie, a product of Roadless Traction Ltd in Hounslow, had been replaced by one of the War Office type. The half-track vehicle had been extensively tested by the Mechanical Warfare Experimental Establishment (the MWEE) at Farnborough in the role of gun tractor and, with a maximum speed of 14 mph, was judged to be too slow. The R.46, with the engine turning at the same 1,300 rpm, had a speed of 25 mph.

A more sophisticated development was the prototype R.6.T, built specifically for the War Office under contract V.1806 in 1928. Like the R.46, this six-wheel-drive gun tractor employed a version of the War Office bogie. It was rigorously tested by the MWEE through much of 1929 and despite minor failings it was judged to have good potential.

The R.6.T Prototype

The prototype R.6.T had a wheelbase of 10 feet measured from the front axle centreline to the mid-point of the rear bogie. The bogie axles were 4 feet apart and the overall axle spread was thus 12 feet. The chassis had an overall length of 18 feet 10 inches and width of 7 feet 6 inches, while the frame had a height of 3 feet 4½ inches and a depth of 8 inches. The tyres were 42 inches by 10.5 inches on demountable rims attached directly to the wheel hubs. The wheel-track measured 5 feet 11¾ inches; the ground clearance under the axles was 12 inches.

The engine was the six-cylinder side-valve Dorman 6JUL Mark 2. Of 100 mm bore and 140 mm stroke, the engine had a swept volume of 6,597 cc. It developed 57.5 bhp at the 'normal' speed of 1,300 rpm and 78 bhp at 2,000 rpm. The engine combined most of what would be seen as desirable features in a mid-1920s design. The crankcase was cast in aluminium, the crankshaft carried in four main bearings and the camshaft driven by Reynold silent chain from the front of the crankshaft. Both the cylinder block and cylinder head were one-piece castings cast in high-grade cast iron, the cylinder head having combustion chambers of the Ricardo pattern. A Still tube radiator ensured that the engine was adequately cooled.

The engine, clutch, gearbox and transfer gearbox were assembled as a single unit and carried in a sub-frame. This sub-frame was carried in the main frame on a three-point mounting, thereby obviating any problems which may have arisen with flexing of the chassis over rough ground.

The transmission comprised a four-speed main gearbox and a two-speed transfer box. The main gearbox had ratios: 1st, 4.46:1; 2nd, 2.98:1; 3rd, 1.75:1; 4th, 1:1; and Reverse was 4.46:1. At 1,300 engine rpm, these provided forward road speeds of 3.5, 5.3, 8.9 and 15.6 mph. The ratios provided in the transfer gearbox were 1:1 and 2.78:1, which in the low range provided the following overall gear ratios: 1st, 12.37:1; 2nd, 8.27:1; 3rd, 4.86:1; 4th, 2.78:1; and Reverse, 12.37:1. At the same 1,300 rpm, the relative forward road speeds were 1.3, 1.9, 3.2 and 5.6 mph. For normal road work, direct drive in the transfer gearbox was employed and only the rear axles were driven. In cross-country conditions, engagement of the lower range of gears in the transfer gearbox brought the drive to all three axles. Changing back into the high range automatically disengaged the drive to the front axle. The drawbar pull on first gear in the low range was 5.27 tons or 11,800 lbs.

As with the earlier R.46, the rear suspension closely followed the arrangement devised for the War Office. This was so arranged as to allow free up and down movement of any wheel up to 18 inches without spring or frame distortion and similarly, the bogie axles were allowed the same 18 inches of rise or fall relative to each other. Two pairs of inverted semi-elliptic leaf springs were employed in the bogie, one pair each side. One spring was mounted directly above the other and each spring pair could rock about a central pivot bracket. The axles were attached to the outer ends of the springs in a swivelling joint. The front springs were anchored at the rear end and shackled at the forward end to a transverse central pivoted rocking beam. This allowed one wheel to be raised 12 inches above the other, again without transmitting stress to the chassis frame.

In terms of ratio, all three axles were identical. The primary reduction was through a bevel gear set with a ratio of 4.31:1 and a secondary reduction in the wheel-hubs (via epicyclic gearing) had a ratio of 56/24 or 2.33:1. The overall reduction was thus 10.05:1. The drive to the front axle was conventional but that to the rear axle, because of the ultra short wheelbase of the R.6.T and the high degree of axle articulation, demanded radical thinking if propeller shaft angularity was to be kept within bounds. By carrying the propeller shafts over the top of the axles and driving the axles from behind through drop gears, the propeller shaft lengths were maximised and angularity was limited to 23 degrees.

The R.6.T's brakes were typical of 1920s practice. Neither footbrake nor handbrake had any form of servo assistance. The footbrake acted through an externally contracting band on a transmission drum and the handbrake operated conventional internally expanding shoes in drums on the four rear wheels. A patented compensating toggle linkage was claimed to provide increased leverage for the handbrake.

The steering gear was of the Marles type.

The winch was mounted transversely above the chassis frame immediately behind the driver. It carried 350 feet of ¾-inch diameter steel rope and had an automatic laying-on device which ensured that the rope was wound evenly on to the drum. The drum could be driven through any of the four gears in the main gearbox and the rope speed and pull varied according to the gear selected. The maximum pull on the top layer of rope was 7.3 tons and on the bottom layer 9.5 tons. Disconnecting the drum from the gearing allowed the rope to be payed out by hand. The winch rope passed through fair leads and rollers at the rear of the chassis and could also be brought forward through a rope guide should conditions so demand. A powerful band brake ensured control under all conditions.

As first built, the prototype R.6.T had a timber body with dimensions 8 feet 10 inches long and 7 feet 6 inches wide. Two spare wheels were carried transversely in a special gantry just forward of the body, raised or lowered by a hand-operated winch. The body was covered by a canvas tilt and a canvas hood covered the forward part of the vehicle. This body was changed for one of steel construction, probably in advance of the vehicle being handed over to the MWEE. Spare wheel stowage was changed, such that the wheels were now carried longitudinally and a canvas hood, supported at the rear on two pillars, covered the body.

Prototype Testing

The prototype R.6.T was generally identified by its civilian registration number MT 6275 but it also carried the military number T20246. It had been built under War Office contract V1806. Its chassis number was S2105 and within the MWEE it was identified as vehicle 176. MT 6275 had been received by the MWEE on 8 April 1929 and was the latest in a series of FWD vehicles to be tested by this military establishment. At the time of it being received by the MWEE it had already covered 350 miles and by 30 September 1929 the total recorded mileage was 2,125.

During testing at Farnborough and manoeuvres at Wool, the road mileage covered was 1,569 and the cross-country mileage 206. The fuel consumption, taken over the 1,776 test miles, was 3.06 mpg. Running solo, a 2-mile cross-country course in Long Valley was covered at an average speed of 14.4 mph and the flying mile on hard road was covered at a speed of 31.05 mph. No. 6 slope on Miles Hill at Farnborough (gradient 1 in 2.3), again running solo, was climbed without difficulty. With a towed load of an AA gun the speed on level hard road was 18 mph. With this same towed load, it proved impossible, even with both foot and hand brake applied, to hold the vehicle on a gradient of 1 in 6, despite the handbrake lever having been lengthened.

The winch gear was thought to be highly satisfactory. During cross-country trials at Wool, several six-wheeled vehicles weighing from 7 to 9 tons were winched out of bog with ease. At Farnborough, a 60-pounder gun and limber was hauled up No. 7 slope of Miles Hill (gradient 1 in 3) without difficulty but attempts to haul the same load up No. 6 slope (gradient 1 in 2.3) initially failed due to the driving chain jumping over the sprockets. After adjustment, this was also successful.

The performance of the Dorman engine was generally satisfactory but repairs were required to a failed big end bearing. The water pump gland, which was difficult to access, also required frequent re-packing.

Comparative Tests

In November 1929, comparative tests were made between three six-wheel-drive tractors, the Hathi, the Scammell and the R.6.T. The Hathi had an unladen weight of 7 tons 5 cwts 3 qrs, the Scammell weighed 8 tons 17 cwts 1 qr unladen and the R.6.T 8 tons 11 cwts 3 qrs. All three carried an imposed load of 1 ton and towed a 3-inch gun trailer weighing 6 tons 2 cwts. The Hathi was quickly eliminated with engine failure and took no further part in the trials. The Scammell and R.6.T were thought to have about equal performance. The R.6.T had been somewhat handicapped in greasy conditions, having comparatively smooth Dunlop tyres whereas the Scammell was fitted with Goodyear tyres with a very pronounced tread pattern.

Beacon Hill (gradient 1 in 10) was climbed by both the Scammell and the R.6.T with the gun trailer in tow, the Scammell in 2nd gear at an average of 3.7 mph and the R.6.T at 3.9 mph in 3rd gear in the low box. The Scammell proved able to hold the vehicle and trailer with either footbrake or handbrake on this gradient. The R.6.T proved successful with the footbrake but just failed with the handbrake. Overall, the R.6.T was adjudged the better vehicle on account of it having a six-cylinder engine, a more orthodox design, a shorter wheelbase and an efficient winch. Winching trials had not been made with the Scammell as the winch was thought to be unsafe.

The AEC Engine

A series of tests were made with this same prototype chassis in May 1930, the original Dorman engine having been replaced by a 100 mm bore six-cylinder AEC A136. Additionally, a set of 40 inch by 9 inch bar tread tyres had been fitted. The object of the test was to determine the maximum weight of armour that could be imposed on the tractor in addition to the normal load of eleven men, equipment and an AA gun in draught before its cross-country performance was adversely affected.

The tests were made over a 2-mile circuit and additional loading of 1½, 2½, 3½, 4 and 4½ tons progressively made. Early in the tests, a smooth climb had been made to very near the top of Miles Hill (gradient 1 in 5) with plenty of power and no wheel spin, when the engine cut out due to lack of petrol. A similar failure occurred later on Beacon Hill. (In later tests, this was diagnosed as having been caused by a vapour lock in a coil in the petrol pipe where it passed close to the exhaust pipe. Re-routing the petrol pipe overcame the problem).

Circuit times varied randomly between 15 minutes 5 seconds and 15 minutes 45 seconds with loads up to 4 tons but increased to 16 minutes 45 seconds when the load was increased to 4½ tons. Lower gears than had previously been needed were required and the vehicle failed in heavy sand due to wheel-spin and digging in.

The overall performance was thought to be impressive and when not starved of petrol, the engine pulled very well. It was considered that with an AA gun in draught, loads up to 4 tons could be carried without nullifying the performance of the vehicle as a tractor. Taking the weight of eleven men and equipment as 1 ton, there remained a margin of 3 tons for armour. The stop on Miles Hill had however again demonstrated the inability of the brakes to hold on gradients steeper than 1 in 6.

Production

The production tractor was readily distinguished from the prototype by the angular front mudguards, the taller radiator and the flat-topped driver's scuttle. The wheelbase had been reduced by 3 inches to 9 feet 9 inches and the frame depth increased by half an inch to 8½ inches. The chassis featured the six-cylinder AEC A136 engine, which produced 95 bhp at 2,500 rpm (the later AEC-built chassis had the 124 bhp A162T engine), together with an AEC clutch and four-speed D119 gearbox.

The main gearbox provided the following ratios: 1st, 4.37:1; 2nd, 2.69:1; 3rd, 1.59:1; 4th, 1:1; and reverse 5.11:1, which at 2,000 engine rpm in the high range of the transfer gearbox gave road speeds of 5.47, 8.9, 15.1 and 24 mph with reverse 4.7 mph. The low range provided a ratio of 2.78:1 and the relative speeds were 1.97, 3.19, 5.43, 8.63 and 1.71 mph. The braking system had also been re-worked, such that the transmission brake, which had been operated by the foot pedal on the prototype chassis, became the hand-brake and the rear axle drum brakes, now servo-assisted, were operated by the foot pedal. Early production chassis retained the smooth road pattern 42 inch by 10.5 inch low-pressure tyres but later chassis had Dunlop 9.00-22 Trak-grip tyres.

An initial production order under contract V1982 for nine AEC-engined R6T tractors for the War Office (now identified as the R/6/T) was completed in March 1930 and a further eight were supplied under the same contract number toward the end of 1930. Six R/6/Ts were built during 1931 and early 1932 under contracts V2138 and V2264. Slough-built R/6/Ts for the War Office, together with the prototype, totalled twenty-four. A single R/6/T chassis, numbered 3029, built in November 1931 was dismantled in October 1935. It is thought that this was the chassis exhibited on the Hardy stand at the Commercial Motor show in November 1931. At this time, the R/6/T carried a list price of £2,950.

The move to Southall

The board minutes of Four Wheel Drive Motors show that throughout the second half of 1931, the financial situation of the company had been cause for increasing concern. This was confirmed when the accounts presented at the second Annual General Meeting on 18 December 1931 showed that trading over the seventeen months ending 31 October had resulted in a loss. A brief board meeting had been held on 11 January 1932 to discuss the results for November and December 1931 and it was decided that a further meeting would be held two days later, on 13 January, when the situation would be discussed more fully.

At this meeting the chairman, Charles Reeve, pointed out that further considerable losses would be incurred should the company continue to operate under its present organisation. General discussion followed but no solution could be found which would allow the company to continue on a satisfactory basis. It was therefore resolved that manufacturing at Slough should cease and the premises be vacated as soon as possible. As there was some possibility that the American company might be interested in the name, it was resolved that the company should not go into liquidation but that, if possible, arrangements be made for AEC to manufacture at Southall such of the FWD's products as were profitable to produce. London office staff were to be given notice and the offices vacated. With the exception of such assets as would be of value at Southall, all plant, machinery, jigs, tools, patterns, furniture and fittings were to be sold.

By 7 April 1932 the necessary agreements were in place and all of the FWD's design, productive and selling operations were in the process of transfer to Southall. In consideration of the drawings, materials and plant taken over by AEC, AEC would advance FWD the sum of £10,000, which in the parlance of the day 'would enable the Company to liquidate the whole of its liabilities'. In recognition of this assistance, Messrs Nyberg and Cleaver would, for a nominal consideration, transfer the whole of their FWD shares to the AEC. AEC would then, either of itself or through its nominees, become sole shareholder in FWD. (The 30,600 A shares and 10,200 C shares held by the UERL had been transferred to AEC in April 1931.)

There was a caveat insofar as after two years the situation could be reviewed, whereby Messrs Nyberg and Cleaver could return to their previous shareholding position, but in the meantime work done by AEC for FWD would be charged at cost plus 12½ per cent. On 13 April 1932, Nyberg resigned his directorship in Four Wheel Drive Motors, but Cleaver stayed on.

Southall production

With production transferred to Southall, the R/6/T was identified as the AEC Type 850. Eight chassis, 850001–008, were built on AEC's programme EG and War Office contract V2392 in January 1933 and were bodied by Medley Brooker & Smith. Chassis 009–015 were built under programme FQ, contract V2504, in September and October 1933 and chassis 016–021, programme JH and contract V2639, were built in December 1934, all with bodywork by Duple. Under this same programme chassis 850022 was built for the Royal Laval Transport Company in February 1935. The last batch of eleven chassis, 023–033, were built under programme LO, War Office contract V2760, in April and May 1936.

The invoice price for the six chassis built under contract V2639 in 1935 was £2,135 each. The bodies, three breakdown and three anti-aircraft, were charged separately at £145 and £165 respectively. By comparison, the final batch of eleven chassis supplied in 1936 under contract V2760 (four breakdown and seven anti-aircraft) were invoiced at £2,283 15s od each and the bodies at £160.

Further MWEE Tests

MG 9549 had been assigned to the MWEE on 4 November 1930. With military identification T21011, it also carried the MWEE No. 253 and FWD chassis number 2112. This was one of the production R/6/T tractors and was fitted with 100 mm bore by 130 mm stroke AEC A136 engine. It had a Solex 40MOVL carburettor, a Simms magneto and a power output of 95 bhp at 2,500 rpm. The tyres were Dunlop Trakgrip 900-22s inflated at the front to 50 lbs/sq inch and at the rear to 45 lbs/sq inch.

Taking part in the trials at Bala in North Wales during April 1931, it had an unladen weight of 8 tons 11 cwts 0 qrs 14 lbs and carrying an imposed load of 2 tons together with 3 tow ropes, 2 scotches, 5 gallons of oil and 2 spare wheels, it had a gross laden weight of 10 tons 19 cwts 1 qr 7 lbs. Additionally, it had a load of 6 tons 16 cwts in tow. The maximum gradient climbed with this load was 1 in 5.2 and solo 1 in 3. Tests at Farnborough had shown that the limiting slope (due to wheel-spin) was 1 in 2.3 and that its maximum speed was 31 mph. Fuel consumption on the North Wales exercise was 3.43 mpg and oil consumption 316 mpg. The 48-gallon petrol tank gave it a range of 164 miles.

Following the trials, this same vehicle was fitted with a new AEC six-cylinder petrol engine of 110 mm bore. It returned to Bala in July 1931 and further tests were made to compare its performance with earlier results. The results are shown in the table below and the relevant report is quoted directly.

FWD 6WD TRACTOR WITH LARGER ENGINE
WALES TRIALS JULY 1931
COMPARED WITH TRACTORS ON WALES TRIALS APRIL 1931

APPENDIX B AVERAGE SPEED AND PETROL CONSUMPTION

	FWD 110mm Petrol	FWD 100mm Petrol	FWD Compr. Ign.	GUY 8-wheel	SCAMMELL	LEYLAND
Mileage	158	158	158	158	158	158
Time	8h 52m	9h 37m	9h 24m	8h 58m	8h 51m	8h 46m
Average Speed MPH	17.82	16.43	16.81	17.62	17.85	18.02
Maximum Speed MPH	26	31	26	27	25	30
Fuel Consumption MPG	3.40	3.43	5.08	2.80	3.59	3.04

The larger engine has increased the average speed and in particular the speed on hills by a considerable amount, although the maximum speed is not increased. It is considered in any case that a maximum speed of 30 mph is adequate for a heavy vehicle towing a 7-ton load and would only be possible on first class main roads.

The cooling is now considered inadequate for hot climates as temperature rises exceeding 100°F occurred on all test hills.

On the re-start tests a higher gear could be used with the larger engine. The brakes were the same as before, i.e. the foot-brake was good but the hand-brake was useless.

22/7/31

E. Barn.

Capt.

for Lt. Colonel & OME

(MWEE)

HX 6114 was another R6T tractor which had gone to North Wales to take part in the trials at Bala in April 1931. (Its other relevant identification numbers were T21544, MWEE 282 and chassis number 2123.) HX 6114 was different in that it was powered by one of AEC's very new six-cylinder 110 mm by 142 mm oil engines, A155/35. More than half a ton heavier than its petrol-engined counterpart, it had an unladen weight of 9 tons 3 cwts 0 qrs 7 lbs. Laden to 11 tons 3 cwts 0 qrs 7 lbs and with the same 6 tons 16 cwts in tow, its fuel consumption was 5.05 mpg. Lubricating oil was consumed at the rate of 216.9 mpg and the 48-gallon fuel tank gave it a range of 240 miles. Its maximum speed was 26.5 mph and the maximum gradient climbed was 1 in 5.2.

A memo dated 26 February 1932 shows that at a mileage of 2,055, engine A155/35 was removed and replaced by A161/35. The two engines were basically similar, the A155 being of 110 mm bore and employing the Acro combustion system while the A161 had a bore of 115 mm and a combustion system developed by Ricardo. Engine A161/35 was removed for examination in June 1934 at a vehicle mileage of 9,317 (engine mileage 7,262) and replaced by A165K/747. The vehicle was handed over to the COO Chilwell in July 1938.

Resume

From the best information available, it appears that the War Department was supplied with the single prototype R.6.T and twenty-three production R/6/Ts built at Slough together with thirty-two Type 850s from Southall, a total of fifty-six. One R/6/T was built at Slough for exhibition at Olympia in 1931 and later dismantled and one Southall-built chassis, 850022, was supplied to the Royal Laval Transport Company. The total build therefore appears to be fifty-eight.

Survivors

It has been said that the Army lost many, even most, of its R6Ts in the evacuation from Dunkirk in 1940. It has not been possible to verify this but a few did survive into the post-war years. The writer recalls seeing one in the Service Department at Southall in the early 1950s when it came in for attention. Two were seen in the yard of CVS Ltd at Drighlington near Leeds in the late 1970s, one suffering the indignity of being fitted with a Bedford TK cab. AMP 80, chassis number 850009, was more fortunate. This, one of the anti-aircraft type, has survived and when first seen in March 1995 was part of the A. F. Budge collection at Gamston near Retford. Privately owned, it now resides in the Imperial War Museum at Duxford.

The R.68 Chassis

The R.68, a rigid six-wheel-drive 8-tonner, had been constructed by the Four Wheel Drive Lorry Company during the closing months of 1929 and exhibited at Olympia in November of that year. It was a direct development of the R.46 and, as the commercial equivalent of the R.6.T military tractor, had a wheelbase of 14 feet 9 inches and a body-space of 18 feet. Unlike the R.6.T, which at its introduction had been powered by the Dorman 6JUL engine, the R.68 was from the outset fitted with the 95 bhp six-cylinder AEC engine, the first FWD chassis to be so equipped. The drive was taken through the AEC's standard four-speed gearbox and FWD transfer box to the spiral bevel driven axles. As with the R.6.T, the drive to the front axle was automatically engaged with the selection of the low range in the transfer box. The transfer box provided ratios of 1:1 and 2.78:1 and the axles had a final drive ratio of 7¾:1. The tyres were 38 inch by 9 inch singles all round.

While the chassis lacked the hub reduction gears and the specialised military equipment of the R.6.T, laden to capacity, it proved able to traverse rough waterlogged ground with a 5-ton trailer in tow and without the trailer, with an overall gear reduction of 95.5:1, could surmount gradients as steep as 1 in 3½. Geared for 14.78 mph/1,000 engine rpm on top gear, on good hard roads it had a usable top speed of 35 mph with 40 mph just possible. In the range of its abilities, the vehicle was described as 'extraordinary'.

The chassis, which appears to have been the sole example built, was placed in trial service for a month with the Great Western Railway for evaluation and is thought to have ultimately been sold to the Griffin Engineering Company in Johannesburg. A price list dated November 1931 shows the R.68 to have carried a list price of £1,885.

Returning from FWD at Slough after modification in October 1929, this tractor was the latest development of the half-tracked FWD Roadless, now with the epicyclic wheel hubs. Identified by the Mechanical Warfare Experimental Establishment as B4E1, it is seen here with a 60-pounder gun in tow. With 73 bhp available from its four-cylinder engine, it had a top speed of 14 mph on the hard road and half of that cross-country. It was judged not suitable as an artillery tractor in its present form. (*Photograph: Imperial War Museum KID1209*)

The Dorman-powered prototype R.6.T chassis had been built during the latter part of 1928 and here demonstrates the extreme articulation afforded by the War Office-pattern bogie. Similar flexibility was provided at the front axle where the springs, anchored at the rear, were contained at the front within vertical guides and controlled by a centrally pivoted rocking beam. The block on which the front tyre stood was 12 inches high and the diagonally placed blocks at the rear were 18 inches high. At those angles of articulation, there was no distortion of the chassis frame. (*Photograph: Imperial War Museum, KID2031*)

MG 9550, T21012, was the last numbered of seventeen similar tractors delivered to the military under contract V1982 in 1930. In October of that year it was demonstrated before the Royal Marines at Eastney Barracks near Portsmouth. It is seen here hauling a heavy naval artillery piece over the sand dunes at Portsea. Of note are the tyre chains, a necessary aid to traction with the smooth tread Dunlop road tyres. (*Photograph: Royal Marines Museum 213*)

HX 6114, T21544, MWEE number 282 is thought to have been photographed at Bala in April 1930. Powered by the A155 oil engine, this R/6/T was externally indistinguishable from its stable mates except for the AutoVac carried above the nearside mudguard. For these tests it has been fitted with 900-22 Trakgrip tyres in place of the usual road-pattern 42 inch by 10.5 inch tyres and has the usual 3-inch anti-aircraft gun in tow. On a dismal day, with minimal protection, the soldiers have their greatcoat collars turned up against the weather. (*Photograph: Public Record Office, WO 194/12*)

Following the transfer of operations to Southall in April 1932, in the period to May 1936 AEC built a total of thirty-three R6T chassis in batches of eight, seven, six, one (for the Royal Laval Transport Company) and eleven. BMM 572, H341094, seen here, was one of the batch of six, numbered 850016–021, built under contract V2639 in December 1934. (*Photograph: Imperial War Museum, H291*)

9

The Ranger Types 665, 670 and 650

THE TYPE 665 RANGER

A short paragraph in the AEC Gazette of June 1930 introducing the Ranger described it as 'created to meet the demand which exists for a single-deck high-powered bus or coach chassis of the driver-behind-engine type.' A photograph of the chassis appeared in the Gazette in the following month. No price was given but in November 1931 the list price was shown as £1,050 – the same as that of the Regal.

In all essential details, the Ranger was a bonneted version of the Regal. Indeed, as first built in right-hand drive form, the Ranger and Regal shared the same 17-foot wheelbase frame (Y146), petrol engine (A145), semi floating rear axle (F129) and radiator (N132). It differed from the Regal only in respect of gearbox (D123), steering gear and in the positioning of the driver's controls.

The six-cylinder A145 engines of chassis 665001 and 004–031 were of 110 mm bore and produced 110 bhp at 2,500 rpm. Chassis 002 and 003 carried the smaller 100 mm bore A137, which produced 95 bhp at the same speed. Chassis 032–044 were fitted with the 110 mm bore, 120 bhp 'high-power' A162 engine, as were chassis 049–051, 053 and 054, 057–060, 081–086, and 091–101. Chassis 0665045–048, 052, 055, 061–080, and 087–090 were fitted with the 130 bhp 8.8 litre A165 oil engine. The odd one out was chassis 0665056, which had the 115 bhp 7.7 litre A171.

Early chassis were fitted with the D119, D122 or D123 four-speed sliding mesh gearbox. The gear selector cover, arranged for direct operation, was interchangeable with the remote gear designed for the forward control vehicles. Later chassis are shown having the D126, a similar gearbox to the D123 but with the constant mesh 'silent third' gear. The D135, which featured on a number of late chassis, had the same internals as the D126 but had a cast iron case. One chassis only, 0665052, was fitted with the AEC-built D132 epicyclic gearbox. The gear ratios provided in the so-called 'crash' gearboxes were: 1st, 4.38; 2nd, 2.69; 3rd, 1.59; and 4th, 1:1. Reverse provided a ratio of 5.33:1. The ratios in the D132 gearbox were: 1st, 4.15; 2nd, 2.36; 3rd, 1.56; and 4th, 1:1. Reverse was 6:1.

The rear axle was the semi-floating type F129, F131 or F145, having the final drive gear offset to the English nearside as on the Regal and Regent chassis. The primary reason for the adoption of the semi-floating axle was that the brake shoes could be removed and relined without disturbing the wheel bearings. Fears in respect of the security of the wheel-hubs and the load bearing ability of the half shafts appear to have been unfounded; nevertheless, the semi-floating axle gave way to the fully-floating type F156 from the early months of 1933. Chassis from and including 0665045 were so equipped. The worm gear on axles F129, F131, F145 and F156 had a standard axle ratio of 6½:1 with alternative ratios of 5 1/5, 5¾, 6¾, 7 1/3, 8 1/3, and 9 1/3:1. Chassis 0665046 and 047 are recorded as having an axle ratio of 4.6:1. On 38 inch by 8¼ inch tyres and with an axle ratio of 5 1/5:1, 52 mph was attained at an engine speed of 2,500 rpm.

Brakes were provided on all four wheels in drums of 17-inch diameter and on the first three chassis were operated through a single vacuum servo. Chassis 004–044 had a triple servo layout where the rear brakes continued to be operated directly from the master servo and the front brakes, still rod operated via the hollow king pins, were each energised by separate slave servos. Servo-assisted hydraulic brakes, which had been optional from the early months of 1932, became standard from November 1933 and chassis 045 and subsequent chassis were so equipped. The brake shoes, twelve in number, were 3¼ inches wide and interchangeable. The handbrake operated one set of shoes in the rear brake drums and the footbrake one set in both front and rear drums. With the arrival of the F156 axle, the rear brake shoes became single units, 6 inches wide. A single camshaft was now employed in place of the previous twin camshaft system.

While the Ranger had been developed primarily for export territories, forty-nine of the 101 type 665 chassis built went into the domestic market. In this application, United Kingdom regulations limited the overall length to 27 feet 6 inches and the width to 7 feet 6 inches. Export chassis, with a wheelbase of 19 feet, had an overall length exclusive of the bumper bar of 29 feet 4 3/8 inches and a maximum width of 7 feet 11 inches. The chassis frame had a maximum depth of 11 inches at mid-wheelbase and a laden height of 1 foot 9¼ inches. The easy riding road springs were 4 feet 2 inches long at the front and 5 feet 2 inches long at the rear. The steering gear normally fitted was of Marles manufacture but chassis 665050, 052, 053 and 054 together with 061–080 are, rightly or wrongly, noted as having the AEC-manufactured worm and nut gear.

Production Details

The first of the Type 665 Ranger chassis had been built in May of 1930 and twenty-two were built in the year to December 1930. Chassis 001, together with chassis 002 and 003, which had been built in July, were despatched to The Griffin Engineering Company Ltd, in Johannesburg, South Africa, from where they were sold to Johnston of Germiston. (Chassis 001 was converted to forward control in November 1932 and had its original engine, A145/19, changed for oil engine A161/88, probably at the same time. Chassis 002 and 003 received Leyland oil engines in March 1941, as also had 045 in the previous year.)

Chassis 004–009 were built in August. Chassis 004, registered MV 346 with a twenty-six-seat Park Royal coach body, served as a demonstrator until November 1931, when it was sold to W. P. Robinson of Dundee and the second demonstrator, 008, MV 347, with a twenty-six-seat Harrington body, was sold, also in November 1931, to W. Law of Tipton. Chassis 005 and 006 were despatched to Oswald Tillotson in Burnley in October and bodied by Burlingham. They apparently remained unsold until February and March 1932, when they were acquired by A. F. Hancock of Bamford in

Derbyshire. (In 1935 Hancock's business was taken over by the BET, becoming part of its newly formed subsidiary Sheffield United Tours Ltd.) Chassis 007 was completed with a twenty-four-seat Duple body and was exhibited at the Scottish Show in Glasgow in November 1930 and was subsequently sold to Dick Bros of Dalkeith, Midlothian. Chassis 009, with a twenty-six-seat Metcalfe All-Weather coach body, went to Parr & Higgs in Birmingham, later passing to Essex County Coaches of Leyton, London E10.

Chassis 010, 011 and 012 were built in September 1930. All three were of 19-foot wheelbase and 010 and 011 had left hand steering. They were the only two of the Type 665 so built and were exported to Canada for Montreal Tramways. Chassis 012 was one of five export chassis which went to Agar Cross & Co. for the British Empire Trade Exhibition held in Buenos Aires in March 1931. (The other chassis were two narrow-tracked Mercurys, 640034 and 640061, Majestic 666026 and the prototype 4x4 Hardy 4-tonner.) Both the Ranger and the Hardy were ultimately returned to Southall, the Ranger passing to Oswald Tillotson, AEC's northern agent, in April 1936 and ultimately to Sudlow in Liverpool.

Chassis 013–021 were built in October and November 1930 and 022 in February 1931 and were sold to Timpson of Catford, London SE6. All received twenty-six-seat coach bodies by Harrington and were registered GN 7302 – GN 7311 but not in sequence. Chassis 023, built in December 1930, had been ordered by the unusually named Glasgow & Paris Omnibus Company of Maryhill, Glasgow but went in to service with Hunter & Nelson of Arbroath.

Chassis 024–031, of 19-foot wheelbase, built in February 1931, went to Johannesburg Municipal Tramways and 032–034, built in November 1931, also of 19-foot wheelbase but fitted with the then-new 120 bhp A162 engine and D126 'silent third' gearbox, went to Pretoria Tramways. Both lots were supplied through the Griffin Engineering Company.

Griffin Engineering took 035, built in February 1932. This chassis was of 17-foot, 6-inch wheelbase, the same as the recently introduced 'longer' wheelbase Regal. Chassis 036 and 037, built in June 1932 with the previously standard 17-foot wheelbase, went to Halifax Corporation. With unusually large 40 inch by 9 inch Goodyear tyres and bodies by EEC, these were registered JX 49 and JX 50.

Chassis 038, with a 19-foot wheelbase, also built in June 1932, went to Griffin Engineering for Brakpan Municipality and this was followed by three similar chassis, 039–041, built in November 1932 for Pretoria. It is noted that 041 was written off following a collision with a train.

Five only were built in 1933. Chassis 042 and 043, built in March, were supplied to South Wales Transport, with twenty-seat All-Weather coach bodies by Harrington. Also built in March was chassis 044, supplied to W. Howe of Stockport, which, supplied through Oswald Tillotson, had a twenty-six-seat Duple body. Chassis 045, built in December, went to Griffin Engineering, destination unknown, and 046, built in the previous month, went to the Marques de Sales in Madrid. Both chassis were of 19-foot wheelbase and featured the A165 oil engine, the F156 fully floating rear axle and Lockheed brakes.

In 1934 no fewer than thirty right-hand drive Rangers were built, of which twenty-three were A165-powered. In this year, many were built out of sequence. Chassis 047, of 19-foot wheelbase with A165 engine, was built in March for the Marques de Sales (destination unknown) and in April 059 and 060, a pair of A162-powered 17-foot, 6-inch wheelbase chassis, went to join 005 and 006 at Hancock's establishment in Bamford. Registered AWA 336 and AWA 335 respectively, they had twenty-six-seat coach bodies built by Craven in Sheffield. Chassis 049, A162-powered, had been built in May, bodied by Burlingham and delivered to W. Herd in Edinburgh. Chassis 048, 050 and 051, also of 17-foot, 6-inch wheelbase, went to the Texas Oil Company. Built in June, chassis 048 was powered by the A165 engine and 050 and 051, built in July, had the A162. Taking the role of the now discontinued Mandator, each carried a stylish three compartment 1,500-gallon elliptical tank, built by Thompson Bros of Bilston.

In August and September, twenty A165-powered 19-foot wheelbase chassis numbered 061–080 were built for the East London Transport Department. These had been ordered through the Griffin Engineering Company, the same company being responsible for building the thirty-four-seat front entrance bus bodies. Also supplied through Griffin was 19-foot wheelbase chassis 052, built in September with A165 engine and D132 epicyclic gearbox, which went to Pretoria. Devon General had 053 and 054, built in November. These, a pair of 17-foot, 6-inch wheelbase chassis with A162 engines, were bodied by Harrington.

Nine Type 665 Rangers were built in 1935. In February, chassis 087, of 19-foot wheelbase and with A165 engine, was built for the Spanish operator Garcia Martin and in the following month chassis 081–086, of 17-foot, 6-inch wheelbase and with A162 engines, were built for Arthur Kitson Ltd of Sheffield, soon to be identified as Sheffield United Tours Ltd. With twenty-six-seat front entrance bodies by Craven, these were registered AWJ 232 to AWJ 237. Chassis 055, of 19-foot wheelbase and with A165 engine, was built for the Marques de Sales (date not recorded) and chassis 056, with 7.7 litre A171 engine, was built for Agar Cross & Co., despatched to the London docks (Blakes wharf) on 5 September.

Chassis 057 was built in February 1936 and completed as a horsebox for Capt Boyd Rochford of Newmarket and 058, built in April, carried an enclosed 900-gallon tank built by W. P. Butterfield Ltd of Shipley for the Albion Sugar Co. of Woolwich for the carriage of liquid glucose. Both were A162-powered 17-foot 6-inch wheelbase chassis. Four 19-foot wheelbase A165-powered chassis, 087–090, were shipped to Spain for Garcia Martin.

Ten Rangers, 665091–100, were built in 1937. All had the A162 petrol engine and the 17-foot 6-inch wheelbase frame. Of these, Westcliff-on-Sea had two, 091 and 092, built in March and April, both with bodywork by Duple. Chassis 093–100 were built in October and November for Devon General. These were fitted with bodies built by Harrington and were placed in service in March, April and May 1938.

The last of the type, 665101, was built for Westcliff-on-Sea on 30 March 1938. It had a 17-foot 6-inch wheelbase frame, A162 engine, D126 gearbox (actually listed as a D124) and the F184 fully-floating rear axle which had been designed for the 1938 Regent.

THE LEFT HAND DRIVE TYPE 670 RANGER

With the exception of two chassis, all the 1931 Type 670 Rangers, i.e. up to 670048, were powered by the 110 mm bore, 110 bhp A145 engine. The two exceptions were

670011 and 012, which had the A155 oil engine. Two others, 670024 and 025, were rebuilt with A162 engines in the early months of 1933. The 120 bhp A162 engine was fitted from April 1932 through to May 1935 and a single chassis, 0670066, was fitted with the A165 oil engine in October 1934. The first of the A171 oil engines was fitted to chassis 067 in June 1935 and remained the preferred fitment thereafter.

All the 1931 chassis had the four-speed D122/D126 spur gearbox. In May 1932, two Rangers had been built for Gray Coach Lines, a subsidiary of the Toronto Transportation Commission, equipped with the Daimler-built D128 fluid transmission and Lockheed hydraulic brakes. Lockheed brakes went on to become a standard fitting and the fluid transmission was again specified for the next Gray Coach Lines intake. The British Columbia Electric Railway Co. took delivery of two chassis fitted with the AEC-built D132 epicyclic gearbox but specified the more familiar D126 'crash' box for later deliveries.

Though the F156 fully-floating axle became the standard fitment on the right-hand drive Rangers from December 1933, the F144 semi-floating axle with the central transmission line remained standard for the left-hand drive Ranger throughout its production life. Ultimately a fully floating axle, the F185, was designed in prospect for the 1938 Type 670 Ranger but never achieved production status.

An analysis of the seventy-nine chassis built shows that seven chassis were of 17-foot wheelbase, thirty-seven of 19-foot and thirty-five of 20-foot.

Production details

During 1931, no fewer than forty-six Type 670 chassis had been constructed. Chassis 670001–012 had been built with Duple twenty-nine-seat bus bodies for the Societe Electrique, Athens, and chassis 013, 016–023, 034–039 and 041–048, with bodywork by the Canadian Car & Foundry Company, went to Montreal Tramways. Chassis 014 and 015 were supplied to the British Columbia Electric Railway Company. Chassis 026 and 028 went to the Three Rivers Traction Company, 027 to the Ottawa Electric Railway Company and 029 and 031 to the London Street Railway in Ontario. The Canadian Transfer Company had chassis 030 and chassis 032 was exhibited at the Copenhagen Show and later dismantled. Chassis 033 and 040 are reported as not having been built.

In 1932, chassis 049 and 051 were supplied to Gray Coach Lines for a new long-distance coach service between Toronto and Buffalo. With fleet numbers 600 and 601, these had luxurious bodywork by the Canadian Car & Foundry Co. and were the first chassis in Canada to feature the fluid flywheel and Wilson epicyclic gearbox. Chassis 050, 052 and 053 went to Montreal Tramways, bringing their fleet of Rangers up to twenty-eight.

Chassis 024, with Duple bodywork, went to Gray Coach Lines in May 1933, becoming No. 602 in that company's fleet, and chassis 025 went the Ottawa Electric Railway Company in July 1933. (Chassis 024 and 025 had apparently been first built in August 1931 and rebuilt with A162 engines and Wilson gearboxes in the early months of 1933.) Chassis 054 and 055 had been built in April 1933 and, with Duple bodywork, went to Canadian-American Coaches Ltd (later named Canadian American Trailways) to work between Buffalo and Detroit. Chassis 056, built in November 1933 with Wilson gearbox and Duple bodywork, became Gray Coach Lines No. 603.

In March, June and July 1934, chassis 670057, 064 and 065 were built for the Ottawa Electric Railway Company and chassis 0670066 was built for the British Columbia Electric Railway Company. This last chassis was the sole example of the Type 670 Ranger with the A165 oil engine, and additionally had the AEC-built D132 epicyclic gearbox.

Chassis 059, 060 and 061, the last to be powered by the A162 petrol engine, were supplied to the Rumanian State Railway in May 1935 and 067 and 068, with A171 oil engines, went to the Ottawa Electric Railway Company a month later.

In March 1936, chassis 058, 062 and 063 were built for the British Columbia Electric Railway Company, A171 powered, and in June and July 069, 070 and 071, similarly powered, went to the Ottawa Electric Railway Company.

The last of the type, a group of ten, 19-foot wheelbase A171-powered chassis, were built in June 1937. Numbered 0670072–081, they went to the British Columbia Electric Railway Company.

THE TYPE 650 RANGER

Only two examples of the Type 650 Ranger were built. Both were built on chassis of 17-foot 6-inch wheelbase and both were powered by the 80 bhp, A168 four-cylinder oil engine. Chassis 0650001, with D126 gearbox and F156 fully-floating axle, was built on 27 June 1934. Carrying a twenty-six-seat Brush body, it went into service with Burton-on-Trent Corporation in August 1934. Chassis 002 was built on 27 July 1936 and supplied to Centro Proprietarios de Omnibus in Montevideo. It was similarly specified to chassis 001 save that both the gearbox casing and the final drive casing were of cast iron rather than aluminium. The type numbers therefore changed to D135 and F171.

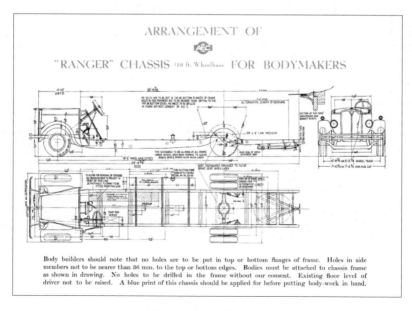

Arrangement drawing of the Ranger chassis Type 670 taken from the AEC sales brochure No. 112, dated October 1931. (*Drawing: AEC, Author's collection*)

Built to specification XU420, the first two left-hand drive Ranger chassis were unique. Not only were they numbered in the 665 series but also the transmission line followed to the English nearside. They had been built for Montreal Tramways in September 1930 and, of 19-foot wheelbase, were numbered 665010 and 011. Though subsequent left-hand drive chassis were numbered in the 670 series, the original designation of these chassis was 665/2. (*Photograph: AEC, Author's collection*)

This close-up photograph of the Montreal chassis' driver's controls shows the pedal gear to be slightly at variance with later versions. In this instance, the clutch and brake pedals straddle the chassis frame member. On later versions both were inside the frame. The photograph was taken outside the experimental department (before the building of the new engine research facility). In the background are seen the six boiler-house chimneys. Further distant are the chimneys from the heat treatment furnaces and the water tower. (*Photograph: AEC 3395, Author's collection*)

TJ23748, 665027, was one of eight Rangers supplied to Johannesburg Municipal Tramways via Griffin Engineering in February 1931. Functional no doubt, built on the 19-foot wheelbase chassis, its long, low appearance gives the vehicle true presence. The body, built by Millhouse, seated thirty-six. (*Photograph: AEC, Alan Townsin collection*)

Ranger JX 90, with twenty-seat body by English Electric of Preston, was one of two supplied to the Halifax Joint Omnibus Committee in the summer of 1932. Chassis 665037 had been built on 13 June 1932 and had engine A162c/484, D125 'silent third' gearbox and triple servo brakes. Geoffrey Hilditch, Halifax's one-time general manager, reports that these two vehicles each cost £1,270 and, demoted early to training duties, were retired in March 1945. (*Photograph: Author's collection*)

Formerly the province of the Mandator, when that chassis was withdrawn from production, its place was taken by the Ranger. Eye-catching, Texaco's BLC 886 carries a three-compartment, 1,500-gallon spirit tank by Thompson Bros of Bilston, which company also built the cab and bodywork. The chassis, 17-foot 6-inch wheelbase 665050, had been built on 12 July 1934. It had engine A162c/991, D126 gearbox, F156 rear axle with a ratio of 7 1/3:1 and Lockheed brakes. Its unladen weight was 6 tons. (*Photograph: AEC, Author's collection*)

AWJ 232, 665081, with coachwork by Cravens Railway Carriage & Wagon Company, was one of six placed in service by Sheffield United Tours in 1935. The 17-foot 6-inch wheelbase chassis had been built on 15 March 1935. Intended for long distance touring, it featured the A162 petrol engine, D126 gearbox, F156 rear axle and hydraulic brakes. (*Photograph: AEC Author's collection*)

10

The A155, A161, A164 and A165 Oil Engines

Origins

A leading article in the Commercial Motor dated 29 December 1925 opens:

> The great increase in the employment of Diesel engines on ships and for stationary plant, etc., and the substantial economies which have been effected through their use have induced many designers to turn their attention to the production of Diesel motors sufficiently compact and flexible as regards control to be suitable for employment as power units on commercial vehicles.

At the summer meeting of the Verein Deutscher Ingenieure at Mannheim in May 1927, Professor Dr-Ing. R. Stribeck of Stuttgart presented a paper relative to tests carried out on a single cylinder 'Acro' type engine of 125 mm bore and 180 mm stroke. Dr Skilbeck had explained that the patents for the engine were held by the Acro AG, of Kussnacht a. R., Switzerland. The sole right to grant licences had been acquired by the Robert Bosch AG of Stuttgart, who had carried out the tests described in the paper. The report in The Engineer of 10 June 1927 went on:

> The progress of the heavy oil engine in the direction of higher speeds of rotation is naturally bound up with the question of the rate at which the injected fuel can be mixed with the air charge in order to ensure the completion of combustion within a sufficiently short length of time. For transport purposes it is also necessary that the combustion should take place with reasonable efficiency over a wide range of speed. It is in connection with possible improvements in the flexibility of such engines that Professor Stribeck's paper is especially interesting.
>
> Fig. 1 shows the special design of piston at top dead centre in the cylinder of an engine of the ordinary four-stroke type. In this position the clearance volume consists of four parts: a, the compression space in the piston; c, the compression space between the top of the piston and the cylinder head – the volume of this space naturally changes as the piston moves down the stroke; b, a Venturi or funnel-shaped passage connecting a and c, of which d is the orifice or neck. The fuel is injected into the space b. The engine tested was a single-cylinder engine of 125 mm. bore and 180 mm. stroke, with a connecting-rod/crank ratio of 3.8 and with a normal speed of 800 r.p.m. These dimensions gave a swept volume of 2209 cu. cm. The total clearance volume was 140 cu. cm., divided as follows :- a, 98

cu. cm.; b, 10 cu. cm.; c, 32 cu. cm., or 70, 7, and 23 per cent. of the clearance volume respectively. The cross section of d was 1.17 sq. cm.

The engine was an ordinary high-speed 'airless' injection engine, which was only altered as far as the cylinder head and the piston were concerned. The fuel was injected in the ordinary way directly into the Venturi-shaped space b, the fuel valve closing at about 15 deg. after top dead centre.

The subjects of pressure differences, air-flow velocities and temperatures were considered at length. Peak temperatures in the order of 1,600 degrees C were recorded in the Venturi (at about 40 degrees after tdc) and the highest mean indicated pressure was 101 lbs/sq inch at 400 rpm. The report continued:

The investigations upon the engine show that the Venturi-shaped portion is of great importance: ignition and the greater part of the combustion take place in it. The air necessary to maintain combustion passes from a, the storage chamber, to the Venturi, the hot gases passing away into c. The restriction of the combustion to a small part of the compression space results in a clear separation, during the process, between the new air and the exhaust gases, and thus a high temperature of combustion may be reached. This restriction of the combustion and the adjustment of the air flow to the engine speed are the essential characteristics of this type of engine. Its adaptability for high speeds of revolution and its suitability for automobile work follow from them.

In conclusion, Professor Stribeck remarked that little could be said at present on the relative volumes and shapes of the three parts of the compression space. At top dead centre space c is of no importance as an air space, and its shape is unfavourable to use as a combustion space. Since the combustion begins before top dead centre, this space is needed to accommodate the exhaust gases. The Venturi space need not be large; its shape and the best size of its orifice can as yet only be found by experiment. The greater part of the air for combustion is stored in a, the volume of which depends upon the compression ratio required. For higher speeds the degree of compression should be greater than smaller.

Research at Southall

It was against this background that research at AEC was first undertaken. Under reference XA9 in an experimental department engine parts index dated 16.10.28, we find the entry 'Diesel type engine (Piston venturi)'. This is the earliest documented evidence we have in respect of AEC's oil engine research but the sales brochure describing the 1930 A155 engine indicates that work on the project had started 'early in 1928'. The crankcase of this first oil engine was based on that of the six-cylinder A121 petrol engine. The rest was new. It featured a one-piece cast iron cylinder block, overhead valves in three separate cylinder heads which were operated via push rods and rockers from the crankcase-mounted camshaft. The Acro pattern combustion chambers were located in the piston crowns and the injectors were carried in the cylinder heads. Bosch was responsible for the manufacture of the injectors and the fuel injection pump.

In the Modern Diesel, Sixth Edition 1941, Iliffe & Sons Ltd., it is written, somewhat dismissively, of the piston venturi type of engine:

> Of the type of air-cell engine in which the cell is located in the piston it is rather difficult to form any other opinion but that this was a passing phase planned chiefly with a view to avoiding costly production changes in existing types of power unit. When higher speeds are being sought it is desirable to reduce piston weight as much as possible, whereas the air cell increases it.

AEC's prototype Acro engine was first installed in one of the AEC's own Type 506 lorries and, laden to a gross weight of 10½ tons, fuel consumption varied between 10 and 10½ mpg. By December 1928 the engine had been transferred to the 104-seat 'LS' type works bus, serving to transport employees on their daily journey between Walthamstow and the new Southall factory.

AEC board minute No. 1670 of 3 January 1929 is relevant:

> Diesel Engine
>
> The General Manager reported that for purposes of test this engine has been fitted into one of the six wheeled omnibuses used in the transport of employees between Walthamstow and Southall: that in prior tests on the bench a few minor mechanical defects had been disclosed, which had since been corrected: that it will be found necessary to design and test various types of cylinder head before final satisfaction with this type of engine can be expressed.

Research at Chiswick

Parallel with the work being carried out by the AEC, the LGOC had embarked on its own research programme. In February 1929, three Junkers SA9 two-cylinder opposed piston two-stroke engines had been acquired for evaluation, two of which were installed in Chiswick-based lorries. These were joined by a further two vehicles, a six-ton Mercedes-Benz and an AEC 5-type powered by a four-cylinder oil engine described simply as an Acro-Bosch. The Mercedes-Benz lorry is thought to have been the one sanctioned for purchase by the AEC board in October 1928 for use by the experimental department. Data relative to these test vehicles were contained in a paper by G. J. Shave, read before the Institution of Automobile Engineers in November 1930. The details provide a ready point of reference and are here reproduced in full:

> Mercedes-Benz.
>
> The engine has six cylinders, 105 x 165 mm., and yields 75 b.h.p. at 1,300 r.p.m. It has a maximum speed of 2,000 r.p.m. and develops a brake mean effective pressure of 87.2 lb. per sq. in. at an injection pressure of 950 lb. per sq. in. The engine employs a Bosch fuel pump, and when tested in a demonstration lorry yielded 11.56 miles per gallon on a mixture of fuel oil and gas oil, equivalent to 101.1 ton-miles per gallon. The acceleration and power at low speeds were good, and it proved possible to start the engine from cold and to get away under load within one minute.

Junkers.

This is a two-cylinder opposed-piston design operating on the two-stroke cycle. The bore and stroke of each piston is 80 x 150 mm. and 45 b.h.p. is developed at 1,100 r.p.m.

Acro-Bosch.

The engine tested had four cylinders 115 x 180 mm., with a compression ratio of 15.7:1. Its nominal output is 45 b.h.p. at 1,100 r.p.m. A Bosch pump is employed for fuel injection and a pre-ignition chamber is provided in the piston. On test, this engine yielded an average fuel consumption on German gas oil of 12.3 miles per gallon or 92.5 ton-miles per gallon, although, on a straight non stop run, 125 ton-miles per gallon was obtained.

Developments at Southall

Charles Edwards had left AEC in February 1929 but it was his claim to have been responsible for the design, development and research into the first diesel-engined bus to run in London (AEC's 104-seat 'LS'). Research continued under the hand of Cedric Dicksee, who had joined AEC as an engine designer in 1928. It was he who brought the oil engine project to fruition. Returning to the experimental department engine parts index, under XA10 we find the reference 'Diesel type engine (Cyl. Head Venturi) Xptl 1.1.29'. This reference, XA10, signalled a new line of development where the combustion chamber was contained within the cylinder head.

The cylinder head venturi line of development almost mirrored that of the Saurer company of Arbon in Switzerland. In principle, the Acro air cell conformed neither to the open chamber direct injection genre nor to the precombustion chamber type but aimed to combine the best features of both. The direct injection engine had the advantage of fuel economy but suffered from pronounced diesel knock while the indirect injection types were smoother in operation but suffered from the pumping losses inherent in all engines of that form. In all three types the fuel was injected into a highly compressed and predominantly stationery air mass, the fuel thereby having to search out the oxygen in which to burn. In this respect, the Acro cell probably had an advantage as, with the piston at tdc, the volume of the Venturi in which the combustion was propagated comprised only about 7 per cent of the total clearance volume. It did, however, suffer the same pumping losses as the indirect injection types.

With a compression ratio of 15.5:1, the compression pressure was in the order of 520 lbs/sq. inch or roughly the same value as the peak pressure generated in a contemporary high-efficiency petrol engine. The temperature of the air under compression reached about 600 degrees centigrade. The elapsed time between the injection of the fuel and the commencement of ignition, identified as the delay period, affected not only the height of the pressure rise but also its rate of increase. Put simply, the longer the period before the onset of combustion, the more violent was the reaction when all the fuel injected to that point ignited at the same time. The reduction of the delay period was therefore of vital importance and could be affected as much by fuel quality as by engine design. The injection timing was usually so arranged that the peak cylinder pressure occurred about 10 degrees after tdc and that the fuel injected beyond that point burned in a controlled manner on a falling pressure gradient.

It is clear from its layout that this second oil engine (the A155 prototype) had been designed for installation in a chassis which pre-dated the Rackham-designed chassis. The flywheel was exposed and the engine's rear mounting arrangement was of similar design to that found on AEC, ADC and LGOC engines of earlier generations. Further, the boss on the left side of the crankcase on which the gear-change mechanism was mounted on the Rackham-designed petrol engines was absent on this Dicksee-designed prototype.

This indicates to the writer that the engine's intended destination was in one or other of the AEC's six-wheeled works buses. Whether or not this in fact occurred is not known. It may well be that in this form the engine was unique but a photograph exists of it on test in the experimental department.

AEC Board Meetings

The board report of 3 October 1929 (below) reveals that the new-design oil engine was now extant and ready for test. An extract from Minute 1840 of that date reads:

> Designs and Experiments
> Mr Reeve also submitted reports as to:-
> (e) the completion of the new Diesel engine having an estimated power output of 85/90 H.P. and its early submission for test and report to the Bosch Company: also the design for the purposes of laboratory experiments of a single cylinder Diesel engine.

At that same meeting, Charles Reeve reported on the signing of an agreement with the Bosch company in respect of the Acro licence and the royalties payable. These were to be paid as a percentage of the selling price of each engine built but with a minimum payment in the first year following such sale of £500. In the second year this would rise to £1,000 and in the third and fourth years to £2,000 and £4,000 respectively. In the fifth and each succeeding year the sum would be £6,000.

At the board meeting on 3 April 1930, it is recorded under Minute 1993 that the chief engineer (John Rackham) reported to the board:

> with regard to the completion of the first six cylinder heavy oil engine and the performance obtained therefrom.

Six months had elapsed since Reeve's first report on the engine and the chief engineer's report was clearly in reference to the engine in its latest form, ready for production.

Minute 2005 of the meeting held on 1 May 1930 under the heading 'Heavy Oil Engine – Manufacturing Programme' reads:

> Heavy Oil Engine – Manufacturing Programme
> The Managing Director submitted a request for authority to incur such expenditure

as might be necessary to produce 100 complete Heavy Oil Engines, together with the necessary spares, the engines to be of the type recently tested, upon which favourable reports have been made by the Chief Engineer. It was resolved that the authority requested be and the same is hereby granted.

Relative to Minute 2005 above, Minute 2015 reads:

Special Expenditure
The Managing Director submitted Requisition for approval as follows: Requisition No. 911/344.
Estimated cost of production of 100 Heavy Oil Engines, together with the necessary spares as submitted in Minute 2005 hereof:-

Patterns, Tools, Jigs etc., approximately	£ 6,000
Material, Labour and Establishment Charges	£35,000
	£41,000

It was resolved that this Requisition be and the same is hereby approved, the expenditure to be charged to production.

Ricardo Agreement

It transpires that even in advance of the building of the first of the A155 'Acro' engines, the terms agreed with Bosch were seen to be too costly and that alternative arrangements were necessary.
    Minute 2006, also of 1 May 1930, reads:

Heavy Oil Engine Development – Ricardo Agreement
The Managing Director submitted the terms of an Agreement proposed to be concluded between this Company and Ricardo & Co. Engineers (1927) Ltd., whereby Mr. H.R.Ricardo is appointed a consultant to the Company for a period of two years at an annual fee of £500 (Five hundred pounds), this Company being responsible also for the payment of out of pocket expenses and the cost of designing work undertaken.

    It was resolved that the terms of the Agreement, as explained by the Managing Director be and the same are hereby approved and that further, the Secretary be authorised to affix the seal of the Company to any documents in connection therewith.

The A155 Engine

It was on 30 October 1930 that AEC unveiled the A155 oil engine, though it is known that prototypes had been subject to extensive testing for some months in advance of that date. It was required that the engine had comparable operational characteristics and a similar power output to the petrol engine. The dimensions of the oil engine were 110 mm bore and 142 mm stroke, its six cylinders giving a swept volume of 8,097 cc.

With the outer cylinder centres at 760 mm, the A155 had somewhat greater bulk than the then-standard A136 petrol engine.

The crankcase of the A155 was a robust, deeply skirted aluminium alloy casting which carried the crankshaft in seven main bearings. The long, dual-purpose, main bearing bolts passed through the top face of the crankcase and served also to secure the cylinder block to the crankcase. The crankcase, in this manner, was relieved from gas pressure loadings. The crankshaft was of the fully drilled type, the crankpins being of 75 mm diameter and the main bearing journals 85 mm. The main bearings were of the steel backed shell type, white metal lined, while the big end bearings were metalled direct into the connecting rods. The connecting rods were two bolt, H section nickel-chrome steel stampings and the heat-treated Y alloy pistons had five rings, all above the gudgeon pin. The gudgeon pins were 40 mm diameter, drilled hollow, each being clamped by pinch bolt to the connecting rod.

The cylinder block was a simple six-cylinder monobloc casting in cast iron with the pistons running directly in the cylinder bores. The Acro air cells were located in the cylinder heads and the Bosch fuel injectors carried in the upper portion of the cylinder block. Pintle type nozzles were employed and the fuel was injected directly toward the throat of the venturi. The two cylinder heads, each covering three cylinders, were detachable, clamping pressure for each head being provided by thirteen studs of 9/16-inch diameter, five studs effectively surrounding each cylinder bore. The overhead valves, of silico chrome steel, were operated via push rods and rockers from the camshaft carried in the crankcase top half. This arrangement was at variance with the then-current AEC petrol engine practice where the valves were directly operated via rockers from an overhead camshaft carried in the cylinder head.

The drive to the camshaft and the auxiliaries was taken by triplex roller chain from the front end of the crankshaft. The Bosch PE6B fuel injection pump was driven at half engine speed in tandem with the exhauster. The injection pump was fitted with 7 mm diameter elements and a manual advance and retard mechanism was incorporated at its forward end. This was to allow for the differing advance requirements of the engine as the speed of rotation increased. A rotary vane exhauster was interposed between the timing case and the fuel injection pump, in order to provide vacuum for the servo brakes.

The water pump, engine governor and dynamo were driven at $1\frac{1}{4}$ times engine speed. As first designed, the water pump had been driven from the rear of the dynamo but was subsequently moved to a new position on the front of the timing case in order to allow for the fitment of a second dynamo. At variance with six-cylinder petrol engine, the gear-type oil pump was driven via skew gears and vertical shaft from the forward end of the camshaft, the main and big end bearings receiving oil at full pressure. The valve rockers were fed with oil at a lower pressure and the camshaft, pistons and gudgeon pins were lubricated by splash.

The engine was governed only in respect of idling speed, and in a perhaps optimistic assessment of the engine's capabilities, the normal operating speed range was 300 rpm to 3,000 rpm. In its production form it produced 95 bhp at 2,000 rpm and 102 bhp at 2,500 rpm with a maximum BMEP of 83.5 lbs/sq. inch at 1,350 rpm. The minimum fuel consumption was 0.43 pints/bhp/hr at 1,000 rpm.

Installation

Though the A155 was 4¼ inches longer overall than its petrol counterpart, its installation in the commercial vehicle chassis created little difficulty. Its accommodation in the Regent, Regal and Renown chassis where the engine was slanted to the nearside was rather less straightforward. In order to maintain adequate clearance between the timing case and the nearside engine bearer bracket, the front of the engine had to be elevated by some 1¼ inches relative to that of the petrol engine. On both the commercial and passenger vehicle chassis, the forward projection of the radiator provided a ready indication of the fitment of the oil engine and its haughty stance in the case of the passenger chassis rendered its presence even more obvious.

Road test data

AEC's claim of fuel economy for the A155 was not without foundation. The experimental department's oil-engined Majestic, laden to 11 tons 7 cwts 2 qrs when tested by Commercial Motor in November 1930 over a 21-mile section of the A40 between High Wycombe and Southall, recorded a fuel consumption of 8.66 mpg. The result was confirmed a month later when, with the same vehicle similarly laden, AEC staff with Capt. Richard Twelvetrees as observer recorded 8.4 mpg on an extended 300-mile test taking in some of Devon's more difficult terrain. The results compare with a test of a petrol-engined Majestic conducted by Motor Transport in October 1931 when, over a 56-mile course in the Chilterns and laden to a gross weight of 11 tons 17 cwts, a fuel consumption of 5.89 mpg was recorded. In terms of both gross weight and terrain the test conditions were strictly comparable, the improvement in fuel consumption of the oil-engined chassis over the petrol-engined type being better than 40 per cent.

Early examples

The experimental department's oil-engined Majestic had been on the road since the early summer of 1930 and Mammoth 667077 with engine A155/5 had been placed with Pickfords for evaluation under operational conditions on 29 September 1930. The newly built Regents 661960, 962 and 964 (the London General's ST462, 464 and 466 with engines A155/2, 6 and 5 respectively) together with AEC demonstrator 661131, MY 2102 with engine A155/1, were on hand on the day of the engine's official launch on 30 October 1930 and on 3 November, Mammoth demonstrator 667045, HX 1782 with A155/4, went to the London, Midland & Scottish Railway Company. Following the launch, it was to the passenger chassis that the bulk of A155 production was directed.

Production engines

Nine oil-engined Renown chassis, 663192–663200 with engines A155/20, 31, 34, 33, 39, 21, 28, 26 and 25 respectively, were built for the LGOC during December 1930 and January 1931, these becoming LT191 to 199. Three of six newly commissioned Green Line Regals garaged at the AEC works, 662712, 770 and 801, received A155s in substitution of their original A145s in May 1931. These, numbered T216, 274 and 305, were, together with petrol-engined Regals T286, 287 and 295, employed on the express coach service between Oxford Circus and Uxbridge and would have provided useful comparative data between the two types. In the period to June 1931 a further twelve oil-engined Regents and two Regals were built, principally for Municipal operators, among which were the Corporations of Birmingham, Glasgow, Leicester, Walsall and Wallasey.

Majestic 666034 with engine A155/30 had been built on 17 December 1930 and delivered to the Gas, Light & Coke Company on 8 April 1931 while 668003, MV 1561, one of the new Mammoth Major demonstrators, had been built with A155/28 on 17 March 1931. Rangers 670011 and 012, with engines A155/52 and A155/65 respectively, were shipped to Athens in June. Records show that the last chassis to be built with the A155 engine was Regent 6611583, built for Portsmouth on 15 June 1931. This engine, A155/63, was however changed for A161/17 prior to delivery in September 1931.

As far as can be judged, there were probably no more than seventy-five A155 engines built.

The AEC Gazette dated June 1931 carried the following leader:

The A.E.C. Oil Engine (Acro Licence), particulars of which were given in last November's issue of the A.E.C. Gazette, has made a strong appeal to operators of road transport. At the time of the introduction of this new engine, it was pointed out that, although very definite and important advance had been made in the design and development of the C.I. engine generally, a development placing it in a formidable position of rivalry with the petrol engine, it was not to be expected that the initial stages of operation would be void of the usual small "teething" troubles, invariably attendant on any new piece of machinery of so revolutionary a design. Chiefly for this reason, and to enable further research work to be carried out, A.E.C. users were frankly invited to give us the benefit of their experience as operators by taking one of these units into their fleet and thoroughly testing it under service conditions. The first production programme, having been dealt with in this way, we should like to remind operators of A.E.C. vehicles, that some time must elapse before further delivery of the C.I. engine can be given. Meanwhile, no expense is being spared on test and research work, further to improve and refine this power unit, which has reached such a high stage of success, and which will do so much to cheapen motor transport.

Ricardo's research

The appointment of H. R. Ricardo as consultant to the AEC in May 1930 recognised his work in the development of the swirl chamber. In his Vortex engine a BMEP of over 100 lbs/sq. inch had been obtained over a wide speed range in engines varying in size from 5½ inch by 7 inch bore and stroke to 7½ inch by 12 inch. The Vortex engine was a four-stroke sleeve valve type with tangentially arranged inlet ports, while the open, cylindrical and flat-topped combustion chamber was formed in the cylinder head. A spiral motion was imparted to the air on its admission into the cylinder, its speed of rotation in the cylinder head cavity at top dead centre being about ten times that of the engine, one revolution of the air mass approximating to the duration of the fuel injection. Fuel was injected across the flow of the air stream, each particle of fuel thereby being provided with an adequate supply of oxygen for complete combustion.

The generation of swirl in the overhead valve AEC oil engine demanded a different approach to that adopted in the Vortex engine. While some degree of swirl could have been generated in the AEC engine on the induction stroke by the use of masked inlet valves, swirl created by the positive displacement of air by the piston seemingly offered a more effective solution. It was in this direction that Ricardo directed his efforts. Not that the swirl chamber was a new discovery. British Patent No. 28753/10 had been taken out by one M. Laurin in 1910 and Ricardo's Comet chamber was a development of it. The Comet chamber was truly spherical in shape, connected to the cylinder by a short tangential passage through which the air was forced by the rising piston. Fuel was injected into the combustion chamber across the rotating air mass in much the same manner as had featured in the Vortex engine except that in the Comet chamber, the speed of rotation was about 2½ times greater.

An important difference between the Comet and Laurin chambers and indeed other swirl chambers, such as the Sanders, Perkins or Hercules, was the so-called hot plug which formed the lower half of the Comet chamber and which contained the communicating passage between the combustion chamber and the cylinder. The provision of an air gap around the hot plug effectively insulated it from the rest of the cylinder head, its resultant temperature under full load conditions being in the order of 700 degrees centigrade. This in turn provided for the rapid vaporisation of the fuel on its injection and a more effective control of its burning thereafter. As with the Acro head, heater plugs were required when starting from cold and pintle type fuel injectors were employed.

The A161 engine

Component lists show that the A161 employed the same basic crankcase assembly as the A155 but featured a new cylinder block, new pistons and new cylinder heads. The cylinder dimensions were 115 mm bore and 142 mm stroke, the engine's capacity thus being 8.85 litres (though one AEC derived document erroneously records the cylinders as being of 120 mm bore). The main bearing caps, previously employing shell bearings, were now steel drop forgings with white metal directly applied and it was thought desirable to add counter weights to the crank webs in order to reduce dynamic loadings on the main bearings. The crankcase, both top and bottom halves, was now cast in Elektron, a magnesium alloy, and some experimental work had been directed toward the use of duralumin connecting rods. This was short-lived, as by November 1931 they were again shown to be alloy steel drop forgings of the usual I section. The pistons were of heat-treated aluminium alloy, running directly in the cylinder block, flat-topped with three compression rings and one scraper above the gudgeon pin and a single scraper below. The gudgeon pins were now of the fully floating type, retained in the pistons by circlips. The engine was governed in respect of both maximum and idling speeds and the fuel injection equipment, as previously, was of Bosch manufacture. The weight of the engine, with the various modifications, had risen by 64 lbs to 1,414 lbs.

The LGOC is reported as having converted its twelve original A155s to A161 (three from the Regents ST462, 464 and 466 and the nine from Renowns LT191–199) in October 1931. The engine numbers allocated to these reworked engines is not recorded.

Engine performance

Ricardo's work had brought the A161 to the very forefront of automotive oil engine development. From the AEC Gazette of November 1931, we learn that its BMEP had been raised from the 83.5 lbs/sq. inch of the A155 by no less than 23 per cent to 103 lbs/sq. inch with a claimed clear exhaust. The engine delivered 128 bhp at 2,000 rpm and 140 bhp at 2,500 rpm, the minimum fuel consumption meanwhile had been reduced from 0.43 pints/bhp/hr to 0.40.

On the road, this translated into an improvement in fuel consumption over that achieved by the A155 in the order of 20 per cent. The LGOC, though rather coy about disclosing specific data, revealed that the overall fuel consumption of its 105-strong Hanwell-based oil-engined Renowns, eleven of which were Gardner-powered, was 82 per cent better than that of its otherwise similar petrol engined vehicles. Testing a petrol-engined Renown under simulated urban service conditions and loaded to 11 tons 18 cwt 1 qr gross, Commercial Motor in March 1932 recorded a fuel consumption of 4.65 mpg. By an extrapolation of this test result, we obtain an overall fuel consumption for the LGOC's oil-engined Renown fleet of 8.46 mpg.

Build numbers

The A161 had received its first major showing at Olympia in November 1931 but delegates to the Municipal Transport and Tramway Association's Conference in Manchester had had the opportunity to inspect it a couple of months earlier in September. All the aspiring oil engine manufacturers were represented at this meeting and in addition to its static exhibits, AEC had taken the LGOC's newly built

Renown 663644, otherwise identified as LT643. The vehicle, initially powered by the standard 110 mm bore A145 petrol engine, had been hurriedly fitted with the A161 oil engine specifically for the demonstration. The chassis record card identifies this engine as A161/6. This was the first of twenty engines built for the LGOC, the nineteen remaining being fitted in chassis 6633751–769, LTs750–768, built between September 1931 and January 1932. The engines were numbered A161/13, 14, 48, 52, 56, 58, 53, 59, 62, 63, 65, 68, 67, 70, 74, 81, 18, 73 and 42. The three engines from the Regents ST462, 464 and 466, now to A161 specification were fitted in LTs 590, 948 and 949.

Of the remainder, we find that engine A161/25 went into Mammoth Major demonstrator 668033 in October 1931 and this was followed by a further fifteen A161-powered Mammoth Majors with engines A161/51, 33, 37, 75, 86, 66, 54, 82, 28, 90, 21, 6, 84, 76 and 77 in the period to February 1932. Mammoth 667217 was built for Talbot Serpell & Co. in December 1931 with engine A161A/19 and two other Mammoths, 667227 for Brett of Canterbury and 667230 for Fairclough & Co. in London, were fitted with engines A161A/78 and 47.

The Scottish Motor Traction's Regal 662839 had received engine A161/20 in exchange for A155/8 in October 1931 and Regals 6621161, 1162 and 1163, built for the Midland Bus Company of Airdrie (a subsidiary of the SMT) in December 1931 and January and February 1932, were fitted with engines A161/71, 79 and 89.

Engine A161/17 had replaced A155/63 in Portsmouth Regent 6611583 before despatch from AEC in September 1931 and engine A161/35 was first fitted in FWD chassis R682, exhibited at Olympia in November 1931. This was subsequently transferred to FWD R6T chassis No. 2123, as described later. A161/66 was fitted in the Leicester Regent 6611156 in June 1932 in exchange for A155/44.

The highest recorded engine number is A161/96, which was rebuilt as A180/1533 on 27 June 1944.

The A164 engine

The A161 was joined by the A164 in March 1932. With no outward differences between the two types, we again have to revert to the component lists. We find that while the A164 had the same crankcase and cylinder heads as the A161, the cylinder block, crankshaft and the piston and con-rod assembly had been subject to detail modification. Whereas with the A161, the pistons had run directly in the cast iron cylinder block, the A164 was fitted with hardened steel liners, requiring that the cylinder block be bored oversize, probably to 120 mm, in order to accommodate them. The connecting rods now had steel-backed shell bearings, the top half lined with lead bronze and the bottom half white metal.

The first of the A164 engines, numbered 1, 2, 3, 7, 8, 9 and 10, were fitted in Majestic chassis 666085–091 for Pickfords, the London hauliers, in March 1932. These were followed by a further three, numbered 47, 48 and 46, in chassis 666098–100 in the following May but it was in the Mammoth and Mammoth Major chassis that the bulk of the A164s were fitted. Mammoths accounted for nine engines, A164/14, 15,

20, 22, 25, 29, 36, 39 and 54, which included Pickford's short wheelbase Carrimore articulated unit 667258 and Fairclough's 667298 (converted to eight-wheeler 0680801 in January 1935). Fourteen engines, A164/16, 17, 21, 24, 27, 28, 30, 31, 34, 35, 40, 44, 50 and 51, were fitted into six-wheeled Mammoth Majors, which included 668099, built for A. & H. Hardy the newsprint carriers in Northfleet, Kent in May 1932, and 668129, built for Cow & Gate of Wincanton in July of that year.

Long wheelbase Regent demonstrator 6611809, MV 2764, with engine A164/19, went to Sheffield in April 1932 and another similar demonstrator, 6611849, KG 1251, with engine A164/33, was built for Cardiff in May. Reid in Dundee had short wheelbase 6611885 with engine A164/26, built in April 1932. Long wheelbase preselective demonstrator 6612050, MV 3749, with engine A164/57, was built for Bradford in August and five short wheelbase Regents, 6611805 and 2065–2068 with engines A164C/58–62, were built for Halifax in November. Four similar chassis, 6612133–2136 with engines A164C/66 to 69, also for Halifax, followed in March 1933. Regals 6621371 and 1372, built in July and August 1932 for Huddersfield Corporation, had engines A164/52 and 55. At a later date, engine A164/52 is shown as having been fitted in Green Line Regal T274 and engine A164/76 was fitted in T305 on 20 April 1933.

The A165 engine

Internally, the A165 was similar to the A164. The crankcase was cast in aluminium alloy rather than Elektron and the cylinder heads were cast in RR50 aluminium alloy. In time, due to cracking, the RR50 heads were abandoned and were instead cast in cast iron. Externally, the A165 was immediately recognisable by the Bosch governor, built in unit with the fuel injection pump. The engine was now more conservatively rated at 122 bhp at 2,000 rpm with a BMEP of 94 lbs/sq. inch, but with a just visible exhaust 135 bhp was available at 2,200 rpm, delivering a maximum BMEP of 103 lbs/sq. inch.

The first A165s, sixty-two examples in total numbered A165/1–65 less 14, 51 and 53, had been built for the LGOC's growing fleet of oil-engined Renowns. These were built in the period May to September 1932 for chassis 6631155–1216 (LTs 1355–1416). The building of the A165 for 'outside' customers commenced in October with engine A165/69, which went into Mammoth Major 668156 for Mac Carriers in Bournemouth. The last of the type to be fitted in a production chassis was A165W/1721 for Halifax Regent 06616601, built on 25 May 1939. The last engine on record is A165/1733, which was rebuilt as A180J/1627 on 4 October 1946.

Reliability issues

While great strides had been made in respect of power output and fuel efficiency, mechanical reliability was hard won. Minute 2288 of the AEC board meeting held on 25 February 1932 provides interesting commentary:

Chief Engineers Report

The Chief Engineer during a report in detail as to the present activities of his department, and in reply to a specific question by the Chairman, recorded his view that while the development of the oil engine has achieved such a degree of progress as to warrant its further development by means of the production for operational purposes, of batches of not more than fifty at a time, its relative inferiority in reliability as compared with the petrol engine will prevent its general production in unrestricted quantities until a much wider experience in actual operation has been first obtained.

Bearing failures

In the Acro engine, the maximum cylinder pressure was around 1,000 lbs/sq. inch, crankpin loadings were in excess of the capacity of the big-end bearings and the failure rate was inevitably high. The adoption of the Ricardo head, with its more controlled burning, brought some relief to the situation. The maximum cylinder pressure had been reduced to around 850 lbs/sq. inch but it was, however, not until the development of lead-bronze by Napiers in nearby Acton and its adoption for the top half of the big end bearings that failures in this area were brought into manageable proportion. Lead-bronze comprised 74 per cent copper, 25 per cent lead and 1 per cent tin, the copper content providing a matrix-like structure in which to carry the lead, while at the same time providing the necessary strength to resist crushing.

Cylinder wear

Equally serious was the high rate of cylinder wear experienced in the upper limits of piston ring travel, thought originally to be a feature of the high cylinder pressures acting on the top ring. Its incidence was variable. It had not shown up on the test bench, nor was it prevalent in the petrol engine. The situation was the subject of much learned discussion and in a paper delivered in March 1933 before the Institution of Automobile Engineers, H. R. Ricardo had said that evidence so far suggested that the rate of wear in the cylinder bore appeared to be almost independent of the conditions under which the engine was operated.

C. B. Dicksee, commenting on the paper, wrote:

With regard to the cylinder-liner wear, I must emphatically disagree with the author's statement that service and engine speed have no bearing on the rate of wear, as experience under actual service conditions shows very definitely that the cylinder wear is greatest on city services and least on vehicles which operate for long distances daily. It certainly appears to be true that the piston material itself has little or no bearing on cylinder wear, and that the piston rings themselves are the culprits, indirectly at any rate. It has frequently been observed that during extended bench tests the wear on the cylinder has been almost negligible, whereas the same engine placed on the road will show from 3 to

4 times the rate of wear in the same period of time, even though the average engine speed and load must have been appreciably less than that at which the bench tests were run.

I am entirely in agreement with the author that corrosion rather than abrasion plays the major part as far as wear is concerned, and I have almost invariably observed that on removing the cylinder head from an engine after test, patches of rust are discernible on the cylinder bores, these being in evidence even in cases where the cylinder head has been removed while the engine is still warm. It is, of course, necessary to remove the head without having previously turned the crankshaft, otherwise the traces of rust will be removed. The appearance of such rust inevitably means the removal of a certain amount of iron, and it stands to reason that the more often this condition arises the more rapid the cylinder wear becomes.

Research would eventually pinpoint low operational temperature as the source of wear in the early oil engines. The appearance of rust in the cylinder bores had given some indication of the presence of corrosive combustion products even where coolant temperatures had been maintained at a moderately high level. Quoting from C. C. Pounder's Diesel Engine Principles and Practice, second edition, 1962, page 8–21:

During the early stages of warming-up – and later if the jacket temperature is too low – the cylinder walls may be below the dewpoint of the combustion products, and increased wear by corrosion may occur. The deposition of acids from the combustion gases may occur during any of the working strokes, including the exhaust stroke and even the compression stroke, from the exhaust residual left behind from the previous cycle. The remedies for corrosive wear are, of course, a quick warming-up technique and the use of a suitable jacket temperature (140°F. to 190°F.).

The LGOC claimed some improvement in bore wear following the adoption of hardened cylinder liners, while research by AEC showed that liner materials containing a proportion of phosphorus provided a considerable resistance to corrosion. By February 1934 it had become the practice of the LGOC to blank off the lower part of the radiator in cold weather, which would provide for an increase in engine temperature and a reduction in the formation of combustion acids. The formulation of high film-strength detergent engine oils in the 1940s would finally overcome this problem of acid corrosion.

Operational experience

Interesting commentary on the performance of engine A161/35 is found in a report dated 22 February 1934, addressed to the Officer Commanding of The Mechanical Warfare Experimental Establishment, Pinehurst Barracks, Farnborough.

The report is centred on a six-wheel-drive FWD R6T tractor, T21544, HX 6114, which had first been placed with the MWEE on 19 March 1931. First powered by oil engine A155/35, it had been placed in service in order for comparison to be made with the standard A162-powered R6T tractor. Clearly, the A155 engine had been found troublesome and after having been returned to Southall on three occasions, the vehicle, with a total of only 2,055 miles run, was finally returned to Slough on 30 September 1931. The A155 engine was replaced by A161/35 and the tractor returned to the MWEE (from Southall) on 26 February 1932. The report reads as under:

Special Report

On

Condition of

A.E.C. 6-cylinder C.I. Engine

in

F.W.D. 6-Wheel-Drive Tractor – W.D. No. T.21544

M.W.E.E. Report No 269(c)

22nd February 1934

Statement.
Owing to the falling off in performance of this engine it was decided to measure the cylinders. These measurements were reported to M.G.O.6. who decided that the engine should be removed from the chassis for detailed examination.

History of Engine.
At a vehicle mileage of 2055 the original engine was removed and replaced by the present engine. The latter was larger and more powerful and was fitted with a Ricardo head. The specification is given at Appendix A.

Engine Mileage to date of Examination.
Road 5934. Cross Country 1328. Total 7262 miles.
Vehicle mileage.   Total 9317 miles.

Defects Repairs and Modifications.
Details of all work carried out on the engine are given at Appendix B.

Condition on Final Examination.
The condition of the engine on final examination together with measurements of engine wear is given at Appendix C.

Conclusions.
This engine cannot be said to have given satisfactory service. It has had several major defects and its general condition is not as good as might reasonably be expected after 7,000 miles.
It is difficult to assign any definite reason for the excessive cylinder wear, but it is understood that this type of engine is now fitted with cylinder liners, which might indicate that other cases of severe cylinder wear have been experienced with engines of this type.

Appendix A

to

M.W.E.E. Report No.269(c)

Specification

Of

A.E.C. 6-Cylinder C.I. Engine

In

F.W.D. 6-Wheel-Drive Tractor – W.D. No.T.21544

Engine No.	A161/35 (Ricardo Head)
No. of Cyls.	6
Bore	115m/m
Stroke	142m/m
B.H.P. (max)	128.6 at 2000 r.p.m.
H.P. (R.A.C.)	49.2
C.C.	8850 cc
Fuel Pump & Injectors	Bosch
Lubricating System	Gear type pump. Pressure feed To all main and connecting rod big end bearings: by-pass from pump to rocker gear. Splash to camshaft and cylinders.
Cooling System	"Still" radiator. Four-blade fan: centrifugal water pump.

Appendix B

to

The MWEE Report No.269(c)

Defects, Repairs and Modifications

At the same time as the new engine was fitted, the cooling system was modified to give increased cooling performance. (57/Vehicles/2484, M.G.O.6. dated 26.2.32 refers)

At 742 miles.
A small blowhole was observed in the cylinder head water jacket.

At 2122 miles.
Cylinder head gasket blown. No2 head cracked and No6 piston marked by valve. New Aluminium cylinder heads of improved Ricardo combustion chamber type complete with valves, springs, bronze seatings for valves, injectors and new gaskets fitted by firms representatives.

At 3641 miles.
A timing chain failed during trials in Wales (vide report No355(e) d/5.10.32).

The following work was subsequently carried out by the firm's representatives:

New camshaft timing wheel and timing chain fitted.

Two new top rings and scraper ring fitted to each piston.

Six new type connecting rods with steel backed big end liners and bronze small end bushes.

New tappets of modified design and new gaskets all round.

One new fan driving shaft and bearings.

At 3939 miles.

An engine oil leak behind fuel pump was observed – oil leaking through two stud holes under pump platform.

At 4939 miles.

New fuel pump fitted. No3 injector replaced by spare.

At 5158 miles.

New KLG heater plugs fitted

At 6825 miles.

Cylinder head badly cracked over No5 cylinder.

At 7262 miles.

Engine completely stripped for examination.

Appendix C

to

MWEE Report No.269(c)

Condition of Engine on Final Examination

All parts not mentioned are in good condition.

Cylinders.

Heavily Worn.

Pistons.

Nos.4, 5 and 6 marked by valve tops. There was evidence that the ball ends of the rockers had been riding on the lip of the cup forming the push rod end. Thus an abnormally high valve opening took place. When the Ricardo heads were being fitted by the makers, the marking now observed had just commenced. The marking and cause was pointed out at the time to the maker's representatives.

Gudgeon Pins.

Slightly slack in pistons.

Big-end Bearings.
No.5 cracked and remainder gritty.

Crankshaft.
Main journals slightly ridged. No.7 main bearing run (pipe partially blocked by copper chip). Remainder rough and gritty. Oil seal badly worn by oil retaining threads.

Valves.
Faces normal but stems slightly loose in guides. Exhaust seatings pitted.

Oil Pump.
Teeth and Casing worn.

Oil relief Valve.
Spring worn on sides.

Timing Sprocket.
Teeth wearing hook shaped.

Dynamo drive chain.
Slightly stretched. Chain guides badly worn.

Cylinder Diameter Wear
Bore - 115mm. = 4.528 ins

A-with gudgeon   B-against gudgeon

Wear at limit of travel of Top Ring

Position	NO.1 Cyl	NO.2 cyl	No.3 cyl	No.4 cyl	NO.5 cyl	No.6 cyl
A	.051	.049	.046	.047	.044	.038
B	.044	.043	.044	.050	.044	.042

Valve bounce appears to be the likely reason for the coming together of the valves and pistons, occasioned either by over-speeding or weak valve springs.

Rotational speed

From the very earliest days of the oil engine development programme, it had been thought vital for the acceptance of the engine that its performance characteristics should be comparable to the petrol engine and any admission by AEC that high-speed operation carried any penalty was perversely resisted. Without identifying the vehicles involved, C. B. Dicksee claimed personal knowledge of oil-engined single-deck coaches having been run at up to 75 mph, a speed which represents 3,800 rpm. (AEC Gazette April 1933, page 170) An inspired guess would suggest that these vehicles were in fact the LGOC's Southall-based A155-powered Green Line Regals.

The LGOC

The general approach by the LGOC to engine speed quickly became more conservative. By December 1932, all of its ninety-four AEC engines had been governed to 2,000 rpm (the LGOC's Gardner 6LWs were governed to 1,700 rpm) and while bearing troubles were not unknown, they were now said to be no more prevalent than those experienced in petrol engines. In the fullness of time, AEC, like the LGOC, limited the rotational speed of the engine and the power output to more moderate values.

1934 and beyond

By 1934 the 8.8 litre engine had been set to develop 130 bhp at 2,300 rpm and the BMEP reduced to a maximum of 94 lbs/sq. inch. The excellent combustion properties of the Comet head provided a high specific power output and the lower maximum cylinder pressures gave the big-end bearings a rather easier time than had been the case with the Acro head. It also showed a wide tolerance to the sometimes indifferent fuel quality. Against this had to be weighed the penalty of a higher fuel consumption than was afforded by the direct injection types, an unavoidable forfeit occasioned by the pumping losses inherent in the indirect injection engine.

With the introduction of the Railcar came a different set of problems. In this application, the engine was called upon to sustain high speed running for long periods, with the result that the lubricating oil became overheated. This had, in some degree, been envisaged, with the result that the special flat-bottomed sump was cast with integral cooling fins. This proved only marginally effective and subsequently the oil capacity was increased and an oil cooling arrangement was devised whereby cooling water from the radiator was passed through a 'still'-type matrix incorporated in the sump.

Late in 1935 a special engine, the A165T, was developed to suit the rather different railcar operating conditions. The light alloys previously adopted in the manufacture of the crankcase were dropped in favour of cast iron and the chain drive for the camshaft and the auxiliaries gave way to a gear set.

All of the A165s (with the exception of the small number of engines converted to petrol for the Australian State Railways in 1933) featured the Comet head. The A165AA, built to the requirements of the Athens Electric Transport Company, was unusual in having cylinders of 103 mm bore. Rather more than half of the A165s built survived to be converted to the direct injection A180 in the 1940s.

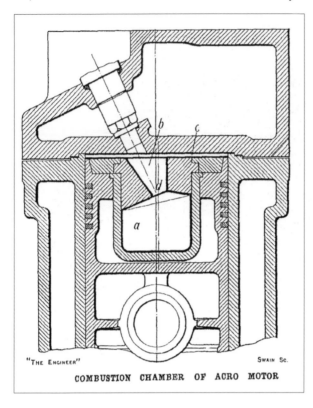

"THE ENGINEER"   SWAIN Sc.

COMBUSTION CHAMBER OF ACRO MOTOR

AEC's research into the development of the high-speed oil engine had started early in 1928. From information then available it appeared that the newly evolved Acro system, the patent rights of which had been acquired by Robert Bosch of Stuttgart, offered a sensible starting point. In its original form, the Acro chamber was formed in the piston crown and it was this arrangement which AEC first adopted. (*Drawing:* The Engineer)

3277.

Charles Edwards is credited with having brought this first oil engine to fruition. The engine was based on the crankcase of the six-cylinder side valve A121 engine. Reflecting its heritage with the camshaft on the right (or the English nearside), the push rod tubes for the overhead valve gear gave the engine a somewhat antiquarian appearance, further emphasised by the back to front fan with its link-type fan belt. The fuel injection pump, of Bosch manufacture, appears linked to a governor assembly driven in tandem with the water pump. The tops of the downward pointing injectors can be seen just below the rocker shaft. (*Photographs: AEC 3277 & 3271, Author's collection*)

3271

Above: Another view of Charles Edwards' oil engine.

Right: Now totally redesigned, the oil engine had the combustion chambers located in the cylinder heads. The A155 is seen here in its production form. (*Drawing:* The Engineer)

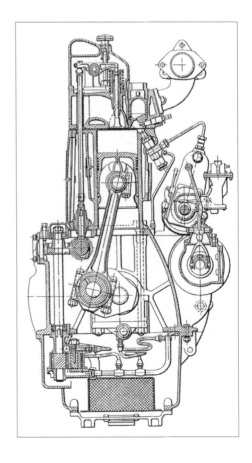

Above and below: By October 1929 the Dicksee designed engine had been built and was ready for test. The engine was of clean modern appearance with the camshaft, fan and auxiliaries now driven by triplex Reynold chain. The water pump, driven in tandem with the dynamo and mounted rearward of it, delivered water into the cylinder block between cylinders four and five, much in the manner of its predecessor. At this point in its development the engine still featured an open flywheel and mountings such as would allow its ready interchange with engines fitted to the LGOC's six-wheeled 'LS' type omnibus. (*Photographs: AEC 3 off not numbered*)

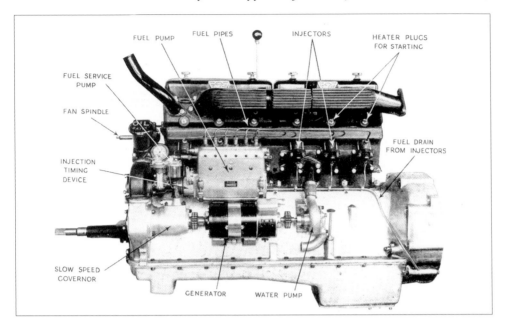

FUEL PUMP   FUEL PIPES   INJECTORS   HEATER PLUGS FOR STARTING

FUEL SERVICE PUMP

FAN SPINDLE

INJECTION TIMING DEVICE

FUEL DRAIN FROM INJECTORS

SLOW SPEED GOVERNOR

GENERATOR   WATER PUMP

Above: In the next development, the engine had progressed to a point where it was being adapted for fitment in the Rackham-designed chassis. The flywheel was enclosed in a bell housing, which would allow the mounting of the gearbox in unit with the engine, and the crankcase bottom half had been re-profiled to suit the range of commercial and passenger chassis then in production. A gear change mechanism was mounted on the offside of the crankcase. (*Photograph:* Tramway & Railway World)

Below: Moving on to October 1930, the engine now in its production form and identified as the A155, the water pump had been moved to the front of the timing case and a vacuum exhauster for the servo brakes interposed between the timing case and the fuel injection pump. The two simple rocker covers and the separate inlet manifold had been replaced by a new, single-piece rocker cover incorporating the air intake passages. (*Photograph:* AEC 3407)

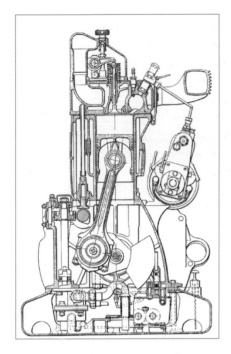

The sectional drawing of the A165 engine for Railcar No. 18 demonstrates how, within the basic structure, the engine had developed from the original A155. The wide and shallow sump casting allowed adequate clearance above the rails. Within the sump, the oil was cooled by means of a longitudinal grid of water-cooled 'Still' tubes, shown just to the right of the oil pump suction pipe. (*Drawing: AEC*)

There were few outward differences between the A161, the A164 and the A165. The immediate distinguishing feature of the A165 was the adoption of the Bosch governor, mounted in unit with the fuel injection pump, whereas the A161 and the A164 (the A155 also) featured a separate AEC designed unit. The LGOC's A161s were fitted with twin crankcase-mounted dynamos and the crankcase on the A165 still retained the two dynamo mountings. Meanwhile, in order to combat the high lighting loads imposed by the double deck Renown, the LGOC had opted for a single chassis-mounted 1250-watt dynamo, jackshaft driven from the timing case. (*Photograph: AEC*)

11

The Trolleybuses Types 663T and 691T

It was announced in the AEC Gazette of April 1930 that in the previous month, AEC and the English Electric Company had agreed to collaborate in the manufacture of single-motor, low-loading trolley omnibuses. AEC was to build the chassis and English Electric the electrical equipment and the bodies. Three types were to be produced which would have direct counterparts in the Regal, the Regent and the Renown. The first built was the three-axled Type 663T.

The chassis specification

The Type 663T trolleybus chassis had a wheelbase of 16 feet 6 inches, measured from the front axle to the centreline of the rear bogie, and the bogie axles were on 4-foot centres. The chassis had an overall length of 26 feet 9 inches and an overall width, over the front hubcaps, of 7 feet 5½ inches. The chassis frame width at the front dumb irons was 3 feet 0¼ inches, increasing to 5 feet just forward of the rear bogie. It had a maximum depth at mid-wheelbase of 11 1/8 inches. The frame, with constant changes in section, curved gently over the axles and had a laden height at mid-wheelbase of 1 foot 10½ inches. Rearward of the bogie, it fell to 12½ inches.

The front axle was of the normal Reversed Elliot pattern with 2¼-inch diameter stub axles, the hubs running on taper roller bearings. The front springs were conventional semi-elliptics 4 feet 2 inches long, fixed at the forward end with swinging shackles at the rear. Luvax rotary hydraulic shock absorbers controlled the tendency of the front axle to bounce on bad road surfaces. The steering gear on the early chassis and on those built for Birmingham Corporation was of the Marles type, but the London United Tramways' Diddlers had the AEC worm and nut pattern, at that time referred to as the LGO type.

The rear axles were of the semi-floating type with 7-inch underneath worm gear and having a ratio of 9 1/3:1. The final drive was offset to the nearside by 1 foot 2 3/8 inches and an inter-axle differential equalised driving loads. The rear suspension comprised two centrally pivoted semi-elliptic leaf springs, one each side, carried on substantial hanger brackets. The springs were anchored at the outer ends in the axle's spring carriers. A torque blade, anchored in the foremost bogie axle, was loosely connected to the rearmost axle in a swivelling, sliding joint. This absorbed all driving and braking stresses and prevented rotation of the axles.

The foot brake operated on all axles and the hand brake only on the bogie axles. The brake drums were of 17-inch diameter and the brake shoes were 3¼ inches wide with ¾-inch thick linings. The hand brake and foot brake shoes were carried side by side in the rear drums and all of the twenty brake shoes were interchangeable. On the prototype chassis, 663T001, the brakes were compressed air-operated, the compressor being driven by an electric motor mounted on top of the traction motor. Two operating cylinders, one front and one rear, served the front and rear brakes.

Chassis from 663T004, and possibly 002 and 003 also, had vacuum servo brakes where the main servo operated the bogie brakes and a slave servo those on the front axle. Two chassis, 663T022 and 023, are noted as having triple servos, i.e. individual servos for the each of the front brake units. The vacuum exhauster was motor-driven in similar manner to the air compressor on chassis 001. An additional electric braking system (type unspecified) could be provided, this operating in conjunction with and in advance of the wheel brakes.

The standard traction motor was a self-ventilating, box-framed 80 hp English Electric D.K. 130-80 operating at 500/600 volts d.c. An alternative, found in twenty-five of the LUT's sixty trolleybuses, was the 82 hp 110-DL built by the British Thomson-Houston Company. The motor was front-mounted in the chassis frame and, like the engine in the Renown chassis, was angled slightly downward to the rear and toward the nearside. The drive was taken, close by the nearside chassis member, by open tubular cardan shafts and Spicer couplings direct to the rear axles. The master controller was of the six-notch variety and was operated by foot pedal. A current limit relay was incorporated which prevented surges of current and controlled the rate of acceleration.

The building programme

Three chassis, 663T001–003, were built for demonstration purposes. 663T001, carrying registration number HX 1460, was despatched to Nottingham on 23 July 1930. The duration of its stay at Nottingham is unknown but it was rebuilt in 1931 with an English Electric half-cab body and shown on the English Electric stand at Olympia in November of that year. Registered JN 2086, it was ultimately sold to Southend Corporation and noted as being 'off float' on 12 June 1933. Chassis 002 was despatched to the English Electric Company on 6 October 1930. It is believed to have been the vehicle which, later in that month, was employed in the preliminary testing of the LUT's new trolleybus system between Twickenham and Teddington. The vehicle was rebuilt in June 1932 and, with a new Brush body, was sold to Birmingham Corporation as 663T070. Chassis 003 was sold to Bournemouth Corporation in March 1933, having also received a new body. In 1936, in an unusual conversion, its electric traction motor was replaced by a standard AEC engine and gearbox.

Two chassis, 663T004 and 005, had been built on 24 October 1930 and were despatched to English Electric on 28 October and 4 November 1930. Identical in appearance to the three demonstrators, these were supplied to Walsall Corporation in May and June 1931.

The LUT's sixty chassis, 663T006–065, were built in the period between December 1930 and September 1931. The bodies were constructed by the Union Construction Company and seated twenty-four passengers in the lower saloon and thirty-two upstairs. They were an interesting amalgam of standard LGOC bus practice with features borrowed from the 'Feltham' tram, which the Union Construction Company had also built. The first of these so-called Diddlers entered service on 16 May 1931. The first withdrawals were made almost seventeen years later, in February 1948. Ten were retained short-term for training duties and these, with one exception which is now in the London Transport Museum, went to the breaker's yard in May 1952.

The supply of traction equipment was split between the English Electric Company and the British Thomson-Houston Company. EEC supplied motors and associated equipment for the first thirty-six chassis and BTH for the remaining twenty-four. The wheel brakes were operated through a normal Dewandre vacuum servo system but 663T065, the last of the group, had Westinghouse brakes. Chassis 042–051 and 065 are shown as having LGO type steering, i.e. worm and nut.

Acceleration and braking

While the traction motors had a nominal output of 80 hp, the characteristics of the electric motor provided a starting torque far in excess of that delivered by an equivalent 80 hp petrol engine. Though the trolleybuses were geared for a maximum of only 30 mph, their acceleration was such that fully laden, a speed of 20 mph could be attained in 10 seconds (and within a distance of 62 yards). Normal rheostatic braking provided a deceleration of about 8 feet per second per second but employing both the rheostatic and the wheel brakes together, the vehicle could be brought to a standstill from 30 mph in about 80 ft. This equates to a deceleration of 12 feet per second per second.

The later Type 663T chassis

Chassis 663T066–069 together with 070, which had been converted from 663T002, were completed for Birmingham Corporation in June 1932. They had front-mounted motors, Dewandre vacuum servo brakes and Marles steering gear. The H33/25R bodies were built by Brush. These, together with eleven four-wheeled Leyland TB2s, remained on the Nechells route all their lives and were withdrawn in 1940.

Development of the trolleybus chassis was constant and ongoing. Two special single-deck chassis, 663T071 and 072, were built for Sydney Corporation in May and June 1933. While retaining a 16-foot 6-inch wheelbase, the frames were so constructed as to provide an overhang forward of the front axle. Like the type 691T built for the LUT (see below), the traction motors were mid-mounted, that of chassis 071 being a BTH BT201 while 072 had an English Electric EE405. The chassis had Westinghouse compressed air-operated Lockheed brakes. Chassis 071 received a transit-type body built by Park Royal, the forward extension allowing for the fitting of folding, front entrance doors under the control of the driver. The exit platform was at the rear. Chassis 072 was despatched to Australia as a bare chassis.

Chassis 073 was built for Huddersfield Corporation in October 1933. Its Y156A chassis frame was of the same type as the five Birmingham chassis, and indeed the sixty built for the LUT, and this, together with the detachable panel on the front of the vehicle, suggests that it also had a front-mounted motor. G. D. Peters supplied the equipment for the direct-acting compressed air brakes. Registered VH 5728, it remained the only one of its type in the Huddersfield fleet.

The Type 691T

691T001, AHX 801, described in the March 1933 issue of the AEC Gazette, was the first 30-foot trolleybus to be seen in the capital. Experimental in nature, it had been built for London United Tramways and designed to replace the tramcar on heavily trafficked routes. Its Chiswick-built body had seating for seventy-four passengers, forty of whom were accommodated upstairs and thirty-four in the lower saloon. At the time of its construction it was claimed to have the highest capacity of any trolleybus in the British Isles. It entered service with the LUT on 27 March 1933 and though it was the only one of its type to be built, many of its features were carried forward to the 30-foot six-wheeled Type 664T. An unusual feature, at least for London operation, was the single centre entrance body with double, driver-controlled, pneumatically operated, sliding doors.

Chassis details

The Type 691T had a wheelbase of 18 feet 7 inches, with front and rear track dimensions of 6 feet 5 inches and 6 feet 2¾ inches respectively. The centre entrance body required some compromise in respect of chassis frame design, the nearside frame member being steeply angled down rearward of the front axle and lower than the offside member by some 7 3/8 inches at mid-wheelbase. Chassis frame aside, perhaps the most significant change (in 1933) was the positioning of the traction motor just forward of the rear bogie instead of at the front of the chassis. The motor was an English Electric EE404 field-controlled, series-wound unit with a nominal output of 80 hp, the drive being taken to the rear axles through a single short tubular cardan shaft with 8-inch Spicer couplings. The remote, foot-operated master controller and the resistances were carried at the front of the chassis and the contactors were mounted in watertight cases on the offside chassis member.

The arrangement of the axles, suspension and the rear bogie were similar to that of the then-current Type 663T chassis and the steering gear was of the now familiar AEC worm and nut type. Operation of the brakes was through a Lockheed hydraulic system, energised by a single Westinghouse compressed air servo, but the arrangement of individual brake shoes for the footbrake and handbrake remained. The bare chassis had a weight of 4 tons 5 cwts 3 qrs and the complete vehicle a laden weight of under

13 tons. By how much was not revealed, but it should be remembered that 13 tons was the maximum weight permitted for a three-axled passenger-carrying trolleybus.

The Type 663T Further Developed

In the summer of 1934, Portsmouth Corporation took 663T074 and 075, with sixty-seat bodywork by English Electric. These are noted as having Y156B frames, English Electric mid-mounted 80 hp motors with regenerative control, worm and nut steering and G. D. Peters compressed air brakes.

AXU 188, chassis 663T076, had been built for the London Passenger Transport Board for evaluation in its forthcoming tramway replacement programme. Like the Type 691T, which had preceded it by some fifteen months, it was built to the maximum legal length of 30 feet and, while combining some of the advanced features of the Type 691T, retained the conventional rear platform. The bare chassis had been despatched to Metropolitan Cammell on 15 May 1934 and delivered to the LPTB on 4 July of that year. It had a wheelbase of 18 feet 7 inches, with the traction motor mounted just forward of the rear bogie and offset to the nearside. The motor itself was a self-ventilating, compound-wound Metropolitan-Vickers MV202. The motor characteristics ensured that automatic regenerative braking provided an even deceleration of not more than 4.5 feet per second down to 12 mph, rheostatic braking taking effect below this speed. Except for its greater length, the basic chassis had much in common with the earlier Type 663T but the wheel brakes were now compressed air-operated, with the brake cylinders on the front axle mounted above the hollow king-pins. The compressed air equipment was supplied by G. D. Peters Ltd.

Chassis 663T077–086 were built for Grimsby Corporation in 1936 and were fitted with attractive fifty-eight-seat centre entrance bodies built by Charles Roe. These chassis, now with fully floating rear axles, are thought, wheelbase excepted, to have been identical to the current Type 664T. The last three of the Type 663T chassis, 087, 088 and 089, with bodywork by Park Royal, went to Canada.

Beyond the Type 663T

Until 1931, except for sporadic short-term tests of the trolleybus, electric traction in London had been the exclusive province of the tramcar. The opening of the new trolleybus system by the LUT in May 1931, in replacement of the existing tramway, marked the beginning of the end for the London tram but it was not until 1935 that tram replacement schemes got under way in earnest.

Experience gained by the LUT and the LPTB with the Type 691T and 663T076 led, in 1935, to the building of the 18-foot 7-inch wheelbase Type 664T, of which 869 were built. Six hundred and fifty-nine were supplied to the LPTB. Other home market operators of the Type 664T included the Corporations of Newcastle–upon-Tyne, Rotherham, Belfast and Cardiff, while beyond British shores, deliveries went to Montreal, Sydney and Durban. Two went to Russia.

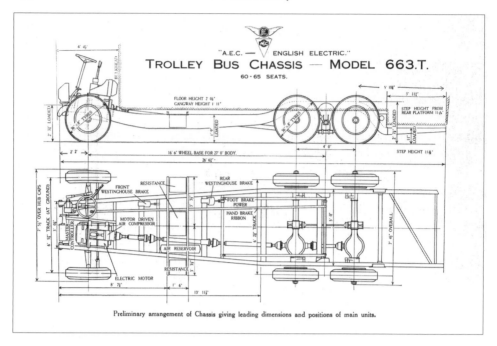

Arrangement drawing of trolleybus chassis type 663T taken from AEC sales brochure No. 91, dated July 1930. (Drawing: AEC, Author's collection)

Chassis 663T004 and 005 were built on 24 October 1930 and despatched to English Electric on 28 October and 4 November respectively. They were delivered to Walsall Corporation on 8 May and 1 June 1931. DH 8312 is 663T005. (*Photograph: AEC, Author's collection*)

Above left: Replacing an existing tramway service in the area around Kingston upon Thames, a new 17-mile trolleybus system was inaugurated by the London United Traction Company on 16 May 1931. Sixty Type 663T trolleybuses, 663T006–065, with fifty-six-seat bodies built by the Union Construction Company, were built to service the operation. MG 186 is 663T040. (*Photograph: AEC, Author's collection*)

AEC built two chassis, one six-wheeled and one four-wheeled, for evaluation by the London Passenger Transport Board for the projected mid-1930s tramway replacement scheme. The six-wheeled chassis, 663T076, like its Type 691T predecessor, was built to an overall length of 30 feet. It was despatched to Metropolitan Cammell on 15 May 1934. As AXU 188, it is seen here on its return to Southall, its seventy-three-seat body notably more austere than the Chiswick-built body on 691T001. (*Photograph: AEC 0013, Author's collection*)

12

The Regal 4 Type 642
1930–1937

Specification

With the exception of the engine, the four-cylinder Type 642 Regal was mechanically similar to the six-cylinder Type 662 and except for the Regal 4 script on the radiator and the four-cylinder engine's forward-mounted sump, readily seen behind the radiator, the two types were indistinguishable. As first built, the Regal 4 would have had the four-speed D119 gearbox, single servo brakes and a semi-floating rear axle. As with the Type 662, the gearbox would give way to the 'silent third' D124, the brakes to triple servo and the rear axle to the fully floating type F156. Latterly, servo-assisted hydraulic brakes would be adopted. Because of the shorter engine, one of the hidden features was that the gearbox and its associated banjo cross-member were carried correspondingly further forward in the chassis frame.

The A139 engine had been first designed for the Mercury and Monarch chassis. Save that it had four cylinders instead of six, its design followed closely on that of the A136 and A137. It had a cylinder bore of 112 mm and a stroke of 130 mm, giving a swept volume of 5.12 litres. Its power output was 38 bhp at 1,000 rpm and 65 bhp at 2,000. With the 'power head', the engine was identified as the A163 and its power output was increased to 80 bhp at 2,400 rpm.

In March 1933, AEC launched the A166 four-cylinder oil engine. Its cylinder dimensions were 108 mm by 146 mm bore and stroke giving a capacity of 5.35 litres. The camshaft drive and overhead valve gear clearly had a close affinity with the A139 and A163 petrol engines and the Ricardo combustion chamber owed much to the A165 six-cylinder oil engine. Its quoted power output was 75 bhp at 2,000 rpm. In turn, the A166 was superseded by the A168, similar in every respect save that the bore had been increased to 120 mm and the power output to 85 bhp.

Production details

The first Regal 4 had been a conversion of 662277, a Hall Lewis-bodied demonstrator registered HX 1271, originally built on 10 May 1930. With the four-cylinder A139 engine installed, it was temporarily re-numbered 642001. Restored to its original specification and chassis number, it passed to Bells Services of Walbottle on 31 March 1931. Chassis 642002 had been built on 15 September 1930. From the outset it carried a four-cylinder engine but it owed is origin to chassis 662480. The chassis card for 662480 reads 'built as Regal 4, see 642002'. With a standard 17-foot wheelbase chassis, it had engine A139/102 and a 6¾:1 final drive. Bodied by Brush and registered UP 4744, it went to Stockton Corporation. Burlingham-bodied 642003, registered WX 5613 and with engine A139/96, went to Severn & Son of Stainforth in October 1930.

Five Regal 4s were built in 1931. Batty of Blackpool had 642004 and 005, both with twenty-six-seat front entrance coach bodies by Burlingham, registered FV1840 and FV 1637 respectively. Halstead of Halifax also opted for Burlingham bodywork for 642006, WX 7668, but favoured a rear entrance layout seating thirty-two passengers. Severn of Stainforth took 642007, with a front entrance thirty-two-seat bus body by Cravens, registered WX 7403. AEC's demonstrator, 642008, had a thirty-two-seat bus body by Short, registered MV 295. This passed to Gelligaer UDC in 1936. It is perhaps worthy of note that during 1931, 1932, 1933 and 1934, AEC built no fewer than eight Regal 4 demonstrators.

Of the 178 Regal 4s listed, in the seven-year period from 1930 to 1937, no fewer than 130 are recorded as purchased by public companies or municipal undertakings. City of Oxford Motor Services was the first major undertaking to take the Regal 4 with chassis 642014–019, built in May 1932, and 642026–031 in January 1933, a total of twelve, all powered by the A163 engine. Reading Corporation took 642032 and 033. East Midland Motor Services had nine, 642038–044 delivered in 1933 and 642034 and 047, delivered in 1934. All were A163-powered. Mansfield and District had 642050–055 in May 1933, again with the A163 engine.

In May 1933, Dublin United had the first oil-engined Regal 4, 0642056 with engine A166/13. This was followed in October by a further five, 0642065–069, also A166-powered. Gelligaer UDC had 0642070 and 071. Great Yarmouth had five, 0642075–077 and 079 and 080, with thirty-two-seat English Electric bus bodies. Scottish Motor Traction took thirty-three in a single order, 0642081–113 with the larger 120 mm bore A168 engine in April 1934, and Dublin United followed with fifteen similar specified chassis, 0642115–129, between April and August of that year. The Gosport and Fareham Omnibus Company (trading as Provincial) took eight, 0642130–137, in October 1934 and Dublin United came back with a final order for twenty-five chassis, 0642138–152 and 154–163, built between November 1934 and September 1935. These, like those built for Provincial, had the A168 engine.

By 1936, sales of the four-cylinder Regal were dwindling. Burnley, Nelson & Colne had 0642165 and 166, with thirty-five-seat Park Royal bodies, and 0642168–173 were exported to South America, presumably in chassis form. Swindon Corporation had the distinction of taking the last three, 0642176–178, in August 1937. These, registered AWV 555–557, had thirty-seven-seat bodies, also built by Park Royal.

Chassis price

The ex-works chassis price of the Regal 4 in January 1932 was £975. The September 1934 data sheet shows the oil-engined Regal 4 priced at £1,100. With a price differential of £180 between the A163 petrol engine and the A168 oiler, the petrol-engined Regal 4 of 1934 would have had a list price in the order of £920.

Except perhaps in the case of Provincial, where the vehicles were employed in a dual-purpose role, the great majority of Regal 4s were employed on stage-carriage work rather than private hire. Where power output was not a serious consideration, the lower cost of operation made the Regal 4 an attractive proposition. The four-cylinder engines could never compete with smooth-running six-cylinder types but where economy was the ruling factor, refinement was perhaps only a minor consideration.

Only the Regal 4 script on the radiator distinguishes this four-cylinder A163-powered Regal from its more powerful six-cylinder stable mates. East Midland's RB 7823, chassis 642040, with body by Brush and built in April 1933, is seen in Mansfield in August 1935. (*Photograph: G. H. F. Atkins via John Banks*)

13

The Mandator Types
669 and 672

THE TYPE 669 MANDATOR

The forward-control Type 669 Mandator was introduced in February 1931. At its launch, the AEC Gazette of that date carried this leader:

> The A.E.C. has for some time observed that there was a definite need for a heavy duty vehicle of the "Mammoth" type, but designed for low loading. There are numerous forms of goods transport service, as, for instance, furniture removing, where loading and unloading from vehicles with a frame height of say 38 ins., is a matter of some difficulty, and involves the loss of valuable time. These drawbacks are remedied in the new low loading model which is now undergoing its final trials.
>
> The new "Mammoth" is fitted with a 110 h.p. engine, but differs from the standard type, in having offset double reduction gearing for the final drive. The standard axle ratio is 9 1/3 – 1, but alternatives of 8 and 10.6 – 1 are available to suit individual circumstances.
>
> The frame when laden is 2 feet from the ground and downswept after the rear axle to 1ft. 2in. A difference of only 1 in. is made between the wheelbase of the new and standard models, that of the low loader being 16ft. 6in. Tyres are 40 x 8, which represents the maximum size that can be fitted to this type of vehicle. The design, in all cases, includes a full cab with controls as used on the "A.E.C. Regent" passenger model.

The 1932 sales brochure went on to describe the Mandator:

> The design of the AEC "MANDATOR" Low Loading Goods Vehicle is a very distinct advance on all previous conceptions of lorries, because, in general performance, high speed and easy control, perfect springing and quietness in operation, it embodies the features of modern touring car and passenger coach practice. Considerable all-round advance in design has been made, which together with greater durability and accessibility throughout, constitutes a freight carrier superior to any that has hitherto been produced.

With the Mandator, AEC was clearly looking to cash in on a niche market where image was all-important. Previous examples can be seen in the purchase by the Anglo American Oil Company of the Regent tanker, 661037, shown at Olympia in 1929 and the three Renown tankers, 664061, 062 and 113, built for the same company in 1931.

A study of the Mandator's mechanical make-up reveals that it had much in common with the then-current Regent and Regal chassis. Its 110 bhp, 110 mm bore A141 engine was only mildly different from the 100 mm bore A136/A137 of the Regent and Regal. It shared with them the same gearbox (D119), front axle (L118), steering box (M128), and radiator (N132). The rear axle (U50191) on the other hand was special, similar to that of the Mammoth and Majestic, save that the driving head was offset to the nearside. The brakes, 17-inch diameter at the front and 20-inch diameter at the rear, were operated by triple vacuum servos.

Though the Mandator had been officially launched in February 1931, the engine number of chassis 001, A141/159, suggests a building date in the middle of November 1930. With a box van body and cab built by Normand Garages, it was registered MV3100. As such it served as a demonstrator with AEC until sold to Crompton Parkinson in May 1935.

Chassis 002 was built in June 1931 and went to A. Harding in Birkenhead while 003, built in the same month, went to C. Watling in Norwich. This carried a large Luton-type van body built by Bayleys.

Chassis 004 was the first to be fitted with the 120 bhp A162 engine and D124 'silent third' gearbox. Built in July 1931 and registered WX9631, it was supplied with a van body to Nicholas Smith of Skipton. The same vehicle was later rebuilt with a new cab and platform body by Tillotson and sold to Pilkington Bros in St Helens.

Chassis 005 appeared at Olympia in November 1931. With a cab by Weymann it carried a dual-purpose insulated van body by Duramin, intended for the carriage of live cattle or meat carcasses. It was supplied to the London and Southern Counties Transport Company of Reigate in December 1931. Chassis 006, 007 and 008 were supplied to the same company in January 1932 with similar bodywork but built by Park Royal Coachworks. In season, these multi-purpose vehicles were employed in the flower trade, transporting Scillian-grown daffodils from Penzance to London's Covent Garden. Chassis 007, registered PJ 2894, like chassis 004, was rebuilt with a new Tillotson cab and body and passed to Pilkingtons in January 1935.

Chassis 009, VY 3511, was supplied to J. B. Harrison of York in April 1932 and later passed to Sutton & Oxtoby in the same city.

Chassis 010, with bodywork by Lee Motors, was supplied to Austin Clark of Minety near Swindon. It had been built in May 1932 but was not sold until May 1935. By this time it had acquired a 7.7 litre oil engine, A171/407, which dates to the end of March 1935.

Chassis 011 had been built for Pickfords in March 1933 and was powered by an 8.8 litre engine, A165c/147. With a box-van body and registered AGO 308, it went to a Pickfords subsidiary, Briers & Son Ltd of Leicester.

The last of the type, 669012, with engine A162c/1079 and again with a Tillotson cab and platform body, was built new for Pilkington in May 1935. It was registered DJ 6622.

THE TYPE 672 MANDATOR

Except that it was bonneted, the Type 672 Mandator had the same mechanical specification as the forward-control Type 669. Seven only were built. Chassis 001–005 were built for the Texas Oil Company in December 1931 and carried stylish bodywork built by Butterfield of Shipley. Their three-compartment spirit tanks had a capacity of 1,500 gallons. Chassis 001, 003 and 005 were registered WX 9637, WX 9639 and WX 9634 respectively. Chassis 002 and 004 are shown to have been registered HG 183 and HG 296 but it is not known in what order.

Chassis 006 and 007 were built for Carless, Capel & Leonard in July 1932 and supplied in September and October 1932. These also had Butterfield bodywork but the tanks were of 2,000 gallons capacity. They carried registration numbers YY 9235 and YY 9236.

It is recorded that in later life, chassis 002 was sold to the Limmer & Trinidad Lake Asphalt Company. Chassis 005 was acquired by the Gosport & Fareham Omnibus Company and was rebuilt in 1944 as a fifty-six-seat Regent look-alike, EOR 251. It was withdrawn from service in 1960. Photographic evidence (London's Lorries by Arthur Ingram, Roundoak Publishing 1990, page 56) shows that one of the Carless, Capel & Leonard Mandators, YY 9235, was acquired by the Limmer & Trinidad Lake Asphalt Company and fitted with a tipping body.

The Mandator in retrospect

Perhaps the niche market that AEC had identified was but a mirage. The road haulage industry, then as now, was driven by hard economics and a new vehicle had to provide much more than image. The low floor afforded by the Mandator clearly had benefits, but in many instances, these were perceived rather than real. The exceptions perhaps were with Pilkington's, where outsize pieces of glass had to be moved, and with Texaco and Carless, Capel, where the smart, speedy bonneted tankers undoubtedly provided the prestige image looked for. The Mandator, with a list price of £1,100, was £100 more expensive than the Mammoth and for this reason alone it was only ever likely to attract the attention of the specialist. The sale of nineteen chassis over a period of four years hardly constituted a niche market. Future requirements for a low-height chassis were adequately covered by the Ranger and Regal chassis.

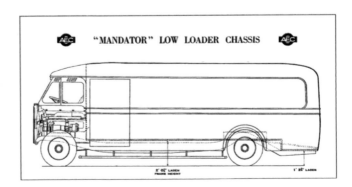

Arrangement drawing of the Mandator Type 669. (*Drawing: AEC, Author's collection*)

While the low-loading frame of the Mandator was similar in many respects to that of the Regent and Regal, the heavy-duty cross member bracing the frame at the rear spring front anchorages gave a clue to the more arduous duties expected. The rear axle, with its double reduction final drive and fully floating wheel hubs, had much in common with that of the Mammoth. (*Photograph: AEC 3437, Author's collection*)

MV 3100, with the sky-light windows set into the van's roof, served until 1935 as AEC's demonstrator. Built in June 1931 and numbered 669001, it was fitted with engine A141/159. With box van body and cab built by Normand Garages of Park Royal, it was sold to Crompton Parkinson in Guisley in May 1935. (*Photograph: AEC 5590, Author's collection*)

Pilkington's Mandator 669004, WX 9631 is seen adjacent to Tillotson's works at Burnley. The chassis was built in July 1931 with engine A162B/14 and supplied through Tillotson's to Nicholas Smith of Skipton in the following December. In its second life it was re-bodied by Tillotson and joined the Pilkington fleet in the haulage of plate glass. Pilkington acquired two more Mandators in 1935, second-hand 669007, PJ 2894, formerly with London & South Coast Transport and 669012, DJ 6622, which was purchased new. These also received Tillotson-built cabs and bodies. (*Photograph: AEC L1803, Author's collection*)

December 1931 saw the building of five bonneted Mandator chassis for the Texas Oil Company. They were despatched to Butterfields of Shipley in January 1932 where they were fitted with stylish cabs and 1,500-gallon three-compartment spirit tanks. Shod on 40 inch by 8 inch Firestone tyres, 672004, WX 9635, engine A162F/116, is seen at the Butterfield works. (*Photograph: Author's collection*)

14

The Mammoth Major Types
668 and 680

Though the Heavy Motor Car (Amendment) Order, 1922 had provided for the operation of a four-wheeled lorry and trailer combination at a gross weight of 22 tons and an articulated six-wheeled lorry at 18½ tons, it was not until 1927 that the rigid six-wheeler, in the Heavy Motor Car (Amendment) Order 1927, was given any official recognition. In the 1927 order, where the vehicle was not employed for the conveyance of passengers for hire or reward, the rigid six-wheeler was permitted a gross weight of 19 tons. A further order, the Heavy Motor Car (Amendment) (No 2) Order, 1930, allowed for the operation of a rigid eight-wheeled vehicle at a gross weight of 22 tons.

The six-wheeled Mammoth Major had come rather late into the field of the maximum capacity goods vehicle. It was officially launched in September 1931 and it had been hoped, at its introduction, that the oil engine would be sufficiently well proven to offer it as the standard power unit. While the 8.1 litre A155 oil engine had featured in the demonstrator, 668003, and the 8.8 litre A161 in a dozen or so late 1931 deliveries, it was not until November 1933 that the engine in 130 bhp A165 guise became the preferred option.

The chassis had been designed for operation at the maximum permitted gross weight for multi-axled goods vehicles of 19 tons. The petrol-engined chassis had a bare chassis weight of 5 tons 18 cwts 2 qrs and the licensing weight complete with cab and flat body would be about one ton heavier. Adding a further 8 cwts for fuel, oil, water and spare wheel, the weight ready for the road would be in the order of 7 tons 6 cwts 2 qrs. The oil-engined chassis would be 5 cwts heavier.

Specification

The prototype chassis had the six-cylinder A141 petrol engine of 110 bhp but the 120 bhp A162 was in production in time for the official launch in September 1931. Chassis 001 had the D119 four-speed crash gearbox but subsequent chassis were fitted with the 'silent third' D124. New for the Mammoth Major was the D125 constant mesh auxiliary gearbox, which provided a step down ratio of 1.58:1. This was mounted as a separate unit in the chassis and required a separate gear lever for its operation. This resulted in the interesting 'two-stick' gear change where the auxiliary gearbox was always the first to be taken on a downward change and the last on an upward change. This twin gearbox combination provided a very effective five-speed range of gears and remained a feature of AEC's heavy goods chassis until the advent of the five-speed constant mesh D153 gearbox in 1949. The D124/D125 combination provided the following ratios: 1st, 6.92:1; 2nd, 4.25:1; 3rd, 2.51:1; 4th, 1.58:1; and 5th, 1:1. Reverse was 8.41:1. At 2,400 engine rpm, with an 8.1:1 axle ratio and on 40 inch by 8 inch tyres, the road speeds in the various gears were: 1st, 5.26 mph; 2nd, 8.57 mph; 3rd, 14.5 mph; 4th, 23.0 mph; and 5th, 36.4 mph.

The rear suspension comprised two centre-pivoted inverted semi-elliptic leaf springs, one each side, 4 feet 5 inches long, the ends of which were secured in the axle spring carriers. The gunmetal bushed pivots were carried on the end of an I-section beam, which in turn supported the chassis on a deep central cross member. Torque arms ensured correct vertical movement of the axles and absorbed all driving and braking forces. The first bogie axle (type F141) had the same heavy-duty double reduction final drive with spiral bevel and double helical gears as fitted to the Mammoth chassis. The standard ratio was 8.1:1, with alternatives of 7.1:1, 9 1/3:1 and 10.6:1. The rearmost axle (type F143) was un-driven.

The footbrake and handbrake mechanisms operated independently on each of the four rear wheels. The brake drums were of 20-inch diameter and each wheel hub had two pair of shoes, 3 inches wide. All the brake shoes were interchangeable. One pair of shoes in each hub were operated by the footbrake via twin Dewandre vacuum servos and the other pair by a powerful multi-pull hand lever.

The front axle was a simple I-section beam of the reversed Elliot pattern and the front hubs were carried on stub axles of 2¼-inch diameter. Early chassis were without front axle brakes. The steering gear was by Marles.

The chassis had a 12-inch-deep nickel steel frame with 3½-inch flanges and a thickness of 5/16 inches. Alternative wheelbases of 14 feet 10½ inches and 16 feet 10½ inches were available. A chassis of 18-foot 6½-inch wheelbase was introduced in 1933. The 16-foot 10½-inch wheelbase chassis had an overall length of 27 feet 2 inches and the 18-foot 6½-inch chassis a length of 30 feet. The front track measured 6 feet 3 inches, the rear track 5 feet 8 5/8 inches and the overall width was 7 feet 5 inches. The mid-length chassis provided a platform length of 22 feet 6 inches and the long chassis 24 feet 8 inches.

The tyres were 40 inch by 8 inch on 24-inch ten-stud disc wheels, singles at the front and twin rears. Tyres of 13.5 inch by 20 inch section were also available in single formation, but where these tyres were specified, front axle brakes could not be fitted.

The chassis list price was £1,400.

Production

Records show that the main impetus of production of the Type 668 six-wheeler finished with chassis number 0668360 in February 1935 but export orders took production to 0668371, the last in February 1939. Two chassis, 668283 and 324, are recorded as not having been built and the cards for 668310, 317 and 347 are missing. 668275 was a show chassis, dismantled in September 1934 with the parts returned to surplus store.

The prototype chassis had been built in November 1930 and another half dozen, 668002–007, were built as demonstrators in the period March to May 1931. Chassis

003 had one of the very early oil engines, A155/28, and the remainder had the then-standard A141. Chassis 007 was the first of the short wheelbase types and had a Weymann cab and a three-way tipping body by Bromilow & Edwards.

Sixty-eight chassis were built in 1931. The A141 petrol engine had, by this time, given way to the A162 but eleven chassis were powered by the second-generation oil engine, the A161. From the number of engine changes made, it is clear that oil engine reliability was, at this time, still patchy.

The year 1932 saw 101 chassis built. Bouts Bros, having taken three Type 668s in 1931, took a further seventeen chassis in 1932, Bowaters took nine and Mac Carriers six. Seventy-three chassis were petrol-engined and twenty-seven oil-engined, of which five engines were of Type A161, fourteen of A164 and eight of A165.

One hundred and nineteen chassis were built in 1933, though three, chassis 668273, 290 and 299, had been converted from Mammoth four-wheelers 667251, 007 and 130 respectively. Growth in the larger fleets was quite dramatic. Bouts Bros had added a further fourteen, Bowaters eleven and Mac Carriers six. Pickfords took six. The Anglo American Oil Company took fourteen chassis in a single batch, 668218–231, and Marston Road Services, a new customer, took twenty, 0668248–267. An analysis of engine types shows that only Bouts Bros, Mac Carriers and the Anglo American Oil Company took the A162 petrol engine in 1933, fourteen, two and fourteen respectively, and eighty-eight were fitted with the A165. One, 0668173, built for Express Dairies, was fitted with a Gardner engine, presumably a 6LW.

Sixty-two chassis were built in 1934, of which four, 668282, 297, 298 and 300, had been converted from Mammoths 667227, 024, 281 and 264. Marston Road services took six, Bouts Bros had five and Hughes of Hawarden four. The Cement Marketing Company, the Albion Sugar Company and Shell Mex each had two. Sixteen chassis were fitted with the A162 petrol engine and forty-four with the A165 oiler. Four chassis, 282, 297, 298 and 300, had been converted from the Mammoth type 667 and of these, two had the earlier A161 oil engine and one the A164.

Of the remaining chassis, 0668359–371, three were built in 1935, six in 1936, three in 1938 and one in 1939. All were powered by the A165 oil engine. Chassis 359 and 360 were home market deliveries and the remainder were exported. Chassis 0668361 went to the Shell Oil Company in Canada, 362 and 363 to the South African Railway & Harbour Board and 364, a bonneted vehicle, thought to have been sent out CKD, went to the Commonwealth Government of Australia. Chassis 0668365–370 all went to South Africa. Chassis 0668365 was supplied to Griffin Engineering, 366–369 went to the Coronation Brick & Tile Company and chassis 370 went to J. & T. Paynter. Chassis 0668371 went to Agar Cross in Montevideo. A feature of the exported chassis, 0668361–371, was that they were all fitted with the heavy-duty Kirkstall rear bogie.

The eight-wheeled Mammoth Major

It has to be said that AEC was not the first company to produce a rigid, maximum capacity, load carrying eight-wheeler. That must go to the credit of Sentinel, which had built the first of eight eight-wheeled DG8 steam lorries in August 1929. Built for overseas territories and in no way complying with United Kingdom domestic regulations, the Sentinel had an unladen weight of 10 tons 18 cwts and was designed to carry a 20-ton payload. Nor was Sentinel first in the field with twin steering axles. Bradford Corporation's six-wheeled trolleybus No. 522 of 1922 was so equipped and both Morris Commercial Cars and Guy Motors produced experimental double front-axled eight-wheel drive vehicles for military evaluation in the late 1920s and early 1930s.

The first Mammoth Major 8 was built in November 1933 for the Liverpool Cartage Company. Chassis 0668216, a standard six-wheeled, A165-powered Mammoth Major with Lockheed hydraulic brakes, had been built in October 1933. A second front axle (L131), together with special steering controls, was added at Southall on 3 November 1933 and the vehicle, with Park Royal cab and body, was delivered to the customer on 6 January 1934.

Its construction had come about as a result of an idea put forward by a Mr S. B. O'Neill, chief mechanical engineer of Coast Lines Ltd, a shipping company with extensive road transport interests on the Liverpool waterfront and of which the Liverpool Cartage Company was a subsidiary. Perhaps having a specific requirement for a vehicle of greater carrying capacity than was afforded by the standard six-wheeler, he had suggested that the addition of a second front axle to the Mammoth Major was feasible.

Details of the eight-wheeled Mammoth Major had appeared in the Technical Press in February 1934 and on April 14th Modern Transport reported on its first few weeks of operation with the Liverpool company. The vehicle had started work on 10 January and by 25 March had covered 9,500 miles with a fuel consumption of 9.36 mpg. Lubricating oil was consumed at a rate of 309.5 mpg and the running costs, inclusive of fuel, oil and the wages for its two drivers, were 4.22d per mile. Accompanying the vehicle on one of its journeys was a correspondent from the technical journal Modern Transport. He wrote:

> The A.E.C. eight-wheeler is the most comfortable machine of its size we have ever encountered. The steering is so light and accurate that it must be tried to be believed, for, apart from the perfect castoring of both sets of wheels, their easy gliding motion induces a freedom of steering action that does not exist in models of the conventional type.

The detailed requirements for the fitting of the second front axle were listed under XU1108, dated 8.11.33. Whereas Sentinel, Morris and Guy, each with their individual designs, had allowed for a high degree of articulation and interaction between the bogie wheels, AEC had adopted a simpler approach. The two front axles of the Mammoth Major were wholly independent in respect of suspension (each of the four front springs were fixed at the front spring eye and had swinging shackles at the rear) but interconnected in respect of steering linkages.

The first of the factory-built eight-wheeled Mammoth Majors had come off the assembly line in May 1934. In that month Bouts Bros took five with the A162 petrol engine, chassis 668312–316, and Marston Road Services had six with the A165 oiler, 0668336–341. Chassis 0668342 was built for C. W. Hewson in June 1934, 343 for F. Edlin, also in June, 346 for A. E. Davey in July and 353 for Agar Cross in October.

In addition to these, a further eighteen existing six-wheeled chassis were converted to eight-wheel, predominantly in 1934 and 1935.

The Type 680 Mammoth Major was identical to the eight-wheeled version of the Type 668, the new chassis code having been introduced in June 1934 to differentiate between the six-wheeled and eight-wheeled variants. Three more chassis were converted from Type 668, namely 668320, 325 and 267, becoming 0680001, 010 and 034. Factory-built chassis 0680002–009 and 011–024 were constructed between July and December 1934 and 025–028 in January and February 1935. Chassis 033 was built in July 1935 and 029 in June 1936. Chassis 013, 014, 025 and 033 were petrol-engined.

Four four-wheeled Mammoth chassis, 667298, 317, 359 and 360, were converted for Fairclough to eight-wheel Mammoth Major specification in the early months of 1935. These were renumbered 0680801–804. One Mammoth, petrol-engined 667251, built for J. H. Clapcott of Parkstone in February 1932, was rebuilt as A165-powered six-wheeler 0668273 in September 1933. It received a second steering axle (retaining the same chassis number) in February 1935.

AEC's data sheet of 1934 reveals that the A165-powered eight-wheeler had a bare chassis weight of 6 tons 13 cwts 2 qrs. Adding one ton for the cab and body and 8 cwts for fuel, oil, water and spare wheel, the weight ready for the road would be in the order of 8 tons 1 cwt 2 qrs. As shown at the Glasgow Show in November 1934, the chassis, again with the oil engine, had a list price of £1,860 and with Park Royal cab fitted, £1,920.

The Crocodile

Three special low-loading eight-wheelers were built for Pickfords in July, September and October 1935 and, in chronological order, were numbered 0680032, 031 and 030. They were designed for the carriage of indivisible loads of up to 18 tons in a well measuring 12 feet by 7 feet 6 inches and having a loading height of 2 feet.

The chassis was of fabricated construction. The two main-frame members in the highly stressed well each comprised two 12 inch by 3½ inch rolled steel channels back to back, joined at the top and bottom flanges by full length 7-inch-wide steel plates. All were riveted together to form an I-beam of 12 inch by 7 inch nominal section. Fabricated cross members extended to the full width of the well and further longitudinal members reinforced the outside edge of the loading area. The front and rear sections of the frame were also fabricated, such as would accommodate standard AEC components and were attached to the well section by substantial gussets and angle plates.

The engine was a standard 8.8 litre A165, set to produce 110 bhp at 1,700 rpm and the gearbox was a near-standard four-speed D124. The special auxiliary gearbox provided extra low 1st and reverse gears and the low-level gearbox output flange allowed for the cardan shafts to pass below the floor level of the well. The rear bogie, with its semi-floating axles, was 'borrowed' from the Type 663/664 Renown passenger chassis. A third differential was fitted and the underneath final drive worm gears had a ratio of 10 1/3:1.

The front axle was a standard production unit but the second axle was specially produced. Normal semi-elliptic springs were employed on the front axles while at the rear, the suspension was provided by a pair of centrally pivoted semi-elliptic springs, the ends of which were anchored in the axle's spring carriers. A torque blade, with a swivelling and sliding joint at one end, loosely connected the two axles. This absorbed all driving and braking forces and prevented the rotation of the axles.

The brakes were of the normal internally expanding type with a total frictional area of 672 sq. inches. Footbrake actuation was through a twin circuit, vacuum servo-assisted Lockheed hydraulic system, operating on the front and rear brakes independently. The handbrake was of the multi-pull variety, operating the rear brakes only.

A special low ratio worm and nut steering gear was fitted to ease steering loads when fully laden.

The tyres were low-pressure 12.75 inch by 20 inch ones in single formation. The road speeds obtainable at 1,000 engine rpm ranged from 1.8 mph on the lowest ratio to 12.7 mph on direct drive top gear. Low reverse provided 1.5 mph. Governed to 1,700 rpm, the maximum speed was 21.59 mph.

The crocodile had a wheelbase of 23 feet 3 inches (measured from the front axle to the rear bogie centreline) and an overall length of 30 feet. The length of the well was 12 feet 2 inches and had a loading height of 2 feet. From the back of the cab to the front of the well measured 4 feet 2½ inches and from the back of the well to the end of the frame was 8 feet 8 inches. The height of the rear deck was 3 feet 9 inches.

With a licensing weight of 7 tons 16 cwts, its maximum laden weight was an arbitrary 26 tons. When not engaged on special duties, it fully complied with Ministry of Transport regulations and could operate normally at a gross weight of 22 tons.

In conclusion

The highest numbered chassis in the 668/0668 series was 0668371. From this total, two were listed as not built and the cards for another two were missing. As first built, 341 had been built as six-wheelers and eighteen as eight-wheelers. Additionally, seven Mammoth chassis were converted to Mammoth Major 6 and re-numbered in the 668/0668 series. The total which can be accounted for is thus 367.

Of this total of 367, twenty chassis were converted from six-wheel to eight-wheel, of which seventeen retained their original chassis number and three (as noted below) were renumbered in the 0680 series.

Thirty-eight chassis were numbered in the 680/0680 series. Twenty-eight had been built as eight-wheelers, three were converted from Type 0668 (as noted above) and four from Type 667. Three crocodiles, as already detailed, were built for Pickfords.

Built in the same vein as the Mammoth, the Mark I Mammoth Majors suffered from an excess of weight. Whereas before the imposition of the Road and Rail Traffic Act, 1933, loading limits had been seen as a subject for individual assessment, the penalties which were inherent in the Act required that the operator look more carefully at his operation. AEC in turn responded by introducing the considerably lighter Mark II range of chassis in November 1934.

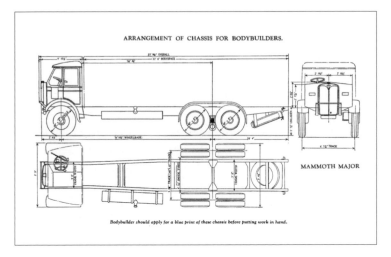

ARRANGEMENT OF CHASSIS FOR BODYBUILDERS.

MAMMOTH MAJOR

Bodybuilder should apply for a blue print of these chassis before putting work in hand.

Arrangement drawing of the Mammoth Major 6 chassis taken from the AEC sales brochure No. 153, dated November 1933. (*Drawing: AEC, Author's collection*)

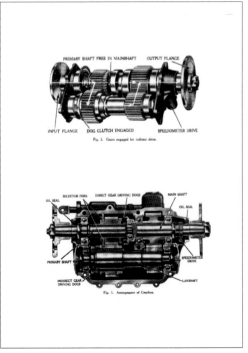

Above left: The prototype Mammoth Major chassis had been built in November 1930 but it was not until the Commercial Motor show at Olympia in November 1931 that it received its first public showing. Six pre-production chassis had been built in March 1931 and the first production examples in August 1931. (Photographs: AEC 3467, Author's collection)

Above right: With the Mammoth Major had come the auxiliary two-speed gearbox. Identified as the D125, it provided ratios of 1:1 and 1.58:1 and in conjunction with the standard four-speed D124 provided a low first speed ratio of 6.92:1. The gears were in constant mesh and engagement was by means of dog clutches. It was also adopted as a standard fitment on the Mammoth chassis and optional on the Matador. (*Illustration: AEC, Author's collection*)

Yeoman's of Canterbury already had Mammoth 667186 when this Mammoth Major arrived. The chassis, 668011, had been built on 30 September 1931 and was powered by petrol engine A162A/41. Typical of its day, the detachable dropsides allowed the carriage of bulk commodities but were easily removed when not required. (*Photograph: AEC L710, Author's collection*)

Travel-stained and weary, RH 4445 is 668056, built 9 November 1931 with oil engine A161A/54. First supplied to Willey & Sons in Hull, there is nothing as will identify the owner at the time the photograph was taken. The cab was built by the local coachbuilder Barnaby. With short trousers, wrinkled socks and cap at a jaunty angle, the youngster is clearly taking a keen interest in the technicalities of photograph taking. (*Photograph: Author's collection*)

Purchased by Pickfords, GX 2275, 668100, is seen in the livery of its parent company, the Hay's Wharf Cartage Company Ltd. The chassis had been built on 24 March 1932 with engine A164A/31 and was unusual in having Dunlop 13.50 inch by 20 inch tyres on the front axle as well as on the rears. With the body built for the carriage of meat carcases and the cab built by Duramin, it had an unladen weight of 9 tons 0 cwts 1 qr. (*Photograph: AEC L988, Author's collection*)

Mammoth Major 0668216 had been converted from a six-wheeled to an eight-wheeled chassis on 3 November 1933. As built on 23 October 1933, the chassis was standard in all respects with servo-assisted Lockheed brakes and had engine A165K/359. Of particular note in this photograph is the steering geometry, where the wheels on the second steered axle are turned less sharply than those on the front axle. (*Photograph: AEC, Author's collection*)

The arrangement of the steering linkage to the second axle and the difference in camber and weight of the front springs are clearly shown. Axle loading was in direct proportion to the relative strength of the springs and here it can be seen that the front axle would always carry more weight than the lighter sprung second steer. Other points to note are the absence of brakes on the second axle, the multi-pull handbrake lever which was also adopted as standard on the Mammoth and the separate gear levers for the main and auxiliary gearboxes. (*Photograph: AEC 3607, Author's collection*)

Badged ACLO and shod on 40 inch by 8 inch Firestones, chassis 0668353 was shipped out to Agar Cross & Co. in Buenos Aires on 14 November 1934. With locally built cab and body, this eight-wheeler joined three Centenario-owned bonneted Matadors, 0646004, 005 and 006. (*Photograph: AEC L1810, Author's collection*)

15

The Four and Six Wheel Drive Hardy Vehicles

Hardy Motors Ltd

Hardy was the name adopted for the new range of AEC-derived vehicles built at Slough by Four Wheel Drive Motors Ltd. The name Hardy emanates from Hardy Rail Motors Ltd, an associate company of the Four Wheel Drive Lorry Company, which had been formed to market the rail-borne vehicles built by FWD. As we have seen, Four Wheel Drive Motors Ltd had been set up to take over the business of Four Wheel Drive Lorry Company Ltd on 31 October 1929, following the making of an agreement with AEC for the supply of engines earlier that month. The Underground Electric Railways Company of London Ltd (the UERL), proprietors of the AEC and the LGOC, had subscribed a controlling 51 per cent shareholding in Four Wheel Drive Motors Ltd. Hardy Rail Motors Ltd, effectively only a trading company, came under UERL control in the following month.

It did not take long for the new masters to stamp their authority on Four Wheel Drive Motors. By 30 April 1930, it had been decided that the then-standard range of FWD vehicles was outdated and that demand was not sufficient to keep the factory on full time. The works director, Charles Cleaver, was urged to complete, as soon as possible, the designs for a new range of four-wheel drive chassis employing standard AEC mechanical units. AEC would supply these units at cost and profits deriving from sales would be divided between the two companies in relation to input costs. Minute books reveal that while Four Wheel Drive Motors Ltd would market the new chassis, a new identity was to be provided for them under the brand name Hardy. Clearly the new management not only saw the old FWD chassis as obsolete but that the initials FWD also projected the wrong image.

The name of the company Hardy Rail Motors Ltd had been changed to Hardy Motors Ltd on 12 December 1930 and the new range of the Hardy-branded vehicles was launched in February 1931. From this time, Hardy Motors became the marketing front for the AEC-powered chassis built by Four Wheel Drive Motors. Remarkably, a price list appearing in one of the Show issues of the Commercial Motor, dated 3 November 1931, contained separate entries for Hardy Motors Ltd and Four Wheel Drive Motors Ltd. The Hardy entries detailed the AEC-engined chassis (including the military R/6/T tractor) and the FWD entries those of the old pattern chassis with the four-cylinder T-head engines. This perhaps indicates that sales of these old pattern FWD chassis had continued to form a material part of the company's dwindling business right through to the transfer of operations to Southall in April 1932. FWD board minutes dated 24 January 1934 show that all Hardy Motors transactions made in the year to 31 October 1933 had been conducted through the books of Four Wheel Drive Motors Ltd. The same was probably true of earlier transactions.

Though the FWD name had quietly faded with the introduction of the Hardy brand, the company and its title, Four Wheel Drive Motors Ltd, remained extant until 24 January 1950, continuing then under the name of ACV Sales Ltd.

Hardy Motors Ltd had remained in existence but dormant, seemingly from the early 1950s, as a subsidiary of Associated Commercial Vehicles Ltd, the successors to AEC. A balance sheet for the year ended 30 September 1950 shows that the company had nett assets of £4,479 of which £2,128 was cash at the bank. Under threat of being struck off by the Registrar of Companies because of its continued dormancy, the company was dissolved on 19 March 1974.

The Hardy chassis

The primary difference between the AEC and Hardy chassis was the adoption of the driven front axle and the additional transfer gearbox. As originally envisaged, the new four-wheel drive vehicles would have their direct equivalents in AEC's newly introduced Mercury, Monarch, Majestic and Mammoth chassis and were designated 4/3, 4/4, 6/6 and 6/8. In the event, the Mercury equivalent proved to be a non-starter and the four-wheel drive Monarch was built both as a 4-ton and 6-ton chassis, i.e. 4/4 and 4/6. FWD board minutes dated 28 May 1930 show that design work on the 4-ton chassis was already well in hand and that it was resolved that material for five chassis be ordered, of which two chassis would be demonstrators.

Henry Nyberg, FWD's managing director, had good contacts in Norway and he also accompanied John Rackham on a sales mission to Canada in June and July 1930. Resultant on the Canadian visit, it was decided at the board meeting on 6 August 1930 that a single, bonneted, six-cylinder left-hand drive tractor, suitable for hauling a 12-ton semi-trailer, should be built for demonstration in that country. The chassis was to be designated the 6/T.

At the board meeting on 3 November 1930 it was decided that production of the new models should not proceed until the experimental chassis had been fully tested but the works director was nevertheless instructed to obtain material prices for a further ten 4-ton 4/4 chassis.

In May 1931 it was reported that the design of a new six-wheel drive chassis employing the latest AEC units was in hand, prospectively for sale in Norway. It was proposed that two such vehicles, designated the R/6/8, be constructed.

Hardy chassis records are unfortunately incomplete. The first chassis built was numbered 3001 and the last 3031. Within these numbers, record cards exist for seventeen Hardy chassis together with two for the R/6/T. Photographic evidence exists for two further chassis, a type 4/6 and the well-documented Canadian type 6T, which leaves ten numbers in the 3000 series without detail.

Specification – the Type 4/4

The Type 4/4 had a wheelbase of 12 feet 1inch and an overall length, excluding the starting-handle, of 18 feet 4 5/8 inches. This allowed for a platform length of 14 feet. The front track measured 5 feet 10 inches, the rear track 5 feet 7 inches. The chassis frame was of nickel steel, 5/16 inches thick and having a maximum depth of 8 inches with 3-inch flanges. At 42 inches wide it was 6 inches wider than that of the standard AEC commercial chassis frame, necessarily so for the accommodation of the driven front axle. The laden frame height of 44 inches was 10 inches higher than that of the AEC's Type 641 Monarch.

The radiator was AEC's N133 and the engine the 65 bhp four-cylinder A139. The clutch and main gearbox combination, J138 and D119 respectively, were exactly as fitted to the Monarch chassis. A short Spicer jointed propeller shaft took the drive from the main gearbox to the transfer gearbox, which was carried at approximately mid-wheelbase. This was so arranged that for normal highway operation, only the rear axle was driven. The engagement of the low range of gears automatically brought the front wheel drive into operation. Alternative low-range ratios provided a gear reduction of 1.86:1 (standard) or 2.3:1.

The overhead worm, semi-floating rear axle was of similar pattern to that of the Monarch and had the standard ratio of 7.25:1 with alternatives of 8.25:1 and 9.33:1. The brakes, provided only on the rear axle, were vacuum servo-assisted and had drums of 17-inch diameter. The footbrake and handbrake shoes operated independently, side by side. The brake shoes were 3¼ inches wide, which provided a frictional area of 176 sq inches for each system and 352 sq inches in total.

The front axle was the design of Charles Cleaver and was built at Slough. The overhead worm gear, again of standard AEC design, was offset to the offside of the chassis centreline by some 10 inches. The axle ratios, of course, matched those of the rear axle. The drive was taken to the front wheels via open universal joints, these being concentric with the steering pivots. The design of the hubs was such that there was no room for front wheel brakes. The steering gear was of the Marles type and the steering box was so mounted that the motion of the drop arm and drag link was across the chassis, with the drag link connected directly to the steering lever on the nearside hub. This arrangement clearly allowed for a better steering lock than would have been possible with the conventional set-up, bearing in mind the wider than normal chassis frame.

The standard tyre equipment was 38 inches by 7 inches, singles on the front and twin rears. With an axle ratio of 7.25:1 and the engine turning at 2,000 rpm, the maximum road speed was 31.2 mph. The Type 4/4 had a payload rating of 4 tons and was designed to haul a 6-ton trailer.

Production details

Chassis 3001 was unveiled at Southall on 28 November 1930, preparatory to being shipped to Agar Cross & Co. in Buenos Aires. From there, it was to be exhibited alongside other Southall-built chassis at the British Empire Exhibition in that city in March 1931. The AEC Gazette of December 1930 described the chassis as an ACLO-FWD. It differed from subsequent chassis of this type insomuch as it was fitted with single Dunlop 38 inch by 9 inch tyres on centre dished wheels all round. So fitted, the front and rear track measurements were almost identical, which allowed the vehicle to traverse cart-rutted roads with greater ease. In the fullness of time, this vehicle returned to Southall and, fitted with a Park Royal cab and Medley body, was sold at an unknown date to the Demolition & Construction Company of 74 Queen Victoria Street, London EC4. Many years later its bare chassis, minus engine, was discovered in Scotland.

W. & C. French took eight Type 4/4 chassis, numbered 3002, 3004, 3005, 3006, 3007, 3009, 3012 and 3013. They are recorded as having been built between March and November 1931 and were delivered to French's in April and May 1933. Axle ratios varied. Four had axle ratios of 7.25:1 and four had 8.25:1. Tyre sizes also varied; chassis 3002 and 3004 had 36 inch by 8 inch tyres and the remainder were carried on 40 inch by 9 inch tyres. All had hydraulic tipping gear, of which five were noted as being of Patterson manufacture. Most were noted as having Medley cabs and bodies but on chassis 3012 both cab and body had been built by Weymann.

Chassis 3008 had been built in June 1931 and went first to A. G. Auden & Co. of Charlotte Street, Walsall, delivered to them via Birmingham Garages in November 1932. It then went to Chandlers Motors in Boscowan Street, SW8, thence to Chambers in February 1935. This chassis had an axle ratio of 7.25:1, 36 inch by 8 inch Dunlop Trak-Grip tyres and a three-way tipping gear and body built by Bromillow & Edwards. It had an unladen weight of 6 tons 1 cwt.

Mechanisation Ltd of 188 Walmer Road, SW11, took 3010. This had been built on 19 October 1931, was delivered to the coachbuilder (unspecified) in July 1935 and to the customer in the following month. It had an 8.25:1 axle ratio, 36 inch x 8 inch tyres and was fitted with a winch.

Chassis number 3011 had been despatched to the Mechanical Warfare Experimental Establishment at Farnborough in January 1932. With civilian registration HX 6736 and the military identification L.22032, it took part in extensive proving trials with the MWEE but remained the only one in military service.

Chassis 3018, a Type 4/4, had been built in February 1932 and went to J. Ross of Portway, West Ham, in November 1935.

Chassis 3019 was built on 30 October 1931. Fitted with a Park Royal cab and flat body, it is thought to have been one of the vehicles exhibited on the Hardy stand at Olympia in November 1931. It went to Broad & Co, of 4 South Wharf, Paddington, W2, in July 1933. It was later sold to Willment Bros of Twickenham. An entry on the chassis record card dated October 1946 shows that it been converted to a six-wheeler with an un-driven axle fitted forward of the rear axle.

Military tests of 4/4 No. 3011, L.22032, HX6736

Comparative tests were undertaken at Farnborough with 4/4 chassis 3011 and the six-wheeled double-drive Leyland Terrier L.21285 which, already tested by the MWEE, provided the then-current benchmark for the 3-ton medium class load carrier. HX 6736 had the AEC 5.123 litre, 65 bhp A157 engine, which was identical to the A139 except that it was fitted with an electric starter. The Leyland engine was rather larger, with a swept volume of 5.9 litres and an output of 73 bhp. In those tests where power was all-important, the Leyland had a clear advantage. Quoting directly from the report:

> It is seen that the Hardy was slower than the Leyland 6-wheeler on the roads. The cross-country performance was practically equal to that of the Leyland. The ditch crossing capacity was superior to the Leyland. The Hardy was slightly slower than the Leyland on rough going.
>
> A further test established that the cross-country performance of the Hardy was due chiefly to the front wheel drive and not to the twin 900-22 tyres on the rear wheels.
>
> The engine fitted to the Hardy was not as suitable as the Leyland for cross-country work. The cooling was inadequate.
>
> Generally however this vehicle is considered suitable for cross-country work.

It should be noted here that it was a requirement of the War Department that the maximum water temperature should not exceed 100 degrees F above the ambient temperature.

With a 3-ton nominal payload, the Hardy had a gross weight of 8 tons 1 cwt and the Leyland 8 tons 8 cwts. The Hardy made a successful climb of the 1 in 3.23 gradient of Miles Hill with the engine close to the limit of torque but failed two thirds of the way up the 1 in 2.49 due to lack of power. The Leyland was successful on both climbs. Further tests were made with the Hardy's front axle drive disconnected and in this instance it failed on the 1 in 3.23 slope due to wheel-spin.

The flying mile was covered at an average speed of 28.75 mph and the Leyland at 32.6 mph, while the relative speeds on the two-mile cross-country circuit were 15.3 mph and 16.8 mph respectively. In normal highway operations, the Hardy chassis returned a fuel consumption of 7.13 mpg. In braking tests, the Hardy was brought to a standstill from 20 mph in 27 feet 10 inches, the Leyland in 32 feet 2 inches.

The Type 4/6

There is photographic evidence of the existence of one Type 4/6 chassis but there is no record card for it. The Type 4/6 had the same mechanical specification as the Type 4/4 but had a wheelbase of 15 feet, a platform length of 16 feet 6 inches and an overall length of 21 feet 5 5/8 inches. The chassis frame had a maximum depth of 10 inches as compared with the 8-inch frame of the Type 4/4. The standard tyres were 36 inch by 8 inch singles at the front and twin rear. Its load capacity was 6 tons, with the additional capacity to haul a 6-ton trailer.

The Canadian Type 6T

No record card exists for this Type 6T chassis but it is thought to be chassis 3003. Built for operation in Canada, it was fully described in the Commercial Motor of 30 December 1930. This left-hand drive type articulated tractor unit had a wheelbase of 13 feet 0½ inches, 2 feet shorter than on the proposed standard 6-ton chassis, a front track of 5 feet 8¾ inches and a rear track of 5 feet 8 inches. It had an overall length of 19 feet 6 inches and an overall width of 7 feet 2 inches. The frame was 3 feet 6 inches wide and parallel from the front to a point just rearward of the transfer gearbox rear crossmember, tapering thereafter to 3 feet between that point and the rear spring front hangers, from where it remained parallel to the end of the frame. Its section was 10 inches by 3 inches x 5/16 inches thick and had a laden frame height of 3 feet 1¼ inches. The tyres were 40 inches by 8 inches, singles at the front and twins at the rear.

The engine was a near standard six-cylinder AEC 110 mm bore unit, which delivered 56 bhp at 1,000 rpm and 110 bhp at 2,500 rpm. It had a front-mounted sump to allow clearance for the driven front axle. As with the 4-tonner, the engine was carried close to the left-side frame rail and was therefore markedly offset from the chassis centreline. The front axle's worm gear was similarly offset to the right and was as described for the 4-ton chassis. The rear axle was similar in most respects to that of the Majestic and Mammoth chassis but the double reduction final drive gearing, housed in the early two-piece casing, was offset to the left side in order to provide a more nearly straight driveline from the transfer gearbox. The axles had a ratio of 8.25:1, which in the high range of gears provided a speed of 29.4 mph at an engine speed of 2,000 rpm. The gearbox was AEC's then-standard D119 and the FWD-built transfer gearbox provided ratios of 1:1 and 1.86:1.

The footbrake was vacuum servo-assisted, operating only on the rear axle in 20-inch diameter drums. The footbrake and handbrake shoes were 3¼ inches wide and operated independently side by side, each providing a frictional area of 213 sq inches (426 sq inches in total). The steering gear was by Marles, with the column near vertical and the drop arm swinging in an arc beneath the chassis frame rail. So arranged, this allowed free movement of the drag link in the conventional fore and aft plane without limiting the steering lock.

Shipment to Canada and return

Almost from the outset, there was discussion as to how the chassis would be paid for. At the FWD board meeting on 29 January 1931, it was reported that AEC (Canada) Ltd was not prepared to pay cash against shipping documents and had asked that it be sent to them on a consignment basis. The managing director (Nyberg) was adamant that the vehicle should be bought outright. Ultimately, it was agreed that AEC would ship it to Canada on AEC's own consignment terms.

Harry Pick, a past president of the AEC Society and one-time manager of the AEC's West Bromwich depot, reports that the Canadian demonstrations were not without drama. While demonstrating its capabilities on a frozen lake, the ice gave way and the vehicle settled on the lake bed. Driver Bill Burford (later general foreman in the Southall service department) and his passenger escaped and the vehicle was subsequently recovered. In due time, the vehicle returned to Southall. Here it was extensively rebuilt. The petrol engine was replaced by an A165 oil engine and the steering controls converted to right-hand drive. With a new cab and workshop body, an overhead gantry and a set of 5-ton chain blocks, it became AEC's new heavy breakdown vehicle, first at the North Road depot, later at Southall.

Known by all as 'The Mammoth' (which technically it was not), its pulling power was legendary. It was also slow, with a reported maximum speed of 22 mph, which indicated an axle ratio of 9.33:1. It remained at the Southall service department until 1954, when it was transferred to AEC's newly opened West Bromwich depot. It was replaced at Southall by an 0853 Matador and was retired from West Bromwich in 1956 when, in turn, that depot also received a Matador.

The 6-ton and 8-ton chassis

Bonneted chassis number 3028, simply marked as 'Built at Slough', had a six-cylinder A136 engine, a D123 main gearbox and an FWD-built GB26 transfer gearbox, vacuum servo-operated rear brakes and Goodyear 40 inch by 8 inch tyres. This went to the Demolition & Construction Company in January 1937. Identified as a Type 6/6 with a 6-ton payload rating, its specification, with the exception of its wheelbase (13 feet 0½ inches), was similar to that of the Canadian tractor above. Its D123 'silent third' gearbox suggests a building date after August 1931.

Chassis 3015 was also noted as having been 'Built by FWD Slough'. With a six-cylinder A141 engine and D124 gearbox, it was carried on Goodyear 42 inch by 9 inch tyres. It went to J. Ross of West Ham in November 1935. This was a four-wheeled, forward-control 8-ton chassis. Designated the Type 6/8, it had its equivalent in the AEC Mammoth. The axles had a ratio of 8.25:1. Like chassis 3028, its D124 gearbox suggests that it was also built after August 1931.

The R/6/8 six-wheeled chassis

Despite encouraging enquiries from Norway in the design stage, the R/6/8 chassis, number 3031, was to be the only one of its type built and was in fact the last chassis to be built at Slough. It was exhibited at the Commercial Motor Show at Olympia in November 1931 alongside a Type 4/4 and a military R/6/T. This six-wheeler, variously identified as the R/6/8, the R6/8 and, in the Commercial Motor, as the R682, should not be confused with the FWD R.68 of 1929. That chassis had a broadly similar designation, the same engine and gearbox combination and the same 8-ton carrying capacity but in other respects followed the specification of the R/6/T with the War Department four-spring rear bogie.

A study of the specification shows the standard power unit for the R/6/8 was the six-cylinder 120 bhp A162 petrol engine but as exhibited at Olympia, it was fitted with the AEC's latest oil engine, the 115 mm bore 130 bhp A161. It was coupled, through AEC's 16-inch single plate clutch, to the D124 four-speed main gearbox. First gear had a ratio of 4.38:1; 2nd, 2.69:1; 3rd, 1.59:1; and 4th 1:1. Reverse was 5.33:1. The FWD-built two-speed transfer gearbox provided ratios of 1:1 and 1.86:1. As with the other Hardy chassis, in the high ratios, only the rear wheels were driven. The front wheel drive was automatically engaged when the low ratio in the transfer gearbox was engaged. The wheels and tyres were 38 inch by 9 inch singles all round and the axles had a standard ratio of 8.25:1, which in the direct drive top gear provided a road speed of 28.4 mph at 2,000 engine rpm. With the lowest ratio engaged, the road speed at the same 2,000 rpm was 3.5 mph. The tractive effort in this lowest ratio was 8,900 lbs. The optional axle ratios were 7.25:1 and 9.33:1.

The forward end of the chassis followed the practice set by the forward control six-cylinder four-wheeled Hardy chassis, with the engine and gearbox offset to the left of the chassis centreline by 5 inches to allow clearance for the front axle's overhead worm gear. The frame was 3 feet 6 inches wide at the front and parallel with a depth of 10 inches, tapering amidships to 3 feet just forward of the rear bogie front cross-member. From this point, it remained parallel to the end of the frame. The frame was also down-swept between the transfer gearbox front cross-member and a point 18 inches forward of the rear bogie front cross-member. The laden frame height at the forward end was 3 feet 10 inches and at the rear 3 feet 2 inches. The elevated portion of the chassis behind the engine formed a convenient platform on which to mount the winch, should that be required. The chassis had a wheelbase, measured to the mid-point of the bogie, of 16 feet and the bogie had axle centres of 4 feet. Its overall length was 24 feet 7½ inches, the width 7 feet 2¼ inches and had a clear platform space of 19 feet 8 inches.

The chassis was notable in that it featured a new Cleaver-designed two-spring rear bogie which permitted articulation of the axles of up to 18 inches both longitudinally and diagonally without distortion of the road springs or chassis frame. Each spring was centre mounted on a substantial chair and carried in gun-metal bushes on a central beam. The beam was carried in brackets bolted to the chassis frame and the frame was further reinforced by a central tubular cross-member. The axles were swivel mounted on the ends of the springs and were located by torque rods, which connected the worm gear housings with the central tubular cross-member. The AEC Type 644 Marshal employed the same bogie.

The rear axles were of the familiar AEC semi-floating overhead worm pattern, similar to those employed on the Hardy 4/4 and 4/6 chassis except that the worm gear units were carried centrally in the axles. The internally expanding brakes operated only on the bogie wheels. The brake drums were of 17-inch diameter, with one pair of brake shoes in each drum. (The width is not recorded but those on the Marshal chassis were initially of 3¼ inches) The footbrake was energised by dual vacuum servos and the handbrake was coupled only to the brakes on the rearmost axle. In order to accommodate the extreme angles of axle articulation, the brake linkage connections were spherically jointed.

The front axle was of the same overhead worm pattern as fitted to the other Hardy chassis, with the final drive gears offset to the right by some 10 inches. The track measurement at both front and rear axles was 5 feet 9 7/8 inches. A narrow track version measuring 5 feet 5 3/8 inches was also available, in which case the overall width was reduced to 6 feet 10¼ inches.

The published weights for the R/6/8 in petrol-engined guise were given as follows: bare chassis weight, 4 tons 18 cwts 2 qrs; allowance for cab and body, 1 ton 3 cwts 2 qrs; payload, 8 tons; gross laden weight, 14 tons 2 cwts. Laden front axle weight was 4 tons 10 cwts and laden rear bogie weight 9 tons 12 cwts.

Following the Olympia exhibition, the R/6/8 was returned to its original specification with the A162 petrol engine. In August 1932 it was sold to the Iraq Petroleum Company, which at that time was planning the construction of a 1,200-mile oil pipeline between the Iraqi oilfields and the Mediterranean coast. In conjunction with a tandem-axled dolly trailer manufactured by the Eagle Engineering Company, the vehicle was to be employed in the carriage of steel pipe sections in the desert sands of Iraq and Syria. Tested in the UK prior to shipment, it was loaded with twenty-one such pipes weighing 15 tons 4 cwts.

Scammell's at Watford had supplied the Iraq Petroleum Company with two six-wheeled Pioneer tractive units with tandem-axled pole trailers for similar duties. Ultimately, it was the Scammell which in service proved to be the more successful. Bob Tuck in his book The Supertrucks of Scammell, The Fitzjames Press, 1987, reports that Scammell went on to supply the IPC with twenty-one of these articulated outfits.

Summary

It will be noted that the Hardy chassis listed above were all built in the period December 1930 to February 1932, i.e. before manufacturing operations were transferred to Southall. With the exception of chassis 3011, supplied to the War Department in January 1932, all were sold after the closure of the Slough premises. None were built at Southall. It is thought that the above list probably represents the total of 4/4, 4/6, 6/6, 6T, 6/8 and R/6/8 chassis built.

The quoted chassis list prices in August 1932 were: 4/4, £995; 4/6, £1,150; 6/6, £1,215; 6/T, £1,215; 6/8, £1,265; and the R/6/8 (with petrol engine), £1,585. From December 1933 list prices were not quoted but available on application. One would guess that for those chassis remaining in stock, no reasonable offer would have been refused. The comparable prices for the standard AEC chassis were: Monarch, £800; Matador, £925; Majestic, £1,000; and Mammoth, £1,000.

The Hardy chassis in retrospect

In cross-country operations at Farnborough, the Hardy 4/4, with the driven front axle engaged, had shown itself well capable of climbing out of ditches and bogs, which with only the rear wheels driven had not proved possible. In comparison with the Marshal chassis there was little difference in the hill climbing ability, the Marshal just having the advantage due to its slightly lower gear in the auxiliary gearbox (2.6:1 compared with the Hardy's 2.3:1). Both had a final drive ratio of 7.25:1. Throughout the 1920s and 1930s, little money had been made available to the military purse and there were few applications in peacetime Britain which would warrant the complication and extra financial outlay of a driven front axle. That would all change with the outbreak of war in 1939.

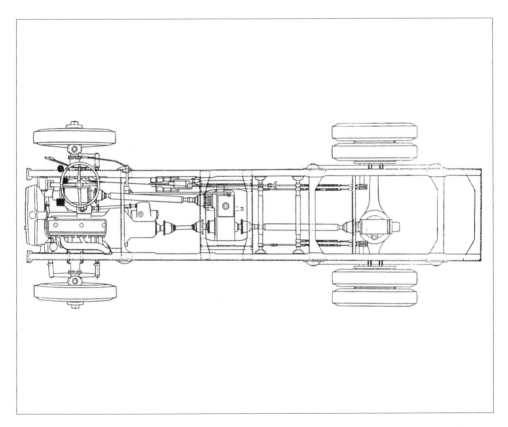

Arrangement drawing of Hardy 4/4 chassis. (*Drawing:* Commercial Motor, *28 April 1931.* *Author's collection*)

Identified as HX 6736 and carrying the Army number L.22032, chassis 3011 is fitted out for trials with the Mechanical Warfare Experimental Establishment. It was received by the MWEE on 22 January 1932 and took part in the War Department Trials at Llangollen in May. (*Photograph: Imperial War Museum KID3710*)

Shown as having been built on 30 October 1931, Hardy No. 3019 was exhibited at the Commercial Motor Show at Olympia in November. By the use of special runners and outriggers, the body floor was no higher than found on a conventional chassis. It was purchased by Broad & Co. of Paddington in July 1933. (*Photograph: AEC, Author's collection*)

16

Trolleybuses Types 661T and 662T

Because of its ten-year production run, the story of the development of the Type 661T trolleybus from the early types with the front-mounted motor through to those with the under-floor mountings necessarily takes us beyond the natural time scale set by the other chapters in this volume.

The first of the Type 661T trolleybus had been built in 1931 and production continued through into the early wartime years, the last being placed in service with the Notts & Derby Traction Company in 1942. Though production of the Type 661T totalled 379 chassis, initial demand had been slow.

As first built, the chassis had a wheelbase of 15 feet 6½ inches, an overall length of 24 feet 10½ inches and a width at the front dumb irons of 3 feet 0¼ inches, tapering outward to 3 feet 11 5/8 inches at a point about 6 feet from the front of the chassis. Like the Regent, the frame curved gracefully over the front and rear axles with ever changing section and had a maximum depth of 11 inches, a laden height of 1 foot 9 inches at mid-wheelbase and 11 inches rearward of the rear spring hangers. The front and rear tracks measured 6 feet 3 1/16 inches and 5 feet 10 3/16 inches respectively and the width over the rear tyres was 7 feet 5 5/8 inches.

The front-mounted 80 hp English Electric DK130 traction motor was offset to the nearside and angled downward so as to provide a straight transmission line to the rear axle. The front axle was the L118 and the rear axle a semi-floating type F129. The M128 steering gear was by Marles. The brakes were compressed air-operated through a Westinghouse system. The brake drums, both at front and rear, were of 17-inch diameter and the brake shoes were 3¼ inches wide. At the rear axle, the footbrake and handbrake shoes worked side by side in the same brake drums. The rear axle ratio was 9 1/3:1. The tyres were 38 inch by 9 inch singles at the front and twin rears.

Production details

Chassis 661T001 and 002 had been built on 19 May 1931. With English Electric single deck bodies, these vehicles were exported to Kyoto in Japan.

Chassis 003 to 006 and 008 to 012 were built for Southend Corporation. They were built between April and November 1932 and had a nearly similar specification to chassis 001 and 002 except that the axles were now the L133 and F145. It is noted that on the rear axles, the handbrake and footbrake levers were now interconnected.

On chassis 008–012, the brake shoes had ¾-inch thick liners and the drums were cast iron in place of pressed steel. Luvax shock absorbers were fitted at front and rear. The vehicles were notable for the full-fronted English Electric double-deck bodywork and dummy radiator grilles.

Chassis 007 was built in November 1932 for Bournemouth Corporation. It had Lockheed brakes, Westinghouse operated, and also carried English Electric bodywork. Like its six-wheeled sister vehicle, 663T003, supplied to Bournemouth at the same time, its motor was exchanged for a petrol engine in 1936.

Chassis 013–027, with half-cab bodywork by MCCW, were built for the Notts & Derby Traction Company in April and May 1933. Still having a wheelbase of 15 feet 6½ inches and front-mounted English Electric 80 hp DK130 motors, these chassis had fully floating F156 rear axles and direct-acting compressed air brakes. The equipment was supplied by G. D. Peters. The F156 axle had one pair of 6-inch-wide brake shoes each side, each being operated through independent footbrake and handbrake linkages.

Long wheelbase and mid-mounted motors

Portsmouth Corporation had chassis 661T028–031. These were of 16-foot 3-inch wheelbase with the traction motor positioned forward of the rear axle and offset to the nearside. The front axle was the L139 and the steering gear AEC's home-produced M134 worm and nut type. The rear axle was the F156 and the compressed air braking equipment was of G. D. Peters manufacture. The chassis were built in April 1934 and with full-fronted fifty-seat English Electric bodywork, they were placed in service in the following August. Chassis 029 is noted as having an unladen weight of 6 tons 13 cwts 1 qr. Chassis 031 was somewhat heavier at 6 tons 18 cwts 2 qrs.

Chassis 661T032 was built for the London Passenger Transport Board. Registered AXU 189, this was the sister vehicle to six-wheeled 663T076, built to evaluate the respective merits of the four-wheeled sixty-seat and the six-wheeled seventy-four-seat trolleybus. Whereas the six-wheeler had Metropolitan Vickers electrical equipment, that of 661T032 was manufactured by English Electric, the traction motor being an EE405. The compressed air equipment was the product of the Westinghouse Brake & Signal Company and the body was built by English Electric.

Bradford Corporation took 661T033–068 in two batches in 1934 and 1935. With sixty-seat English Electric Bodywork and EE405 traction motors, Westinghouse brakes and worm and nut steering, the first batch was similar in most respects to the LPTB's experimental AXU 189. Stress reversals in the rear axle created by the regenerative braking system had revealed a weakness in the worm gear not apparent on the six-wheeled double-drive trolleybus and a new axle (the F167) with modified thrust bearings had been introduced in 1934. Bradford's 1935 batch differed in that the rear axles were fitted with a 9.7:1 spiral-bevel and double-helical double-reduction final drive in place of the standard 9 1/3:1 worm gear. The reliability of the double reduction axle came at the expense of noise and in 1936 a new worm gear with 8½-inch centres was adopted.

Stanley King, in his excellent volume Bradford Corporation Trolleybuses, Venture Publications, 1994, provides interesting insight into the working of Bradford's then-new AEC-EEC trolleybuses. Of them, on pages 37 and 38, he writes:

> They were fast. On the long gradual ascent to Thornton they maintained a good speed at all times; on the return journey they flew like avenging furies. The loud hum of the double-reduction gears increased rapidly in pitch as they accelerated; the trolley-wheels hissed sharply, and at speeds of 35-40 m.p.h. (e.g. from Spring Head Road to School Green) the combination of transmission noise reverberation from the trolley gantry and the vibration of the all-metal body rendered conversation on the upper deck not worth attempting. Driving them was a special skill, as power and electric braking were on the same (left) pedal. To decelerate, the driver slowly released pressure on the pedal; to coast, he removed his foot altogether, and to brake after coasting he applied power quickly and then released pressure, bringing the vehicle to rest with the right foot air-brake pedal. Wrongly used, the system could stop the vehicle violently, with resulting passenger discomfort and complaints – accusations of trolleybus 'jerkiness' dated from this period.
>
> The patent regenerative braking fed power back into the overhead line, thus reducing power costs but occasionally producing spectacular side-effects: descending Leeds Road from Thornbury Depot the new trolleybuses could explode the light bulbs in the Hall Ings tramway shelter; venturing on to the Bolton-Bankfoot route they encouraged the Wakefield Road trams to climb hills like spring lambs.

Chassis 661T069–077 were built for Portsmouth Corporation in June 1935. Their specification, with English Electric bodywork and double reduction axles, closely followed that of the second Bradford batch except that the braking equipment was supplied by G. D. Peters.

In 1936 Reading Corporation took delivery of 661T078, RD 8086, with fifty-two-seat Park Royal bodywork, and eleven, 661T079–089, went to Johannesburg with sixty-seat MCCW bodywork. Portsmouth followed their 1935 intake with a further seventy-six. These, numbered 661T090–165, had fifty-two-seat Craven bodies.

In 1937, twenty went to Adelaide, 661T166–185, and had locally built fifty-nine-seat bodies by Lawton. Chassis 661T186 is thought not to have been built and 661T187, with fifty-eight-seat bodywork by English Electric, went to Bradford Corporation. Cleethorpes took ten, 661T188–197, with fifty-six-seat Park Royal bodies and the Notts & Derby Traction Company had seven, 661T198, 199 and 209–213, with fifty-six-seat bodies by Weymann. Johannesburg added a further eight to its fleet with 661T200–207, having sixty-seat bodywork by MCCW, similar to its 1936 intake.

In 1938, Bradford Corporation added forty-two, 661T208 and 214–254, again with English Electric bodywork, and Adelaide took a further ten, 661T255–264, bodied as previously by Lawton. Cleethorpes added three, 661T265–267, with fifty-six-seat Park Royal bodies and Reading Corporation followed with twenty-five similar vehicles, 661T268–292. Brighton Corporation, new to trolleybus operation, opened with forty-four elegant fifty-four-seat Weymann-bodied vehicles, 661T293–336, registered consecutively FUF 1 – FUF 44.

In 1939, Southend Corporation had six, 661T337–342, with Strachan fifty-six-seat bodies and Brighton, Hove & District took eight, 661T343–350 with fifty-four-seat bodywork by Weymann, similar to those supplied to Brighton Corporation. Chassis 661T351 and 352 were not built.

Later, the Hastings Tramway Company took twenty in 1940, 661T353–372, with fifty-four-seat bodies, ten built by Weymann and ten built by Park Royal; and the Notts & Derby Traction Company had five in 1941 and another five in 1942, numbered 661T373–382, all having fifty-six-seat Weymann bodywork.

The highest numbered chassis was 661T382. Two are listed as not built and a third is unaccounted for.

The Type 662T

Unlike the Type 661T with its ten-year production run, that of the Type 662T did not extend beyond the middle 1930s.

The pattern of building of the Type 662T was similar to that of the Type 661T. The first chassis, 662T001–010, had been built for the Notts & Derby Traction Company in April 1932. The traction motors were front-mounted English Electric DK130-80 or DK130-65, driving the offset underneath worm rear axle through a three-piece tubular cardan shaft. Like the early Regals, the Type 662T had a wheelbase of 17 feet with L133 front and F145 semi-floating rear axles. The worm gear had a ratio of 9 1/3:1. The 17-inch diameter brakes were operated through triple vacuum servos with inter-connected rear brake levers. Luvax shock absorbers were fitted at the front axle. The steering gear was AEC worm and nut. The half cab thirty-two-seat bodywork was built by English Electric and the vehicles were registered RB 6613 – RB 6622 in numerical order.

Chassis 662T011–018 were built for Darlington Corporation. Chassis 011 and 012, HN 9657 and HN 9658, were built in November 1933 and the remaining six, AHN 185 – AHN 190, in June and July 1934. These were of 17-foot, 6-inch wheelbase and like the later Type 661T chassis, the traction motor was mounted forward of the rear axle, driving the rear axle through a single short cardan shaft. They had L139 front axles and chassis 662T011–015 had the F156 fully floating rear axle. Chassis 016–018 had the later F167 axle with the heavy duty thrust bearings on the worm shaft. Both types had an axle ratio of 9 1/3:1. Luvax shock absorbers were fitted on both front and rear axles. The brakes were operated through a Lockheed hydraulic system, without servo assistance, which suggests that more reliance was placed on the electrical braking systems. It is noted that the brake liners were Ferodo MR. The steering gear was by Marles, designated M128. The thirty-two-seat central entrance body, seemingly designed in a previous era, was constructed by Dick Kerr & Co. of Preston, one of the English Electric subsidiaries.

662T019 was built for the Societia Italiana Ernesto Breda in Milan. It had a twenty-two-seat body built by Brush with double pneumatically operated entrance/exit doors on what would be the English offside. The chassis was of right-hand control and had a wheelbase of 17 feet 6 inches. The traction motor was a mid-mounted, 80 hp English Electric EE405 with regenerative controls and the wheel brakes were operated through a Westinghouse compressed air system. Like the Darlington chassis, the front axle was an L139 and the rear axle an F167 with 9 1/3:1 worm gear. The chassis was built in September 1934 and the complete vehicle was despatched to Milan at the end of November 1934.

Chassis 662T020, 021 and 022, with Brush coachwork, were supplied to Darlington Corporation in 1935 and 023–028 were exported to Odense in Denmark.

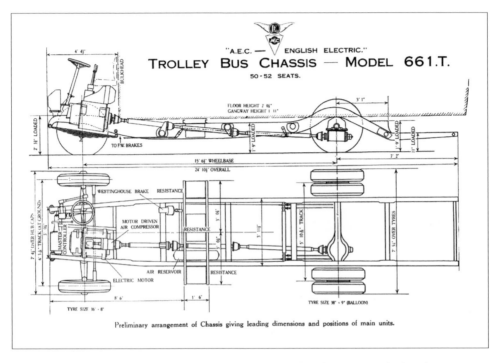

Arrangement drawing of trolleybus chassis Type 661T taken from AEC sales brochure No. 91, dated July 1930. (*Drawing: AEC, Author's collection*)

Trolleybus operation in Southend
had started in October 1925
with the acquisition of two
Railless trolleybuses, followed
in 1928 by the ex-demonstrator
AEC Type 603. The first intake
of modern trolleybuses had been
in 1932 with the acquisition of
four AEC 661Ts with EEC low
bridge forty-eight-seat bodies,
JN 2112 – JN 2115, 661T003–
661T006. A second batch
similarly specified, JN 2817
– JN 2821, 661T008–661T012
followed later in that year. With
the dummy radiator hiding
the electric motor, JN 2819 is
headed for Whitegate Road.
(*Photograph: Author's collection*)

*Semi-plan view of Type 661T A.E.C.-E.E.C. Trolley Bus chassis
with cab mounted equipment.*

This semi-plan view of the
Type 661T taken from the
November 1937 brochure shows
well the general arrangement
of the chassis. Similar in most
respects to LPTB's 661T032,
the chassis depicted has cab-
mounted electrical gear whereas
on 661T032 the contactor gear
was carried in a waterproof
box on the offside chassis rail.
(*Photograph: AEC, Author's
collection*)

Built for evaluation by the London Passenger Transport Board, AXU 189, 661T032, was the first of a new generation of four-wheeled trolleybuses. As on the six-wheeled AXU 188, the traction motor was under-floor mounted and the braking system combined regenerative and rheostatic systems, further backed up by a direct-acting Westinghouse compressed air system. The sixty-seat all-metal body was built by the English Electric Company. (*Photograph: London Transport Museum U15393*)

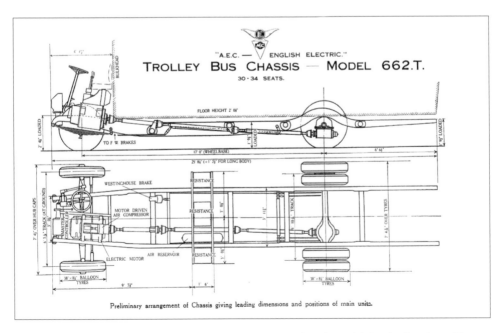

Arrangement drawing of trolleybus chassis Type 662T taken from AEC sales brochure No. 91, dated July 1930. (*Drawing: AEC, Author's collection*)

Resplendent in the sunshine, Notts & Derby Traction's ten 662Ts are lined up for this posed photograph. Numbered 662T001 – 662T010, they were registered in sequence RB 6613 – RB 6622. Both the electrical equipment and the bodies were the product of the English Electric Company. (*Photograph: Alan Townsin collection*)

Darlington's bus No. 34 was chassis 662T012, one of eight delivered in 1934. Its ancient appearance belied the modernity of the chassis with its mid-mounted English Electric traction motor, hydraulic brakes (though without servo assistance), fully floating axles and Luvax shock absorbers. The centre entrance body, built by Dick, Kerr & Co. in Preston, copied closely those fitted to the half dozen English Electric chassis supplied to the Corporation in 1929 and 1930, an example of which follows close behind. (*Photograph: AEC, Author's collection*)

17

The Matador Types 645 and 646

THE TYPE 645 MATADOR

The Matador made its entrance at Olympia in November 1931. Viewed more than seventy-five years on, an engine of 80 bhp in a chassis designed for trailer work appears a most unlikely combination. In truth, however, the Matador was originally conceived as a rugged, no frills 5-ton solo vehicle, which, compared with the Type 641 Monarch, provided an additional 3 feet 6 inches of body-space and one ton of payload.

Specification

Power was provided by the 112 mm bore four-cylinder A163 petrol engine, similar in most respects to the A139 fitted in the Mercury and Monarch chassis, but now having the high power cylinder head. Developed for the Matador, it provided 80 bhp at 2,400 rpm compared with 65 bhp at 2,000 rpm of the A139. The clutch, gearbox and rear axle were as fitted to the Mammoth and the standard final drive ratio was 8.1:1. Alternatives of 9 1/3:1 and 10 2/3:1 were available. The foot brake was assisted by a single Dewandre servo, which, with the handbrake, operated only on the rear axle. The brake drums were of 20-inch diameter and the brake levers were interconnected, such that operation of the footbrake brought the handbrake shoes into operation. The standard wheelbase was 14 feet 6 inches but a shorter 13-foot, 3-inch wheelbase was available for tipper applications. As befitted its 5-ton carrying capacity, the Matador's chassis frame was 9 inches deep, as compared with the 8-inch frame of the 4-ton Monarch. The tyres were 40 inches by 8 inches, singles at the front and twins at the rear.

A road test of the Matador conducted by the Commercial Motor in December 1931 revealed that far from being a sluggish performer, with a 5-ton payload and a gross weight of 10 tons 11 cwts, it had the ability to accelerate from rest to 30 mph in just 30 seconds. The maximum speed recorded was 37 mph. Geared for 15.16 mph per 1,000 engine rpm, this represented an engine speed of 2,440 rpm. Braking from 30 mph required 85 ft and the fuel consumption, over a 21.6-mile undulating course, was 7.27 mpg. As tested, this prototype Matador with its drop-side timber body had an unladen weight of 5 tons 4 cwts.

A second road test of the Matador was conducted by the same journal in November 1932, this time in conjunction with a drawbar trailer. By this time, the Matador had been fitted with front wheel brakes (of standard 17-inch diameter) and an auxiliary gearbox providing a step down ratio of 1.58:1. The effective ratios now afforded were: 1st, 6.90:1; 2nd, 4.25:1; 3rd, 2.51:1; 4th, 1.58:1; 5th, 1; and reverse, 8.42:1. The rear axle ratio remained at 8.1:1 and at 2,400 engine rpm provided road speeds in the various gears of 5.26, 8.57, 14.5, 23, 36.4 mph and, in reverse, 4.33 mph. The Matador, as a chassis and cab, weighed 4 tons 1 cwt and the Eagle drop-side trailer weighed 1 ton 19 cwts. Grossing 15 tons 5½ cwts, acceleration to 30 mph took 62 seconds and braking from 30 mph to a standstill required 90 ft. A stop and restart proved possible on the 1 in 5½ gradient of Harrow Hill. Two measured gallons of commercial spirit were consumed over a 12.49-mile out and return route in the Sudbury and Harrow-on-the-Hill area.

Production

The first production batch of thirty chassis was built in the period January–December 1932 under programme CX. The prototype chassis had been built in September 1931, followed by the first three production chassis in January 1932. Fifteen were built in February; thereafter, there was little more than a trickle. A single chassis was built in April, followed by four in May. Three were built in July, two each in September and November and three in December. Of these, there were a number of multiple deliveries. Mutter Howey & Co. of Edinburgh had chassis 002 and 003, T. J. Bartlam of Stoke on Trent had 006 and 007 and H. Bradley of Baildon had 009, 010 and 011. G. A. Harvey & Co. had 022, 023, 024, 029 and 031 and Silvertown Lubricants had 026 and 035.

Planning well ahead, a second batch of fifty chassis had been sanctioned in January 1932 under programme DG. The building of this second batch commenced toward the end of 1932, continued through 1933 and into 1934. Among this group, H. A. Newport of Fordham near Cambridge had chassis 046, 047 and 074. Hodgson of Beverley, having taken chassis 021 from the first batch, followed with 038 and 049 from the second. By 1933, front wheel brakes had become standard and the auxiliary gearbox, though optional, was a necessary requirement where trailer operation was envisaged. The A166 108 mm bore four-cylinder oil engine had been introduced in February 1933 and the majority of the fifty chassis of this programme were so powered.

The impending 1933 Road and Rail Traffic Act had concentrated the minds of many in the road haulage industry, not least in respect of unladen weight and carrying capacity. In November of that year, an oil-engined Matador with a Duramin light alloy, three-way tipping body had been shown at Olympia. The body was said to weigh 12½ cwts and the complete vehicle under 5 tons.

Following the exhibition, the Feltham Sand & Gravel Company had ordered twenty-four special chassis of 11-foot, 6-inch wheelbase, powered by the A163 petrol engine. Further weight saving was achieved by dispensing with the front wheel brakes, fitting lightweight aluminium brake shoes in the rear hubs and lightening the chassis cross-members. On completion, with the Duramin body and Bromilow & Edwards tipping gear, the vehicles had a licensing weight of 4 tons 7 cwts and a legal payload approaching 7½ tons. The Ham River Grit Company ordered twenty similar chassis but with lightweight steel bodies by Metropolitan-Cammell-Weymann.

During 1932 and 1933 only seventy-seven Matadors, mainly long wheelbase types, had been built but the advent of this short wheelbase tipper provided new impetus. The building of seventy-five chassis under programme FY had begun in December 1933 and coincided with the introduction of the 120 mm bore four-cylinder A168 oil engine. Servo-assisted hydraulic brakes became standard at this same time. Though the oil engine had by this time been declared the standard power unit, of the seventy-five chassis built on programme FY, forty-eight were powered by the A163 petrol engine. Programme GV specifically refers to chassis 0645157–256 inclusive and the trend here was similar. Forty-three of the 100 chassis built had the A163 petrol engine.

In the year 1934, 174 chassis were built, of which 117 were tippers. Additional to the twenty-four delivered to the Feltham Sand & Gravel Co. and the twenty to Ham River, Hall & Co. of Redhill took fifty-seven, Thomas Roberts took twelve and Surrey Sand & Gravel had four. A final programme, HB, dated 14 February 1934, sanctioned the building of fifty chassis, of which only 0645257–263 were completed.

Six chassis were built as six-wheelers with the same four-spring bogie suspension as devised for the Mammoth six-wheel conversions. Chassis 645178, 257 and 258 were built for Express Dairies, 0645241 was supplied to H. C. Thomas of Stamford and 0645259 and 260 went to E. V. Norman of Cambridge. A further seven chassis were converted retrospectively.

The last chassis built was 0645263, supplied to Downer & Co. of Southampton in June 1935, which, like chassis 262, was powered by the six-cylinder A171 oil engine. No records exist for chassis 645067 and 068 and chassis 645081 is recorded as not having been built. Depending on how these facts are interpreted, there was either 260 or 262 Type 645/0645s built.

THE TYPE 0646 MATADOR

This was a small group of seven chassis. Mechanically similar to the forward control chassis, they were of bonneted construction and had a wheelbase of 16 feet 6 inches, affording a clear body-space of 16 feet 4 inches. All featured the four-cylinder A168 oil engine, the D126 gearbox, the heavy F142 Mark 1 rear axle and servo-assisted hydraulic brakes. Chassis 0646001–006 had 40 inch by 8 inch tyres and 007 had 36 inch by 8 inch tyres.

Chassis 001 was built for Shell-Mex on 18 May 1934 and despatched to Thompson of Bilston on the 30th of that month. Chassis 002, built on 29 May, was supplied to H. G. Brown of Leighton Buzzard, registered MJ 4728. It is noted as being fitted with an auxiliary gearbox. Chassis 003, built for Eagle Oil on 30 July 1934, was despatched to Samudas Wharf on 3 August for shipment overseas. Chassis 004, 005 and 006 were built in November 1934 and despatched to Blakes Wharf on 4 December for shipment to Agar Cross & Co. in Buenos Aires. Chassis 007 was built on 8 May 1935 for the Marquis de Sales in Madrid and despatched to London Docks on 14 May 1935.

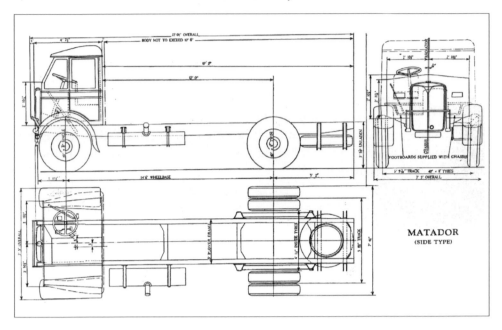

Arrangement drawing of the Matador chassis taken from the AEC sales brochure No. 152, dated November 1933. (*Drawing: AEC, Author's collection*)

With its heavy-duty double reduction rear axle and 40 inch by 8 inch tyres, the Matador could at first view be mistaken for the Mammoth. The immediate point of recognition is the radiator, shorter than that of the Mammoth by 3¾ inches. The primary difference of course, not visible in this view, is the four-cylinder A163 engine. Another point, less obvious, is the depth of the chassis frame, 9 inches deep on the Matador compared with 10 inches deep on the Mammoth. (*Photograph: AEC 3517, Author's collection*)

While forming only a fraction of the overall operating cost, motor vehicle taxation had always been (and so remains) an emotive subject. With a trailer in tow, an increase in payload of 50 per cent or more was possible at a cost of no more than an additional £10 on the annual road fund licence. To many, this had a particular attraction. Dutton's Matador, 645058 with oil engine A168/53, is typical of that line of thought. (*Photograph: Malcolm McNeille, Author's collection*)

As yet unregistered, Dean's Matador 0645073 awaits delivery from Southall. The cab and body were built by Medley, Brooker & Smith of Horn Lane Acton, W3, and while the cab was somewhat lacking in style, the drop-side body looks particularly well made. The short overhang, the sideboards of differing lengths and the extension racks hint at some special requirement – but what? (*Photograph: AEC, Author's collection*)

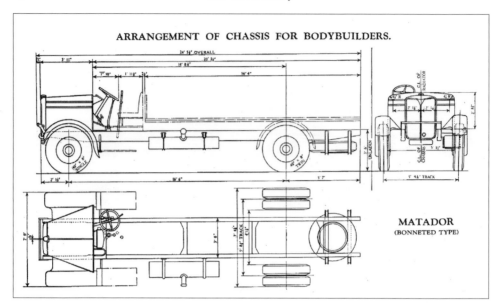

ARRANGEMENT OF CHASSIS FOR BODYBUILDERS.

MATADOR
(BONNETED TYPE)

Arrangement drawing of the bonneted Matador chassis taken from the AEC sales brochure No. 152, dated November 1933. (*Drawing: AEC, Author's collection*)

These bonneted Matadors were two of only seven built. Built in November 1934 and in company with a third example, they were despatched to Blake's Wharf in Fulham for shipment to Agar Cross & Company in Buenos Aires in December. Carrying the unfamiliar 'Aclo Diesel' script on the radiator, they had A168 engines, D126 gearboxes, F142 rear axles, Lockheed brakes and Marles steering gear. The 40 inch by 8 inch tyres were from Firestone. (*Photograph: AEC, Author's collection*)

18

The Q-Types Part One

As with many of John Rackham's design features, inspiration for the Q-type had originated in America. In 1927, the Fageol brothers had devised the Twin Coach, a modern twin-engined, single-decked coach with the entrance forward of the front axle. Two vertical engines were carried, one each side rearward of the front axle, much in the manner of the ill-starred Daimler KPL of 1910. Rackham's design featured a single engine, out-rigged from the offside chassis frame member.

Patents and prototypes

The provisional patent application, numbered 19,302/31, had been filed in the joint names of George John Rackham and the Associated Equipment Company Limited on 4 July 1931 and the full patent specification, under number 380,536, was accepted on 22 September 1932. In this specification it was claimed:

> An advantage of constructing a passenger vehicle according to the present invention is that, in addition to the engine being readily accessible, the space usually absorbed by the engine and bonnet can be made available for passengers since the propelling unit, being located at the side of the vehicle, may lie partially under the passengers' seats.

The prototype Q was single-decked chassis 762001. Its brief first description appeared in the Commercial Motor of 9 September 1932. The chassis had been despatched to the LGOC on 5 May 1932 and the body constructed at Chiswick works. Full fronted, with a front overhang of 4 feet and a well-rounded profile, this thirty-seven-seat bus with a sliding centre-entrance door was quite unlike anything seen in London before.

We learn from Gavin Martin in London Buses 1929–1939 (Ian Allan 1990) that, painted red and working from Hammersmith garage, Q1 was placed in experimental service with the LGOC on route 11E between Shepherds Bush and Liverpool Street on 5 September 1932. It was re-allocated to Nunhead Garage on 28 October, where it was worked on route 621, a local circular route, and following the formation of the LPTB was painted green and transferred to the Country Bus Department in Reigate on 13 February 1934. Initially it was worked on the Green Line service between Redhill and Watford but by 1935 had been relegated to local services, which included routes

439, 447 and 460. It was delicensed on 30 September 1942, stored at Tunbridge Wells and Guildford and sold in January 1946.

Photographs released to the press in October 1932 revealed the emergence of a second chassis, 761001, a double-decker of rather shorter wheelbase, having its entrance platform forward of the front axle. The provisional patent for the body design, numbered 14,345/32, had been filed on 20 May 1932 in the names of Charles William Reeve and the Associated Equipment Company and the full patent, No. 401,739, was completed on 20 November 1933. According to the patent:

> This invention is for improvements in or relating to road passenger vehicles, and has for one of its objects to facilitate the control of the vehicle with respect to the needs and movements of passengers or intending passengers. The invention is applicable to trolley omnibuses as well as to other types of self-propelled road vehicles.
>
> According to the primary feature of the present invention, there is provided a double deck road passenger vehicle having the passengers' entrance to the vehicle located in front of the front axle under the immediate observation of the driver, and having the foot of the only staircase between the two decks immediately adjacent to the said entrance. Therefore the driver will be readily able to supervise the movements of passengers as he will not only be able to see passengers entering or leaving the vehicle but also those passing up or down the staircase. Therefore though the conductor may be in a position where he cannot exercise that supervision or though there may even be no conductor, adequate control of the vehicle in relation to the needs of the passengers or of intending passengers will be possible.

A tramway type lifeguard, approved by the Ministry of Transport, located beneath the 6-foot front overhang was thought to be an important safety feature. Still regarded as experimental, the mechanical details of the new chassis remained a closely guarded secret. Note that the Type 761 designation for the double-decked chassis and 762 for the single-decker were exactly complimentary to the designations for the double-decked Type 661 Regent and single-decked Type 662 Regal.

Specification

Unlike the Fageol and ACF, which were of unitary construction, the Q-type retained a conventional chassis frame. One of features of the Q-type was the adoption of single rear wheels, which, like AEC's Renown, afforded a much wider spring base and thus a greater resistance to body roll. The Q-type's chassis frame had a width of 3 feet 0 1/8 inches over the front springs, splayed outward from a point just rearward of the gearbox front mounting to 5 feet 4 5/8 inches over the rear springs and at the extreme rear to 5 feet 9 1/8 inches. The frame was arched over the front and rear axles to provide clearance and on the double-deck chassis, the nearside member was down-swept forward of the front axle to allow for the passenger's boarding platform. The frame had a maximum depth of 11 inches with 3-inch flanges, the nearside member being 3/16 inches thick while the offside member, carrying the engine and gearbox, was of ¼-inch section. The double-decked Type 761 (and the later 0761) had a wheelbase of 15 feet 10 inches, a front overhang of 6 feet 2 inches and a rear overhang of 3 feet 11½ inches. Its overall chassis length was 25 feet 8½ inches, its width 7 feet 5½ inches and its laden frame height at mid-wheelbase was 1 foot 10 inches. Its turning circle was 60 feet.

The wheelbase of the single-decked chassis has been variously quoted as 18 feet 6 inches and 18 feet 7 inches. The former dimension was the one quoted in most of the contemporary descriptions in the technical press but 18 feet 7 inches was frequently shown on the AEC's chassis record cards. At mid-wheelbase, the single-deck Q had a laden frame height of 1 foot 11¼ inches. The chassis length (for the 18-foot, 6-inch wheelbase chassis) was 27 feet 2½ inches, the width 7 feet 5½ inches and the turning circle 66 feet.

Chassis of shorter wheelbase were constructed to suit specific requirements. Chassis numbered 172–175 and 268 & 269, built for the Christchurch Tramways Board, had a wheelbase of 16 feet, 6 inches and chassis 182 to 261, the LPTB's 5Q5 class, had a wheelbase of 16 feet, 5 inches.

The bare chassis weight for both single and double-decked types was given as 3 tons 10 cwts.

The A167 Petrol Engine

The engine was rubber-mounted and carried on two cantilevered cross-members on the offside chassis frame member. Not immediately apparent was the fact that the engine (and the gearbox) were carried, tail inward, at an angle of three degrees relative to the chassis frame, thereby providing a nearly straight driveline to the rear axle.

The engine was a development of AEC's standard six-cylinder petrol engine, which in its original form had appeared in 1929 for the Reliance as the A130. With 110 mm bore by 130 mm stroke, this 7.4 litre six-cylinder A167 engine developed 63 bhp at 1,000 rpm and 124 bhp at 2,600 rpm on a compression ratio of 5.1:1. The maximum torque was 330 lbs/ft at 1,000 rpm. Though the new engine shared the same cylinder dimensions and cylinder spacing as its immediate predecessor, the A162, there were significant differences between the two types, occasioned both by natural design progression and as a requirement of the engine's new location.

The crankcase was new, with the top face machined at an angle of 18° to the natural horizontal plane, thus tilting the cylinder block outward by the same amount. The crankshaft ran in seven main bearings and was fully counterbalanced. Both the main and big end journals ran in white metal and all were pressure lubricated. The connecting rods were of the usual I-section with the gudgeon pin clamped at the little end. The big end bearings were shimmed to allow for adjustment in service (filing of the rods or caps was strictly forbidden and it was recommended that when re-metalling was required, the rods be returned to Southall). The pistons were flat-topped and carried three compression rings and two scrapers.

The arrangement of the overhead camshaft and its associated valve gear within the cylinder head was similar in most respects to that adopted for the A162. Unlike that engine, however, where the combustion chamber was formed in the clearance volume between the concave piston crown and the cylinder head face, in the case of the Q-type's engine, the combustion chamber was of the bathtub pattern, formed in the cylinder head. Clearance between the flat top of the piston crown and the cylinder head face was minimal.

As previously, the timing case was separate from and positioned in front of the cylinder block. Within the timing case were three shafts, driven by duplex roller chain from the front of the crankshaft. The lower shaft drove the water pump, the dynamo and the magneto, while the intermediate shaft drove the fan. The top shaft carried the camshaft pinion gear and an automatic chain-tensioner ensured that the correct chain tension was maintained. The oil pump was gear-driven from the front of the crankshaft.

With the carburettor, dynamo, magneto and starter all carried on the offside of the engine, the A167 could perhaps have been mistaken for a 'handed' version of the A162. Unusually, at least in an engine employed in automotive work, the A167 ran in an anti-clockwise direction and whereas the A162 had the normal firing order of 153624, that of the A167 was 142635. It was written in the journal Bus and Coach dated 20 October 1933:

> The engine ... rotates anti-clockwise (necessitating a left-hand worm shaft) in order that the torque reaction may oppose the gravity force tending to tilt the chassis to the off side ...

One can only speculate whether or not this was AEC's official line of reasoning and at the same time wonder if the effect of the torque reaction was more theoretical than real. Without doubt, the non-standard features required of both the engine and transmission would add cost and complication to this already unconventional chassis.

The A170 Oil Engine

It was announced in the AEC Gazette of November 1933:

> From this month A.E.C. will adopt the oil engine as a standard fitting to all chassis and regard the petrol engine as alternative equipment.

In that same issue, previewing the Olympia exhibition, it was indicated that the double-deck Q-type, in this instance 761013 for Leeds Corporation, would also be fitted with the oil engine. The chassis, built on 31 July 1933, had been despatched to MCW on 15 August and was at that time fitted with petrol engine A167/16. It was exhibited as planned but the record card shows that it was not until 14 December that 'Oil Engine 1' was fitted. Registered AML996, it was despatched to Leeds on the same day.

The AEC data sheet for December 1933 had listed the Q-type as available with either the 120 hp oil or 120 hp petrol engine, the oil-engined chassis being £300 more expensive than its petrol-engined counterpart. In fact, it was not until July 1934 that the official announcement came that a new six-cylinder oil engine of 106 mm bore and

146 mm stroke had been developed for the Q-type chassis. The quoted power output at that time was 126 bhp at 2,400 rpm. The development of this engine, the A170, and that of its sibling the A171, is studied in a separate chapter.

Demonstrator 761016, AMV 433, had been built on 19 July 1933 and despatched to Park Royal on 8 August 1933. The date of building suggests that this chassis was also petrol-engined as first built and at unknown dates was subsequently fitted with oil engines A170/2, A170/5 and A170/6.

Photographic evidence further shows that the Duple bodied, single-decked demonstrator 762003, BME 130, had by February 1934 received an oil engine, but the chassis record card shows it to have originally been powered by petrol engine A167/6.

Radiator

The forward facing radiator was of the Clayton Still tube type and was positioned immediately behind the offside front mudguard. It was almost totally encapsulated and had a fan not been fitted, there would have been no natural flow of air through it. The fan was cowled and photographs of early vehicles show differing arrangements of ventilation louvres in the engine cover and in the adjoining panel, just rearward of the mudguard. Production chassis carried an inclined air scoop, positioned between the chassis frame rails, which directed the flow of air from beneath the vehicle upward toward the front of the radiator. An aperture cut into the lower part of the front body panel on many of the later single-decked Qs further assisted that respect. From 1935, a new arrangement was adopted where clean air was drawn from the front of the vehicle to the radiator through a duct over the front wheel. Elliott's Duple-bodied Qs 762002 and 005 are noted as having been fitted with high-speed fans (retrospectively), as also were 762028 and 762036. The Grimsby double-decked 761015 and demonstrator 0761016 are also noted as being so fitted. Clearly, engine cooling had been marginal.

Gearbox

762001, the single-decked prototype, was very much a trial chassis. As a chassis, it had passed to the LGOC's coach-building dept in May 1932 and was completed by 30th June. This first Q-type was fitted with a four-speed crash gearbox and plate clutch (which it retained to the end of its days). By the summer of 1932, some idea as to the suitability of the crash (or 'clash' in LGOC language) gearbox would have been assessed and alternative arrangements studied.

When the double-decked 761001 arrived in October 1932, the decision had been taken to equip it with the Daimler-built Wilson preselective gearbox (identified as the D129) and fluid flywheel (J143) which had, since January 1932, been available in the Regent and Regal chassis as an alternative to the D124 crash gearbox. (The fluid flywheel and preselective gearbox are described in subsequent chapter.) Time would show the preselective gearbox to be eminently suitable for stop-start city work but in 1932, the decision to fit it as standard must be seen as a bold step.

Publicity material extolled the virtue of having the engine remote from the driver, where he was free from the heat, fumes and noise of the engine. This freedom from engine noise would certainly make the timing of the gear change on the crash gearbox a less certain operation. Gear changing on the preselective gearbox was certain and foolproof if the gear-change pedal was fully depressed and the operating strut allowed to engage with the bus bar. A rushed change could result in the strut failing to engage and the gear change pedal returning with the full force of the bus bar operating spring behind it. A salutary lesson for the unwary driver. This phenomenon was known and appreciated and on the early applications, the gear change was effected through a vacuum valve and operating cylinder. Instead of the usual heavy-duty pedal, which, with the conventional crash gearbox, would operate the clutch, the vacuum valve was operated through a pedal not unlike that used for the accelerator. Clearly, this arrangement was less than successful and was discontinued.

Like chassis 761001, chassis 002–017 had the Daimler-built fluid flywheel and D129 preselective gearbox, and chassis 018–023, i.e. those built after April 1934, had the AEC-built J148 fluid flywheel and D133 preselective gearbox. Of the single-decked chassis, 762002–006 inclusive and 010 had the Daimler-built equipment and chassis 007–009 and 011 onward had the AEC-built units.

The gear selection mechanism on chassis 761001 was of the Daimler quadrant pattern; all others appear to have had a conventional pedestal type gear selector.

Axles

The front axle was identified as the type L142. It was an I-section alloy steel stamping of the reversed Elliot pattern and because there was no requirement to provide clearance under the engine, the axle beam was almost straight. The king pins were inclined at an angle of 10° from vertical, thus providing centre point steering, and the stub axles were carried on plain bearings with a roller-type thrust bearing to carry the load. Alloy steel was the chosen material for the axle beam and the stub axles. The wheel bearings were of the taper roller type and were adjusted by a special lockable retaining nut. The grease was retained in the hubs by felt washers.

The rear axle, the F161, was of the fully floating type and with its single wheel and tyre formation (as opposed to conventional twins), was unique to the Q-type chassis. The axle casing was a one-piece banjo-type nickel steel drop forging with an 8-inch underneath worm gear off-set as far to the offside of the chassis as the spring carriers would allow. The worm gear was carried in an aluminium alloy casing and a light aluminium cover closed the top opening. The differential gears were of the bevel type and the worm wheel was carried on taper roller bearings in adjustable housings. Uniquely, the worm wheel was cut at an angle of 3° to the worm-shaft. This allowed the worm-shaft to be skewed in the casing so as to reduce the angularity of the prop-shaft between the axle and the gearbox. The worm-shaft was carried in two roller bearings with the end thrust absorbed in a ball bearing. The axle ratios were 5.4:1 for the single decked chassis and 6.2:1 for the double-decker. The wheel-hubs were carried on parallel roller bearings and a spacer between them ensured that the retaining nut could be drawn up tight. Bellows glands provided the hubs with oil-tight seals. The drive to the rear wheels was transmitted via unequal length half-shafts, gear shaped teeth on the half-shaft flanges engaging with similar internal teeth machined in the wheel-hubs. The hubcaps were light steel pressings secured by twelve studs and nuts.

The wheels and tyres were 10.5 inch by 20 inch low-pressure singles on the single-decked chassis and 11.25 inch by 20 inch on the double-deckers. The wheel track at the front measured 6 feet 4¾ inches and at the rear 6 feet 6 inches.

Road springs

The semi-elliptic road springs were all of equal length, 54 inches between centres, and were underslung on both front and rear axles. Wheel loadings varied according to position and the springs therefore varied as to their composition. At the front axle, the springs were 2¼ inches wide, that on the nearside having thirteen leaves, eleven of which were 5/16 inches thick and two of ¼ inches. The offside spring, heavier laden, had twelve leaves, ten at 11/32 inches thick and two of 5/16 inches. The rear springs were the same at both sides, having eight leaves 3½ inches wide, with six leaves 3/8 inches thick and two at 5/16 inches.

Brakes

The brakes were Lockheed hydraulic, assisted by a Clayton Dewandre servo. The brake shoes were cam operated in 17-inch diameter cast iron drums, the front shoes being 4 inches wide and the rears 6 inches. The total effective area was 540 sq inches. The hand brake operated only on the rear drums and had an effective area of 336 sq inches. At the front axle, the Lockheed wheel cylinders were anchored on the brake carrier plate and at the rear axle, on a bracket fixed to the axle casing. The cylinders were pivoted at the fixed end and the pistons were connected directly to the brake camshaft levers. They incorporated AEC-designed ratchet and pawl automatic brake adjusters.

Coachwork

From as far back as the early 1920s, AEC had maintained its own coachwork design office; indeed, in the early days of the development of the Southall factory it had been the intention to set up a coachbuilding department within the factory complex. Vehicles for 'outside' customers (i.e. those outside the London General Omnibus Company) were frequently sold complete, the construction of the body having been sub-contracted to one of the specialist coachbuilders. The LGOC itself also took on outside work at its North Road factory. In later years, Short Bros built the 'camel roof' body to an AEC design for the Regent. In the same way, AEC produced registered designs for both the single and double-decked Q chassis. The registered designs for the single-decked chassis were identified by the numbers 773457 and 773458, and for the double-deckers by 778182 and 778183.

Back in 1919 the AEC and the LGOC had jointly claimed, with some justification, to have taken the design of the motorbus a huge step forward with the introduction of the K type. By placing the driver beside the engine rather than behind it, not only was the driver afforded greatly improved visibility but additional space was released for passenger accommodation. Exactly similar claims were made for the Q-type when compared with the traditional front-engined chassis.

Patent 401,739 brings to the fore the advantage afforded by the removal of the engine from its traditional position at the front of the vehicle in allowing for the positioning the boarding platform adjacent to the driver. Here, he had full view of the passengers when boarding or leaving the bus and additionally, he had an unrestricted view of the nearside kerb. Passenger accommodation was generally increased from fifty-six seats on the Regent chassis to sixty on the Q-type.

Aesthetically, the full-fronted body presented a new, clean and uncluttered frontal aspect, though lack of the radiator at the front resulted in a lack of focus at that point. Yet, particularly in the case of the single-deckers, new features like the central entrance body, the wide windows and sloping window pillars brought a new and refreshing appearance. Duple perhaps built more coach bodies on the Q-type than its competitors but Harrington and Weymann also featured strongly. Accommodation in the coach bodies varied between twenty-nine seats to as many as thirty-seven.

Bus bodies, generally rather more square in appearance than the coaches, usually seated thirty-nine and a wide variety was built, which included the products of Berw, Brush, Craven, Strachan and Walker. The bodies for the London 4Q4s were constructed by the Birmingham Railway Carriage and Wagon Company (BRCW). Those for the 5Q5s and 6Q6s were built by Park Royal.

Into production

Programme EY, dated 7 January 1933, provided for the building of fifteen Type 761 double-deck chassis, five single-decker Type 762s, and one double-decked trolleybus Type 761T, together with four sets of spares. From this, it becomes clear that Rackham's initial thrust with the Q-type was directed toward the municipal operators and was keen to achieve an immediate presence throughout the provinces with the double-decker.

The Double-deck Type 761

Seventeen double-decked Qs from a total of only twenty-three built were constructed before the end of 1933 and were dispersed among virtually all of the AEC's established municipal fleet customers.

Chassis 761001 had been built in the experimental department and there is no indication of the date of its completion. The double deck body was constructed by the LGOC and provided twenty-nine seats on the lower deck and thirty-one on the upper. The first photographs of the vehicle appeared in the November 1932 issue of the AEC Gazette. Its unladen weight was 6 tons 2 cwts. It was despatched to Birmingham Corporation on 26 January 1933 registered AHX 63. Its original petrol engine, A167/3, was changed for oil engine A170/10 in July 1934.

Chassis 002, with engine A167/2, had also been built in the experimental department. With sixty-seat bodywork by Metro-Cammell it turned the scales at 5 tons 17 cwts 1 qr. Registered AMD 256, it became No. 1,000 in the Crossville fleet. Crossville was a traditional Leyland operator and its presence in Chester would have been viewed with some suspicion. Chassis 003, with engine A167/10, was built on 22 June 1933 and again had a sixty-seat Metro-Cammell body. It was delivered to Bolton Corporation, another traditional Leyland operator, on 15 August, registered WH 4850. Halifax Corporation had 761004, JX 1461, built on 2 June 1933. Despatched to English Electric on 11 July 1933, the completed bus was taken into Halifax stock on 21 February 1934.

Chassis 005–013 all had bodywork by Metro-Cammell. Chassis 005, with engine A167/9, built on 10 July 1933 and registered JN 3457, was delivered to Westcliff-on-Sea Motor Services on 3 October. Chassis 006, RH 7747, built on 20 June 1933, went to Hull on 1 September and 007, with engine A167/12, built on 7 June, went to Birkenhead Corporation on 29 July 1933. It was registered BG 1509. Bradford Corporation took 007, built 21 June 1933. Registered KY 5141, it became No. 393 in the Bradford fleet. Near-neighbour Leeds Corporation had 761009, UG 6511, built on 12 June 1933. Originally fitted with petrol engine A167/7, this was exchanged for oil engine A170/7 on 7 June 1935. Chassis 761010 became Newcastle 156, registered ABB 449. It had been built on 21 June 1933.

761011 and 012, with engines A167/21 and A167/17, became Q2 and Q3 in the London Passenger Transport Board fleet. The chassis had been built on 25 August and 16 August 1933 respectively but the LPTB appeared to be in no hurry to take delivery. Ultimately, Q3 was delivered on 25 May 1934 and Q2 five days later. The buses seated twenty-eight passengers on each deck and had an unladen weight of 6 tons 2 cwts. Not particularly beautiful when viewed from the nearside front, the vehicles had a certain elegance when seen from the offside rear.

Chassis 761013 had been built on 31 July 1933 and despatched to Metro-Cammell on 15 August. With thirty-one seats upstairs and twenty-nine below, it had an unladen weight of 5 tons 19 cwts. An erasure on its record card hints that its early history was not as first planned. Originally fitted with engine A167/16, this was exchanged for oil engine A170/1 on 14 December 1933. Registered AML 996, the vehicle was promptly despatched to Leeds. Engine A170/1 was changed for A170/129 on 11 July 1935 and this in turn was converted to direct injection by Tillotson in October 1940.

Chassis 014 was the first of two Weymann-bodied central-entrance Qs for the LPTB, the second being 017. The engines are noted as being A167/1 and A167/8. As Q4 and Q5, registered BPG 507 and BPJ 224, they were allocated to Reigate Garage for country service duties. Like the Central Area Q-types, they seated twenty-eight passengers on each deck.

Grimsby Corporation had 761015, AML 663. This, with a central-entrance dual staircase body built by Charles Roe, seated fifty-six passengers. The building date is unknown but is shown as delivered to Roe on 20 September 1933. It was employed as a demonstrator at the Commercial Show at Olympia in November 1933 and despatched to Grimsby thereafter.

Chassis 0761016 was demonstrator AMV 433, built with oil engine A170/5. Subsequent engine replacements were A170/2 and A170/6. Built on 18 July 1933, it was despatched to Park Royal on 8 August 1933. The body seated fifty-nine and the vehicle is shown as weighing 5 tons 19 cwts 3 qrs. Never finding a permanent home, it is noted as having seen service at various times in Nottingham and Coventry.

Chassis 761018, 021 and 022 had been built on 25, 27 and 28 April 1934. Respectively fitted with petrol engines A167/34, A167/35 and A167/33, they had the AEC-built preselective gearbox, the D133, in place of the Daimler-built D129 fitted to the earlier chassis. All were despatched to AEC Australia for the New South Wales Government Transport Department. In Australia they received front-entrance bodies of similar style to the home market types, built by Syd Wood.

Built at the same time as the Australian chassis were two for Wallasey Corporation. Numbered 761019 and 761020, these chassis carried centre-entrance bodies built by Charles Roe and were similar in most respects to that built for Grimsby. Built on 3 May and 26 April 1934 respectively, they had been despatched to Roe on 10 and 3 May. With petrol engines A167/37 and A167/38 and AEC-built D133 gearboxes, they were registered HF 9399 and HF 9401. The last of the double-deck Q-types was 761023 with oil engine A170/142, built for Cardiff Corporation. Registered KG 7750, it had a body built by English Electric. The engine number suggests a building date of September 1935. The PSV Circle places the date into service as 4/1936.

Road Test

In October 1933, the Commercial Motor conducted a road test of a double-decked, petrol-engined Q; the accompanying photograph suggests that the vehicle was in fact that for Hull, 761006. Laden to a gross weight of 9 tons 17½ cwts (equivalent to a loading of sixty passengers), the vehicle returned a fuel consumption of 6.07 mpg over a mainly level 10.8-mile circular course. A total of thirty-eight stops were made in this simulated city service operation and the average speed was 12.9 mph. A second run was made over a 10.86-mile out and return course with five stops (Southall to Harrow and return) that included two ascents of Harrow Hill. Here the vehicle returned a fuel consumption of 6.4 mpg at an average speed of 16.3 mph. Acceleration to 30 mph took 32½ seconds and the maximum speed recorded was 47 mph. Braking from 30 mph to rest required 75 feet and, fully laden, there was ample power for a stop and restart on the 1 in 6 gradient of Harrow Hill. The tester was fulsome in his praise for the Q-type. Quoting directly, he said:

> The driver's position and range of vision are excellent, and the fluid transmission with epicyclic gearbox add to the final touch of refinement. This was, in fact, one of the most enjoyable driving experiences we can remember ever having had upon the road.

The story of the single deck Q-types is further explored in Chapter 22.

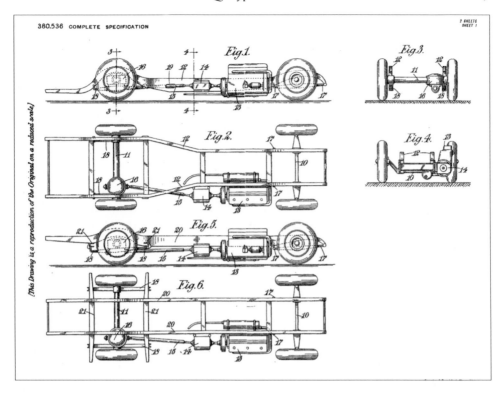

Above and below: The provisional patent for the vehicle we now recognise as the Q-type was filed on 4 July 1931 and the full patent, No. 380,536, was accepted on 22 September 1932. The patent covered both four-wheeled and six-wheeled chassis. A further patent, No. 401,739, in respect of the forward entrance double-deck body was accepted on 20 November 1933. (*Drawing: National Reference Library of Science and Invention*)

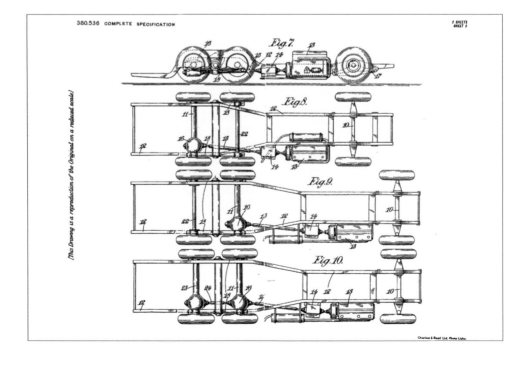

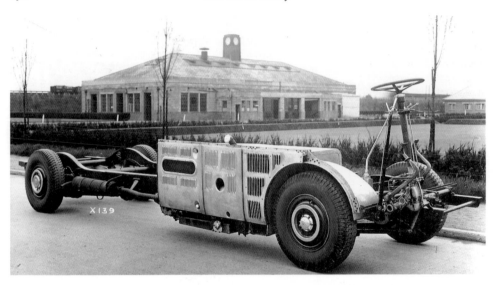

Nothing quite as revolutionary as Rackham's Q-type's chassis had been seen in this country since the ill-starred Daimler KPL of 1910. The chassis had been built amid great secrecy and while the management could not fail to have been aware of its existence, no mention of it appeared in the company's minute book until 2 June 1932. In the background to the photograph is the works canteen and beyond that the Great Western Railway's main line. (*Photograph: AEC X139, Alan Townsin Collection*)

In typical Rackham fashion, the radiator, engine and crash gearbox on this first Q-type chassis formed a single unit, the gearbox apparently a 'handed' version of the then standard D124, Whilst the patent drawings indicate a separately mounted gearbox, it appears likely that no firm decision had been made at that time in respect of gearbox type. (*Photograph: AEC 3522, Alan Townsin collection*)

The Q-type's A167 petrol engine had much in common with Rackham's six-cylinder A162 – the same cylinder dimensions of 110 mm by 130 mm, the same cylinder spacing and a similar arrangement of the overhead camshaft. It differed in other respects. Importantly, the combustion chambers were of the bathtub type and the cylinders were inclined at an angle of 18° from the vertical. This made for easier removal of the cylinder head and at the same time reduced the amount that the engine intruded on the inside of the body. The engine delivered 124 bhp at 2,600 rpm. (*Drawing: AEC, Author's collection*)

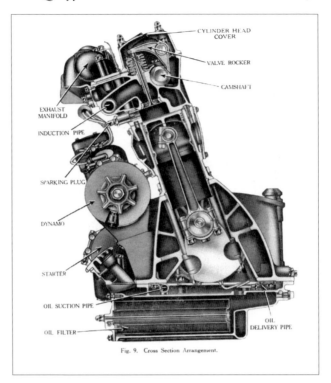

Fig. 9. Cross Section Arrangement.

The arrangement of the Daimler fluid transmission contrasts sharply with the crash gearbox of 762001. Easily visible is the vacuum-operated gear change cylinder, actuated by a valve on the inside of the chassis frame, itself connected to the driver's left foot pedal. Less obvious is the banana-shaped lever on the selection cover, operated through rods and levers from the steering column-mounted Daimler quadrant selector. (*Photograph: AEC 3935, Alan Townsin collection*)

While it is said that inspiration for the Q-type was drawn from the American Fageol Twin-Coach, Rackham had his own very definite ideas on body design. To that end, this model was built, possibly in the AEC's own pattern shop, in order that his ideas may be more readily demonstrated. The photograph was taken at the rear of the experimental department and in the background is the spares building. (*Photograph: AEC M907, BCVM*)

Q1's chassis, 762001, had been despatched to the LGOC's Chiswick coach building shop on 5 May 1932 and the photograph here was taken immediately before being placed in service on 2 September. While the body, with its prominent destination boxes, failed to catch the subtlety of line of the model, perhaps its greatest visual downfall was the positioning of the headlights. (*Photograph: London Transport Museum, U11332*)

Hull Corporation had already taken ten Regals and twenty Regents in 1932 and there was clearly the hope that Q-type RH 7747 would be equally well received. As with most recipients, this Q remained the only one in the fleet. The chassis was 761006, the engine A167/13 and the gearbox a Daimler-built preselector. The body, with twenty-eight seats inside and thirty-two on top, was built by Metropolitan Cammell. (*Photograph: AEC 0876, Alan Townsin collection*)

Wallasey's No. 102 was the third Q-type to receive one of Charles Roe's central entrance bodies and the second purchased by that undertaking. With the exception of the destination boxes, the two Wallasey Q-types appear identical to the Grimsby demonstrator. An unusual feature was the large, rear hinged driver's door, which would make for easy access; the matching quarter light added to the visual attraction. The chassis number was 761020, the engine A167/38 and the gearbox was an AEC-built D133. (*Photograph: Charles Roe P314, BCVM*)

19

The Marshal Types 644, 671 and 673

The Marshal received its first public showing on 14 and 15 July 1932 at Southall, where officers of the Oversea Mechanical Transport Committee and the Comptroller of Overseas Trade had been invited to a demonstration of AEC and Hardy chassis.

The chassis had been conceived as a 3/5-ton six-wheeler, to meet the particular requirements of colonial operation, where metalled roads were often non-existent. Early tests of the Marshal to ascertain its off-road capabilities had been undertaken at the Mechanical Warfare Experimental Establishment proving grounds at Farnborough as early as December 1931. Two prototypes were tested. One was a bonneted chassis with the four-cylinder A163 petrol engine, the second, a forward control type, having the six-cylinder A162.

In May 1932, following the Farnborough trials, AEC's forward control four-cylinder demonstrator, 644001, spent a fortnight with the MWEE. During this time it took part in the War Office trials near Llangollen in North Wales, where it made a successful climb of Alt-y-Bady, a hill of 1,800 yards with a maximum gradient of 1 in 3 and an average gradient of 1 in 6.75. Following the trials, the War Office ordered a single forward control A163-powered Marshal chassis for further evaluation. This, with dual identification of MV5452 and L22605, was delivered to the MWEE at Farnborough in November 1932.

The Type 644 Specification

The Type 644, dependent on whether it was of bonneted or forward control layout, was a three-axled version of the Type 640 Mercury or Type 641 Monarch. The specification had been drawn up under XU604, dated 30.6.31. The chassis was powered by the four-cylinder 112 mm bore by 130 mm stroke 80 bhp A163 petrol engine described in Chapter 6. This drove through a 16-inch diameter single plate clutch to AEC's standard D124 four-speed gearbox. It had forward ratios of 4.38:1, 2.69:1, 1.59:1 and 1:1, with reverse 5.33:1. Forming a single unit with the main gearbox was the D127 two-speed auxiliary. The high range gave a direct drive from the main gearbox while the low range provided a reduction of 2.6:1. The low range gears thus had forward ratios of 11.38:1, 6.99:1, 4.13:1 and 2.6:1, with reverse 13.85:1.

The double-drive bogie was to a patented design by Charles Cleaver, 'borrowed' from the recently introduced Hardy R6/8 chassis. The bogie was, in some respects, similar to that of the Mammoth Major in that it employed two inverted, centre pivoted semi-elliptic leaf springs, one at each side, carried on a central transverse load-bearing member. The outer ends of the springs, in Cleaver's design, were attached to the axles by means of swivelling forks, which allowed a high degree of angular movement between spring and axle without producing any torsional stresses. Ball-jointed links, attached at one end to a central tubular cross member and at the other to the top of each worm-gear case, absorbed driving torque and provided correct location of the axles. Unlike the double-drive axles of the Type 802 'London Six' or the Type 663 Renown, no inter-axle third differential was fitted. This ensured that where adhesion was marginal, wheel-spin on one wheel did not result in total loss of traction. The semi-floating axles had a standard ratio of 7¼:1, which in conjunction with the 9 inch by 22 inch tyres gave a speed of 30.2 mph at 2,000 engine rpm on top gear. Alternative axle ratios of 6 1/3:1 and 9 1/3:1 were available.

The vacuum servo-assisted foot brake operated on the front axle and first bogie axle and the handbrake on the rearmost bogie axle. The brake drums were of 17-inch diameter and the twelve brake shoes, all of which were interchangeable, were 3¼ inches wide.

The front axle was of the reversed 'Elliot' pattern, with stub axles having a maximum diameter of 2¼ inches. The wheel-hubs were carried on taper roller bearings and the steering gear was by Marles.

The Marshal had a wheelbase of 12 feet, 8½ inches, measured from the centreline of the front axle to the centreline of the bogie (civilian chassis were built to a wheelbase of 15 feet 11 inches), a front track of 5 feet 10 inches and a rear track of 5 feet 9 7/8 inches. The bogie had axle centres of 4 feet. The chassis had an overall length of 20 feet 7½ inches and provided a clear body space of 14 feet 6 inches. The maximum width over the front mudguards was 7 feet and over the rear hubs 6 feet 10½ inches. The chassis and cab weight was 4 tons 7 cwts 3 qrs and the maximum laden weight was 11 tons 7 cwts 3 qrs.

Exceptionally, as demonstrated at Southall, the bonneted prototype chassis, 644004, was equipped with a separately mounted auxiliary gearbox from which, via jack-shaft and bevel driven cross shaft, was driven a horizontal drum winch. It carried 280 feet of ¾-inch diameter steel rope and an automatic laying-on gear ensured that the rope wound evenly on the drum. The rope could be paid out under power in reverse gear or, with the drum disconnected from the gearing, could be drawn out by hand. The maximum pull exerted in first gear was 6.3 tons.

Performance

As was the custom of the MWEE, the December 1931 tests of the two prototype chassis were conducted back to back with a fully tested vehicle of similar type in order that direct comparison could be made. In this instance, the two AEC chassis were to be judged against the 3-ton six-wheeled Leyland Terrier L21285. The six-cylinder Marshal had a laden gross weight of 9 tons 5 cwts 2 qrs and the bonneted four-cylinder Marshal, 8 tons 6 cwts 2 qrs 7 lbs. The Leyland was laden to 8 tons

8 cwts. On a road test of 64 miles, the six-cylinder AEC returned a fuel consumption of 5.9 mpg, the four-cylinder chassis 7.5 mpg and the Leyland 7.1 mpg.

The Leyland Terrier had a four-cylinder engine of 4 9/16 inches bore and 5½ inches stroke, a swept volume of 5.889 litres and a power output of 50 bhp at 1,000 rpm. As fitted in the later Retriever chassis and governed to 2,150 rpm, the same engine delivered 73 bhp at 2,120 rpm with maximum torque of 260 lbs ft at 1,150 rpm.

Hill climbing tests on the loose-surfaced gravel slopes with the six-cylinder chassis were negated due to its civilian-pattern tyre equipment. Wheel-spin on the 1 in 3.7 slope brought the vehicle to a standstill and further tests were abandoned. Tests with the four-cylinder chassis fitted with 9 inch by 22 inch trak-grip tyres were more successful. The 1 in 3.7 slope was successfully climbed but it failed on the 1 in 3.1 due to wheel-spin, as did the Leyland. Fitted with Kennedy & Kempe chains on the rear wheels, the 1 in 3.1 gradient was successfully overcome but it failed 7 yards from the top on the 1 in 3 slope due to lack of power. The Leyland failed for the same reason but got within 5 yards of the top. Both the four-cylinder chassis and the Leyland made successful climbs of the 1 in 2.25 concrete slope with no wheel-spin.

The official report, dated 16.12.31, reads:

> Both AEC vehicles put up very good performances and passed the obstacle course with only minor exceptions.
>
> The road speed and petrol consumption were satisfactory.
>
> The cross-country performance of the Marshal 6-cylindered vehicle was adversely affected by the tyre equipment. The power appeared adequate for loads considerably in excess of 3 tons useful load. The makers advertise 7 tons maximum load.
>
> The Marshal 4-cylindered vehicle put up a performance nearly as good as that of the Leyland but the engine has not quite as much power at low speeds.
>
> The braking of both vehicles needs improvement. It is understood from the makers that this is experimental.

Production details

Chassis 644001, following duty as a demonstrator, was assigned to the AEC's service department. The six-cylinder prototype, 671001, which featured in the December 1931 trials at Farnborough, was rebuilt with a four-cylinder A168 oil engine and became 644002. It passed to H. Sainsbury of Fitzroy Square, London in March 1934. Chassis 644003 was built expressly for the War Office under contract V2355. As noted above, it received dual identification of MV 5452 and L22605. The bonneted Marshal became 644004, which, together with the six-cylinder chassis, featured in the 1931 Farnborough trials. Fitted with a winch, it was ultimately seconded to AEC's sales inspection department. A163-powered 644005 was built for the Improved Wood Pavement Company of London EC4 in June 1933. It had 36 inch by 8 inch front tyres and 32 inch x 6 inch rears. Pickfords had three bonneted chassis. 644006 had been built in September 1934 and 007 and 008 in August 1935. These were fitted with the A168 oil engine and had 34 inch by 7 inch tyres, singles at the front and twins at the rear.

Military specification

Criticisms raised following the 1931 tests of the Marshal clearly called for action, particularly in respect of brake performance. To this end, the rear brake shoes were increased in width from 3¼ inches to 6 inches. The footbrake was made to operate on all six wheels and was actuated through a servo-assisted Lockheed hydraulic system. The hydraulic cylinders for the front brakes were contained within the front axle king pins, while at the rear, two chassis-mounted hydraulic cylinders were called upon to operate the four brake units of the bogie axles. The handbrake operated the same brake units through a system of rods and levers.

The radiator was fitted with thermostatically controlled shutters and as befitted a vehicle designed for cross-country operation, the fuel tank, vacuum tank and spare wheel were carried, clear of any obstacle, on a frame behind the driver's cab. Driver protection was minimal, the canvas hood and storm apron being typical of a 1930s War Office specification.

The Marshal was variously equipped as a 3-ton general service vehicle or as a carrier of box girder and bridging sections. Uniquely, the Motor Church of St George was carried on a Marshal chassis and travelled widely across the deserts of North Africa in 1942 and 1943.

War Office contracts

In September 1935, the War Office placed its first production contract for the Marshal chassis. Contract V2780 called for twenty-four chassis, to which a further eight were added two months later. These chassis, 644009–040, were built in April and May 1936. A second contract, V3062, was placed for ninety chassis in July 1936 and these, 644041–130, were built in the period October 1936 to January 1937.

Further War Office orders were placed in March and October 1937. Contract V3062 called for 101 chassis and contract V3165 for 102 chassis. These, 644132–334, were built in the period September 1937 – March 1938. Contracts V3529 of April 1939 and V3561 of September 1939 called for 100 and 200 chassis respectively and were built as 644335–634 between September 1939 and June 1940. In November 1939 a final 300 chassis were ordered under contract V3754. These, 644635–934, were built from June 1940 through to May 1941.

Prices

Unlike other AEC chassis, no list price was published for the Marshal. Military records, however, show that the contract price for the Marshal chassis supplied under contract V3529, complete with cargo body, was £1,165 19s 8d and for those supplied under contract V3754 was £1,309 1s 11d. Comparable contract prices for the Leyland Retriever, supplied in the same periods, were £988 6s 10d and £1,055 15s 3d.

The Types 671 and 673

The Type 671 was of forward control layout and the Type 673 was bonneted. Both shared an essentially similar mechanical specification. The Type 671 was one of the two prototypes tested at Farnborough in December 1931. It differed from the Type 644 principally in that it was fitted with the A162 six-cylinder petrol engine, had a 10-inch chassis frame (that of the Type 644 was 8 inches deep) and a wheelbase of 15 feet 11 inches. The tyres were 11.25 inches by 20 inches in place of the 9 inch by 22 inch tyres of the Type 644. The bonneted Type 673 was built for the Griffin Engineering Company of Johannesburg in March 1933. Only one of each of the types 671 and 673 were built.

A revised specification

In the middle 1930s, a provisional specification was issued for a forward control six-cylinder Marshal chassis, available with either the A165 oil or A162 petrol engine. The clutch and main gearbox were as described for the Type 644 but the auxiliary gearbox, with a low range ratio of 1.6:1, was so arranged as to provide a single five-speed range of gears where 1st gear had a ratio of 7:1; 2nd, 4.3:1; 3rd, 2.5:1; 4th, 1.6:1; and 5th, 1:1. Reverse was 8.5:1. The rear bogie was similar to that of the Type 644. The worm-driven axles, with a ratio of 7¼:1, featured fully floating hubs and an inter-axle differential, which would equalise driving axle stresses. Servo-assisted hydraulic brakes operated on all axles and the handbrake connected with all four of the rear axle drums. As with the Type 644, the steering gear was of Marles manufacture.

The chassis frame was to have a depth of 10 inches with 3½-inch flanges and a wheelbase of 16 feet. The overall chassis length, at 25 feet 2¾ inches, allowed a platform length of 20 feet. The intended tyre equipment was 12 inches by 20 inches in single formation and the chassis was designed for a gross weight of 16 tons 15 cwts. The projected chassis and cab weight for the oil-engined chassis was 5 tons 10 cwts and for the petrol-engined chassis 5 tons 3 cwts.

A single A162-powered chassis of 15-foot 11-inch wheelbase, 644131, was built on 20 October 1937. With a cab and body built by Oswald Tillotson, it was supplied to the Yorkshire Electric Supply Company of Dewsbury for work in the field, in the erection of overhead line equipment and the construction of electric sub-stations. The vehicle was equipped with a winch driven from the gearbox power take-off which, in conjunction with rear-loading ramps, provided for the loading of transformers and other heavy equipment. Two jacks, fitted at the rear of the platform, provided stability during loading and unloading operations. With its six-cylinder engine, a chassis number in the 671 series would have been more appropriate than the 644131 allocated.

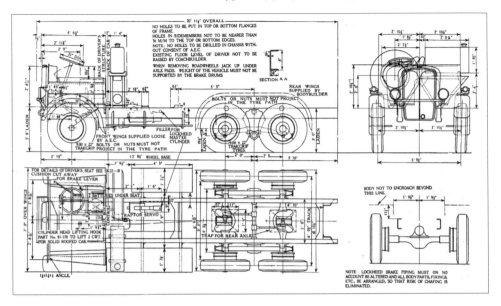

Arrangement drawing of the military-pattern Marshal Type 644 taken from the AEC service manual, dated February 1940. (*Drawing: AEC, Author's collection*)

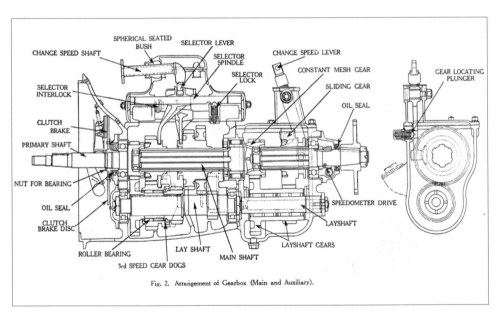

Fig. 2. Arrangement of Gearbox (Main and Auxiliary).

In order to provide the Marshal with adequate cross-country performance, a simple two-speed auxiliary gearbox was built integral with the main gearbox. The high range gave a direct drive from the main gearbox and the low ratio provided a gear reduction of 2.6:1. In the high range the ratios were: 4.38:1, 2.69:1, 1.59:1 and 1:1 and reverse 5.33:1. With the low range engaged, the overall ratios were: 11.38:1, 6.99:1, 4.13:1 and 2.6:1 and reverse 13.85:1. (*Drawing: AEC, Author's collection*)

One of the two prototype Marshal chassis, this bonneted version, 644004, is seen on test at Farnborough. Its ability to negotiate this type of terrain seems quite remarkable and the observer standing on dry ground suggests that the event was not posed. The cab was later removed and winch gear fitted. (*Photograph: AEC, Author's collection*)

The forward control prototype Marshal is seen here with a 3-ton Eagle trailer in tow during the display at Southall on 14 and 15 July 1932. This same vehicle took part in the War Department trials at Llangollen in May 1932. (*Photograph: AEC, Michael Fincher collection*)

Built to the special requirement of the Improved Wood Pavement Co., chassis 644005 had a wheelbase of 15 feet 11 inches. The cab and ultra low body were built by Park Royal Coachworks. The engine was A163/90 and the gearbox a standard D124 without the auxiliary D127. The tyres were by Dunlop, 36 inches by 8 inches at the front and 32 inches by 6 inches at the rear. The chassis had been built on 29 June 1933 and the complete vehicle was delivered on 8 August. (*Photograph: AEC L1340, BCVM*)

Pickfords Marshal BLD 314 was another special, the first of three similar oil-engined chassis numbered 0644006, 007 and 008. Having a 15-foot 11-inch wheelbase and powered by oil engine A168/262, 006, like 005 above, had the D124 gearbox without the auxiliary D127. Dunlop tyres again featured, 34 inches by 7 inches all round with twins at the rear. BLD 314 is seen beside the Thames at Windsor. (*Photograph: John Banks collection*)

Developed as a 3-ton go-anywhere military chassis, the Marshal was typical of the breed. Other vehicles in the same category were the Leyland Retriever, Albion BY1, Crossley IGL8, Karrier CK6 and Guy FBAX. This photograph dates to the spring of 1936, and the Marshal is one from the first production batch of thirty-two chassis, 644009–040, built under War Office contract V2780. Deliveries to the military totalled 925 and the last chassis, 644934, was built on 13 May 1941. (*Photograph: AEC, Author's collection*)

A beautifully evocative photograph this. Well warmed through and with the radiator shutters wide open, the Marshal prepares to ascend to greater heights. The location is thought to be Bwylch-y-groes at the time of the 1936 War Office Trials in North Wales. The Hampshire trade plates and the semi-permanent load perhaps indicate that it is one of the MWEE's long-term test vehicles. (*Photograph: Michael Fincher collection*)

20

The Four-Cylinder A166 and A168 Oil Engines

AEC's four-cylinder oil engine was designed as a direct alternative to the A136 and A163 four-cylinder petrol engines. The 108 mm bore A166 was launched in March 1933 and the 120 mm bore A168 followed in the following December. The engine was intended not only for use in the Mercury, Monarch and Matador commercial chassis but also in the Regal 4. It was also seen as a potential replacement for time-expired petrol engines in non-AEC chassis. Known conversions were made in seven Albion chassis (Baillie Bros, Dumbarton), two Dennis Es (Cardiff Corporation) and seven Leyland Lions (Gosport & Fareham Omnibus Company). It will perhaps be noticed that these three undertakings were already established AEC customers.

Design features

As with the A165 engine, there was a pressing need to keep the weight of the engine as close as possible to its petrol-powered counterpart and for that reason lightweight materials were adopted wherever possible. In the case of the A166, the crankcase was cast in Elektron, a magnesium-based alloy, and the cylinder head in RR50 aluminium alloy. In employing these somewhat expensive alloys, the weight of the A166 engine, complete with bell-housing, flywheel and all auxiliaries, was kept down to 1,170 lbs.

In the design of the cylinder head, the A166 followed that of the A139 and A163 four-cylinder petrol engines (and indeed the A136/A145 six-cylinder types), where the camshaft was carried in the cylinder head, driven via duplex Reynold chain and helical gears from the front of the crankshaft. Like the A165, the A166 employed the spherical Ricardo Comet (Mark I) pre-combustion chamber, into which the air was forced through a tangential passage on the compression stroke. By this means, a high-speed rotational swirl was imparted to the air, across which the fuel was injected.

The cylinder block was a mono-bloc cast iron casting with hardened cylinder liners. The pistons were flat-topped and constructed in 'Y' alloy, a heat-treated aluminium alloy, and had three compression and two scraper rings. The gudgeon pins were hollow, fully floating and ran directly in the piston. The connecting rods were of the four-bolt pattern, bronze bushed at the little end and having white metal-lined steel backed shells at the big end.

The crankshaft had five main bearings of 85 mm diameter and the crank pins measured 72 mm in diameter. Each of the crank-webs was counterweighted, which was claimed to reduce the dynamic loadings on the white metal bearings by 35 per cent. In typical AEC fashion, the main bearing bolts were carried up through the crankcase to form the studs by which the cylinder block was attached. Lubrication was by means of a gear-type pump, gear-driven from the front of the crankshaft and from which oil was delivered under pressure to all the main and big end bearings and to the overhead valve gear. The front mounted sump carried 4½ gallons of oil.

The fuel injection equipment was of CAV-Bosch manufacture and the injection pump incorporated a mechanical governor which controlled both minimum and maximum engine speeds. The idling speed was set at 300/400 rpm and the maximum to 2,000 rpm. The injection pump and the exhauster were driven in tandem from a power takeoff on the timing case while the water pump and dynamo were driven, also in tandem, from a separate power takeoff on the crankcase. The water pump was mounted on the front face of the crankcase, which allowed convenient connection with the radiator.

Dimension & power output

In terms of dimension, the A166 had outer cylinder centres of 502 mm and the centre distance between cylinders 2 and 3 was 188 mm. It was of 108 mm bore and 146 mm stroke with a resultant swept volume of 5.350 litres. The engine had a normal rating of 70 bhp at 2,000 rpm, its maximum torque was 218 lbs.ft at 1,200 rpm, which in turn reflected a bmep of 100 lbs/sq inch. The minimum fuel consumption was 0.42 pints/bhp/hr at 1,000 rpm, rising to 0.46 pints/bhp/hr at 2,000 rpm. The highest numbered A166 engine appears to be A166/323, supplied in Monarch 0641276 to Johannesburg Municipality in May 1936.

Its 120 mm bore A168 stablemate retained the same 146 mm stroke, the swept volume increased to 6.604 litres and the normal rated output to 85 bhp at 2,000 rpm with torque of 265 lbs.ft at 1,100 rpm. The maximum bmep was 100 lbs/sq inch. The highest numbered A168 found was A168/947, which was rebuilt as A186/515. The last A168 actually built into a chassis was A168/907, supplied to the Cement Marketing Company in chassis 0344678 in July 1939.

Development

Naturally, the development work undertaken with the A165 engine was reflected in the development of the A166 and A168 engines. In due time, reliability was dramatically improved by the adoption of lead-bronze for the big-end and bottom half of the main bearings and the cracking experienced in the RR50 aluminium cylinder head was overcome by a change to cast iron.

Verdict

That the four-cylinder engines were still being rebuilt in 1952 is testimony to the fact that they retained a faithful following (not least in the London Brick Company, which had built up a fleet of 168 four-cylinder oil engined Monarchs between 1936 and 1939). The writer recollects that in 1950, a quantity of these A168/A186 engines stood at the rear of the Southall service station, awaiting overhaul. Among them, a number had suffered con-rod failure with resultant extensive crankcase damage.

The engines could never be described as smooth and it is perhaps relevant that they were governed to a maximum of 2,000 rpm. The redeeming feature of the engine, particularly in its A186 guise, was its frugal thirst.

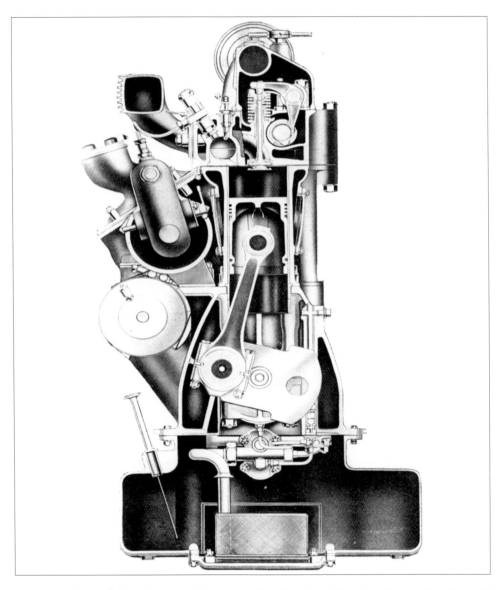

Drawn as if viewed from the rear, this cross section drawing of the A166/A168 oil engine well shows the arrangement of the overhead camshaft and its affinity with that of the four and six-cylinder petrol engines described in Chapters 2 and 6. The Mark I Ricardo swirl chamber is similar in all respects to that of the six-cylinder A165 oil engine described in Chapter 10. (Drawing: AEC, Author's collection)

21

The Colonial Tractor Type 0851

Preamble

The Oversea Mechanical Transport Directing Committee had been set up by the Colonial Office in 1927 to study the problem of transport in the undeveloped regions of the colonies. In due time, the specification of a suitable vehicle was drawn up, the committee having concluded that a vehicle with exceptional cross-country performance was not required as it was envisaged that there would always be earth roads on which to run. It was required, however, that axle loadings be kept to a minimum. Loadings such as were normal in Britain would rapidly lead to the disintegration of what were, in many places, only tracks.

Subsequently, Leyland Motors was invited to build an eight-wheeled, eight-wheel drive tractor, the prime mover in a road train of three vehicles. The two eight-wheeled self-tracking trailers were to be built by R. A. Dyson Ltd of Liverpool. (One of the trailers was exhibited at Olympia in November 1931.) The outfit was designed to carry a payload of 15 tons, 3 tons on the tractor and 6 tons on each trailer. On completion, the laden tractor turned the scales at 10 tons 18 cwts and the trailers each grossed 10 tons. At these weights, each tyre carried little more than 25 cwts. After testing in this country, amounting to some 5,500 miles, the road train was shipped out to the Gold Coast in February 1933. In the nine months to October 1933 it covered a further 8,000 miles in the African bush and was subsequently purchased by the Gold Coast Government.

The Leyland tractor had a petrol engine of 106 bhp, a three-speed main gearbox and a two-speed auxiliary. The final drive assemblies, with inboard brakes, were mounted directly in the chassis frame and the drive was taken to the wheel-hubs by universally jointed half shafts. The wheel-hubs were carried on the outer ends of four centrally pivoted beams and all wheels were steered.

The AEC Tractor

AEC had been commissioned to build a second example, the earliest references to which are found under axle drawing number U61590, dated 15 September 1932, and an XU parts list, XU834, dated 17 September 1932. Designed under the guidance of Charles Cleaver, it was important for reasons both of first cost and future maintenance requirements to employ as many standard production parts as possible. In its general arrangement, the AEC tractor had much in common with its Leyland predecessor. In detail, it was entirely different. Common to both was the eight-wheel drive configuration, the mounting of the two spare wheels on the cab's front panel and the positioning of the oversize radiator behind the engine, where it was protected from damage by brush and more substantial vegetation.

The tractor was powered by the 8.8 litre A165 oil engine set to deliver 130 bhp, driving through a standard four-speed D124 gearbox and a three-speed auxiliary gearbox. In an unusual two-tier arrangement, the engine, gearbox and auxiliary gearbox were carried above rather than within the confines of the chassis frame, such that the crankshaft and transmission centreline was some 5 inches higher than the frame's top flange. The drive was taken from the auxiliary gearbox to the worm-shaft of the rearmost axle through a series of transfer gears carried in an extension of the worm gear case. Thence it was taken forward to the other three axles in turn by means of universally jointed propeller shafts. No inter axle differentials were fitted and the worm gears had a ratio of 8.25:1.

An interlock ensured that direct drive in the auxiliary gearbox could only be engaged when top gear was engaged in the main gearbox and similarly, the emergency low gear could only be engaged with 1st gear engaged in the main gearbox. Separate gear levers were employed for the main and auxiliary gearboxes. The combined gearbox ratios were: 1st, 11.09:1; 2nd, 6.96:1; 3rd, 4.25:1; 4th, 2.51:1; 5th, 1.58:1; and 6th, 1:1. Reverse was 8.41:1. At an engine speed of 2,000 rpm and on 10.5 inch by 20 inch tyres, the relative road speeds in the six forward ratios were 2.56, 4.0, 6.6, 11.3, 17.8 and 28.4 mph. Reverse gear provided 3.48 mph at the same engine speed.

The bogies were of a type similar to that developed for the six-wheeled War Office Marshal chassis. Each bogie was carried on two inverted centre-pivoted leaf springs, the ends of which were attached to the axles by means of swivelling fork-ended joints. In this manner, any tendency for the spring to twist under the articulation of the axles was avoided. Ball-jointed radius rods, which connected the top of the worm gear housings with the central bogie cross-member, absorbed torque reaction and controlled the motion of the axles. Steering was effected on the first and fourth axles, so arranged that if one axle steered left, the other steered right.

Compressed air-operated brakes were fitted on the two middle axles only but with the absence of inter-axle differentials, the braking effort was effective on all wheels. The twin cylindered Westinghouse air compressor was shaft-driven from a power take-off taken from the engine's timing case and delivered air to the twin receivers at 70–80 lbs/sq inch. A pulley on this same shaft provided the drive for the radiator's 33-inch diameter fan. The engine's own 21-inch diameter fan kept surface temperatures within bounds.

The tractor had an overall length of 20 feet 4 5/8 inches, a width of 7 feet 5 inches and the height to the top of the radiator (which was the same as the top of the cab) was 8 feet 9 5/8 inches. The body space was 11 feet 2½ inches and the platform height 4 feet 6 inches. The chassis frame was 3 feet wide and 10 inches deep and the laden height of the frame at the top flange was 3 feet 2 5/8 inches. The bogies each had a wheelbase of 5 feet and the distance between the first and fourth axles was 14 feet. The track of the first and fourth (steered) axles was 6 feet 4¼ inches and that of the second and third axles 6 feet 1 3/8 inches. The ground clearance was 11 inches. The turning circle was 58 feet and the chassis weight, with 50 gallons fuel, oil and water, was 7 tons 19 cwts. With cab, body and 3 tons payload, the laden weight was 11 tons 15 cwts.

The Dyson Trailers

The design of the trailers was such that by switching the position of the drawbar, they could be towed from either end. Each trailer was carried on two identical four-wheeled turntable bogies, cross-linked in such a manner that if, in response to drawbar input, the front bogie was rotated clockwise, the rear bogie would rotate anti-clockwise by the same amount. In this manner, each of the trailers followed exactly the path taken by the tractor. Each bogie was carried on two centre pivoted, inverted leaf springs with the axles located by radius arms. The brakes were compressed air-operated and in order to avoid the trailer snaking when the brakes were heavily applied, one wheel only on each axle was braked, it being so arranged that the braked wheels were on diagonal corners of each bogie. A dual brake valve on the tractor ensured that the trailer brakes were applied in advance of those on the tractor.

The overall length of the road train was 71 feet 8 inches. The trailers each had a loading platform measuring 20 feet by 7 feet 2 inches and a loading height of 4 feet 5 inches. The bogie axles were 3 feet 10 inches apart and the distance between the first and fourth axles was 14 feet 10 inches. The wheel-track was 5 feet 11 1/8 inches.

Proving Trials, 0851001

Proving trials, over a distance of some 3,000 miles, were undertaken at the MWEE establishment at Farnborough, on ground which was judged to be the nearest equivalent in the south of England to what could be expected in the colonies. In the course of these tests, it was shown that fully laden, the road train proved capable of surmounting rough-surfaced gradients of 1 in 6½ and, uncoupled from the trailers, the tractor demonstrated its ability to overcome loose gradients of up to 1 in 2½. A dry concrete slope of 1 in 2.28 proved to be no obstacle and this suggested that wheel-spin only would be the limiting factor on steeper grades. The tractor was shown as 'off float' on 7 June 1933.

In Service

In due course the outfit was despatched to Australia, arriving at Adelaide on the steamship Largs Bay on 3 April 1934. The road train was accompanied by Captain E. C. Roscoe of the Royal Army Service Corps and two sergeant drivers and on arrival in Australia they were joined for the initial trials by Captain E. M. Dollery of the Australian Army. Working first from Adelaide and later from Alice Springs, some 9,387 miles were covered in 29 weeks over terrain that varied from earth roads, bush tracks, deep sand, loose stone, black soil and deep mud, all in a temperature that was never less than tropical. On outward journeys, full loads of 15 tons and sometimes up to 20 tons would be carried but return loads were often minimal. In consequence, the tonnage carried over the 29-week period averaged only 8.72 tons. Over the 9,387 miles, the fuel consumption averaged 3.15 mpg and the overall speed 12.87 mph.

On completion of the trials, the tractor and its trailers were handed over to the Works Section of the Department of the Interior. Working from the railheads at either Alice Springs in the wet season or 750 miles further north at Katherine in the dry season, it served outlying settlements in the interior. Interesting comment on the operation of the road train is found in A History of Road Trains in the Northern Territory 1934–1988 by John Maddock, published by Kangaroo Press in 1988. An extract reads:

> The Payne Report on land use and development in the Northern Territory in 1937 had this comment on the road train:
>
> A development of outstanding importance in inland transport was the introduction three years ago, of a trial 15-ton motor transport unit. This is, in effect, a small road train. After operating less than three years it has succeeded in redeeming its cost paying all working expenses and making a small profit. It is estimated that it could be operated at a cost of about three and one half pence per ton mile without loss if there were both forward and back loading.
>
> The only disadvantage attaching to the transport unit now in use, is its wide gauge, 5ft 9ins. In consequence of this wide gauge, its wheels do not conform to the track made by the ordinary motor vehicles. It is thus only able to use one of the motor wheel tracks, the other set of wheels having to cut a new track outside the existing one. Apart from the damage to the road, this has the effect of reducing the speed at which the unit can travel. The consequent roughness in running is detrimental to the vehicle and in some instances, may entail risk of damage to the freight being conveyed. Any further units introduced would be designed to the standard 4ft 8in. gauge.

A similar criticism was made of the Leyland unit working in the Gold Coast.

Further comment came from Ewan Clough, who was the first regular driver and who drove the vehicle from October 1934 to November 1936:

> The first trip from Katherine to Wave Hill, 287 miles, took three weeks. We had to make new tracks in most places because they had disappeared in some places during the Wet and the river banks were cut away where old crossings had been. My offsider and I had to walk up and down creek beds to find suitable crossings and then sometimes we'd have to dig away part of the bank so that we would get the prime mover across and then haul the trailers over with a long cable.
>
> In boggy or sandy country we would disconnect the trailers, get some planks or tree trunks to put under the wheels of the prime move and drive it out. Then we'd either find or make a new track with the prime mover by running backwards and forwards for some distance to consolidate the surface, and then we'd go back for the trailers and haul them through.
>
> That AEC prime mover would go anywhere and could haul anything – it was like a tractor. In fact it would still be useful on the roads in the Territory today. It was more manoeuvrable than any existing road train.

Fencing wire and pickets, fuel, food and general station supplies were our usual loadings. We were supposed to carry only 15 or 16 tons but as often as not the loading would be heavier. I remember one load of 24 tons, and on another occasion we must have exceeded even that when we took a water boring plant from Alice Springs up to Murranji, which is about 550 miles north of The Alice.

I think the worst feature was that thundering great fan behind the engine. It used to suck air through the cab – which, incidentally, had no windscreen – at such a rate that I had to wear a heavy coat in winter to keep myself from freezing.

You had to be very careful that you didn't let the engine over-rev when going down a hill or into a creek bed. The sheer weight of the prime mover and its trailers tended to push it rapidly downhill if you weren't ready to check it with the brakes. I think that's what happened to it finally; the engine over-revved on a down-grade and a con-rod went through the side of the crankcase.

In terms of reliability, it was noted that the aluminium cylinder heads gave trouble, as did the bearings, and the worm gears in the axles were prone to overheating. This was attributed to variations in the rolling radius of the tyres and the lack of inter-axle differential compensation. More careful matching of the tyres and a change of lubricant appears to have overcome the problem. The mounting of the spare wheels on the cab's front panel was found to be unsatisfactory and an alternative arrangement was devised at the rear of the tractor.

Tractors 0851002 and 003

Tractors 002 and 003 were built for ARCOS Ltd, the agency through which AEC vehicles were sold for undertakings either in or supported by the USSR. Previous sales through ARCOS had been for Russian Oil Products Ltd, the offices of which were situated in Moorgate, London EC2. It is not known whether these two road trains were destined for ROP.

In addition to the two tractors, ARCOS had ordered three Dyson trailers, similar to those previously built, one carrying a 2,500-gallon liquid tank, one with a grain hopper and the third with a two-section side-tipping body. The specifications of the tractors were identical to that sent to Australia, save that each was fitted with a 6,400-gallons-per-hour gearbox-driven Albany pump for use in connection with the liquid tank trailer.

It is recorded that tractor 002 was built on 9 April 1935 and 003 on 10 May. Both were delivered on 2 July 1935, presumably to the docks.

Tractor 0851004

This tractor was built for the Crown Agent for the Colonies on 28 November 1935. The AEC Gazette of April 1939 shows this fourth road train in operation in Tanganyika. Natives and their belongings were being taken from scattered homesteads in the bush where the Tsetse fly had become a problem to a new unaffected location.

In retrospect

Of the four colonial tractors built, it is only the Australian example of which there is any documentation in respect of its working life. Now, seventy-five years on, there are some who would question the original design concept. The road train was a specialist combination designed to perform a particular task. That its payload was only 50 per cent of its gross weight was a function of its design requirements and despite the criticism of its out of track dimensions in the Payne report, the road train had, by 1940, with improving road conditions, been joined by five equally wide Matadors, two Monarchs and a bonneted Mammoth Major 6.

In its twelve-year life in government service, the road train covered approximately 100,000 miles and earned £21,909 for an expenditure of £19,102. The original cost of the tractor was £2,500.

In a final note John Maddock writes:

In 1946 the AEC prime mover and its trailers were sold at a disposal of surplus government equipment at Darwin and were acquired by Territory Timber who used it for some time in the Pine Creek area. A con-rod through the side of the crankcase wrote 'finis' to its career as a haulage vehicle. It was removed to a scrap yard at Berrimah, near Darwin, where it lay derelict for many years. In 1980 it was acquired by the Northern Territory Museums Board.

It is now preserved at the Road Transport Hall of Fame at Alice Springs.

The prototype eight-wheeled tractor on test, towing an artillery piece over the sand dunes at Eastney near Portsmouth, home of the Royal Marines. (*Photograph: Royal Marines Museum, Eastney*)

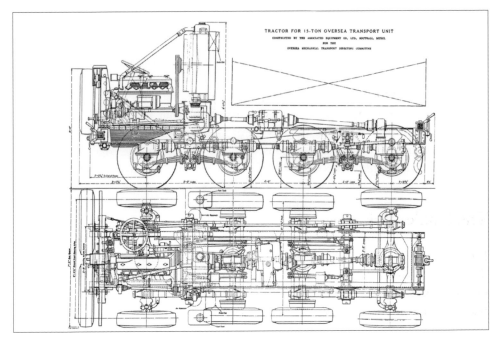

Arrangement drawing of the eight-wheeled, all-wheel drive tractor built for the Oversea Mechanical Transport Directing Committee for use in Australia. The drawing is a reprint from *The Engineer* of 21 July 1933. (*Drawing:* The Engineer, *Author's collection*)

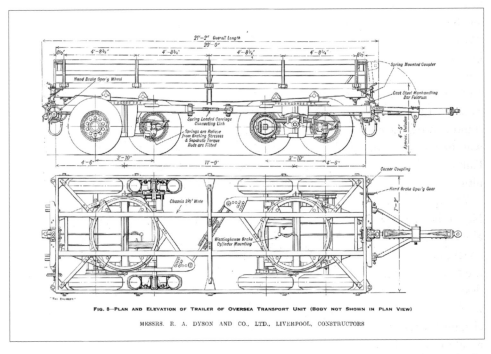

Arrangement drawing of eight-wheeled Dyson trailers with inter-coupled steering bogies built for use with the eight-wheeled tractor above. The drawing is reprinted from *The Engineer*, 21 July 1933. (*Drawing:* The Engineer, *Author's collection*)

22

The Q-Types Part Two

The Single-deck type 762

Mechanically similar to the Type 761, the Type 762 was rather differently proportioned. With a wheelbase of 18 feet 6 inches and an overall length of 27 feet 6 inches, its front overhang at 4 feet 3 inches was almost 2 feet shorter than the double-decker and the rear overhang at 4 feet 9 inches was some 9 inches longer.

Production details

Of the five single-deckers built in 1933, chassis 762002 and 003 had been constructed in July 1933 and despatched to Duple in Hendon. Chassis 002 emerged as LJ 8001 and went straight to Elliott Bros of Bournemouth and was the subject of much publicity, while 762003 became demonstrator BME 130 before being sold to Waltham Abbey Coaches in May 1934. Chassis 004, 005 and 006 were all built in September 1933 in time for the Commercial Motor Show at Olympia in November. Weymann-bodied 004, AMV 124, after serving as a demonstrator was sold to J. Sharp of Manchester in May 1934. 762005, LJ 8600, with a body almost identical to 762002, was shown on the Duple stand and despatched to Elliott Bros on 1 December 1933. Harrington-bodied 762006 was, together with the Leeds Q-type double-decker 761009, exhibited on the AEC stand. Painted in Elliott's livery and said at that time to have been sold to that company, it was ultimately sold to W. Knowles of Bolton in May 1934 and registered WH 5222.

The first single-decked Q-type to be built after the Commercial Motor Show in November 1933 was 762029, again built for Elliott's in March 1934. This carried an alternative high floored thirty-seven-seat body by Duple described as an observation coach, notable for the fact that the longitudinal seat, which previously backed on to the engine casing, had been eliminated. Sadly, the smooth flowing lines of the earlier design had been lost. Chassis 762034 was the fourth for Elliotts. It had been built on 21 April and, as AEL 2, was received by them on 1 June. Its Harrington body, a most elegant thirty-five-seater, featured a stepped waistline, which was to become so much a hallmark of this coachbuilder in the 1930s.

Bracewell's of Colne took chassis 762010 in May with coachwork by Duple. The attractive thirty-five-seat body was built to a design similar in most respects to those built for Elliott's on chassis 002 and 005 in 1933, but with a re-profiled roofline.

Pearson of Liverpool took delivery of 762011 with a thirty-two-seat high floor
Duple body in June. The Belfast Omnibus Company purchased 762022 as a chassis
and built an attractive body for it in their own workshop. Registered CZ 4974, it
passed to the Northern Ireland Road Transport Board in 1935. Chassis 762028 was
built on 4 April 1934 and, with bodywork by Willowbrook, it went to Silver Service
of Darley Dale. Bevan & Barker commissioned Cravens to build a body on 762023
in April 1934 and Skills of Nottingham had Duple build one of the high floor thirty-
seven-seat bodies on 762035. This was registered AAU 946 and was delivered in May.
Hull Bros, trading as Lea Valley Coaches, took an exactly similar vehicle, 762036, in
the same month. The first Q-types to go north of the border were 762012 and 013.
These were supplied to Rover Bus Service of Aberdeen in April 1934 and received
rather uncompromising bus bodies built by Walker in that same city.

Chassis 0762008 and 009 were built on 18 and 26 May 1934. They were notable
in that they were the first single-deckers to be powered by the A170 oil-engine. From
this time, it was the oil engine which became the more usually specified power unit.
The chassis were despatched to Duple in June and were fitted with the same low
floor, high roof body as graced the Q type supplied to Bracewell of Colne. Seating
only twenty-nine passengers, they were delivered to G. Sutton of Clacton-on-Sea
on 16 July. Suttons were to take delivery of a third nearly similar coach, 0762164,
CTW 881, late in 1935. This most attractive vehicle with the 'V'-shaped windscreen
had featured as one of the exhibits on the AEC stand at the Commercial Motor
Transport Exhibition at Olympia in November of that year.

J. Bullock & Sons of Featherstone had two Weymann-bodied thirty-nine-seaters,
762033 and 025. Petrol-engined 033 was delivered in June and 025, with an oil engine,
in August. Chassis 0762030, with engine A170/3, went to Romilly Motors in Cardiff in
June. It was sold to Imperial Motors of Abercynon and received a thirty-nine-seat bus
body built by the Berw Carriage & Engineering Company in Pontypridd. Continuing
in the Welsh idiom, Gellygaer UDC took 0762031, with a thirty-nine-seat body by
Short Bros, in July 1934 and South Wales Transport had the demonstrator 0762038,
BML488, in September, with a thirty-nine-seat Weymann bus body. With a sprag gear
fitted, detailed under XU1189, it was clearly intended for the 1 in 5 Townhill service
in Swansea. David McBrayne of Glasgow took delivery of 0762026 and 024 on 27
and 28 July. Park Royal was the body-builder; 026 is noted as being a thirty-two-seat
coach and 024 a twenty-eight-seat saloon bus. In September, Edinburgh Corporation
took delivery of 0762027, with a thirty-nine-seat Weymann body.

Two chassis, 0762039 and 0762037, had been built, seemingly for stock, on
25 August 1934 and 6 September respectively. Chassis 039 went to Weymanns in
February 1935 and became a demonstrator. It is reported as being despatched to
Dundee in August 1935 and purchased by that Corporation in the following month.
Chassis 037 was despatched to Duple in March 1935. This chassis received a thirty-
two-seat body of the same style as those built for Bracewells and for Suttons and was
supplied to Corona Coaches of Sudbury, Suffolk in May 1935.

Chassis 0762042 was built on 2 November and despatched to Brush Coachworks
on 8 November. Registered WN 8260, it went to South Wales Transport in Swansea
as a demonstrator and was apparently taken in to stock in May 1935.

Out of sequence chassis

Chassis numbers at AEC were allocated in the order in which the orders were received, yet the order of building at times appeared random. Delivery dates were, however, geared as far as was possible to the customer's requirements. Where an order was cancelled, the entry was removed from the list and the number left vacant until a decision was taken, sometimes considerably later, to use up the vacant numbers. Hence, some chassis numbers re-appear well out of date order.

Four chassis so built were oil-engined 0762014 and 015, and petrol-engined 762016 and 020. Chassis 014, built on 12 November 1934, was purchased by Aberdeen Corporation and despatched on the 20th of that month to the coachbuilder Walker in Aberdeen, where it received a thirty-nine-seat rear entrance bus body. Chassis 015 had been built on 12 September and was despatched to Harrington's on the 24th of that month. With a thirty-five-seat coach body, it had been built for Elliotts in Bournemouth and, carrying a fictitious registration number, TH 1935, it is thought to have been intended for exhibition. In March 1935 it found a permanent home with Ripponden and District Motors and was registered AWT 232. Its oil engine, A170/14, was exchanged for petrol engine A167/48 in July 1936.

Chassis 016, built on 6 September 1934, was despatched to Weymanns on 12 September. Having received a thirty-five-seat coach body, its petrol engine A167/41 was exchanged for oil engine A170/17 and was exhibited at the Scottish Motor Show at Kelvin Hall Glasgow between 16 and 24 November. Exhibited in the livery of Stark's Motor Services of Dunbar, it was purchased by that company in March 1935. Petrol-engined chassis 762020 was built on 12 December and, with Burlingham body, was despatched to Dunlop in Birmingham on 2 January 1935.

The first LPTB order

In the period to the end of October 1934, thirty-three Type 762/0762 chassis had been built, hardly an encouraging total. It would have been with some degree of relief that in the November issue of the AEC Gazette, AEC had been able to announce the receipt of an order from the London Passenger Transport Board (the LPTB) for 100 oil-engined Q-types for delivery in 1935.

From this order, two pilot chassis, 0762057 and 058, were built on 18 and 10 December 1934 respectively. Chassis 058 is noted as being despatched to Metropolitan-Cammell at Saltley on 31 December while 057 went to an un-named coachbuilder on 18 January 1935, thought to be the Birmingham Railway Carriage & Wagon Company (BRCW) in Smethwick.

The first Q-type built in 1935 was 0762040, built for Imperial Motors of Abercynon. Ordered through the Romilly Motor Company, it was despatched to that Company in Cardiff and transferred to the Berw Carriage & Engineering Company in Pontypridd, who built its thirty-nine-seat bus body. A second similar vehicle, chassis 0762041, was built for Imperial in March 1935. Chassis 0762021 was built for Ripponden & District on 6 February 1935 and despatched to H. V. Burlingham in Blackpool on the

12th of that month. It's oil engine, A170/33, was replaced by petrol engine A167/47 in June 1936.

Deliveries to the LPTB started in earnest on 15 February 1935 with chassis 0762059 and continued through to 28 September with the delivery of chassis 0762156. The contract for the bodywork went to BRCW. These vehicles were identified by the LPTB as the 4Q4 class and were numbered Q6–105. All were in service by the end of December 1935 with the exception of Q86, which entered service in January 1936. Two additional 4Q4s, Q186 and 187 (0762178 and 179), were added to the fleet in July 1936.

The last Petrol-engined Qs

Summerbee of Southampton took 762044, which was delivered to Harringtons in March 1935, and a similar chassis, 762043, was built in April 1935 for Keith Coaches in Aylesbury. Duple supplied the thirty-five-seat body for this chassis. Chassis 762157, 158 and 159 were despatched to Harringtons in Hove for Westcliff-on-Sea Motor Services in May. Well out of order numerically, 762007 was also despatched to Harringtons on the 26th of that same month for Brown Bros of Sapcote, who took delivery on 29 June.

Scottish and Welsh deliveries

In April and May 1935, the largest single order for the Q-type chassis outside those supplied to the LPTB was completed for Aberdeen Corporation. This order comprised ten chassis, 0762045–054 inclusive. Scott of Aberdeen took two similar vehicles, 0762055 and 056, at the same time. All were fitted with bus bodies by Walker of Aberdeen; those for the Corporation seated thirty-nine and those for Scott thirty-eight. Also built in April 1935 was chassis, 0762017, for Gough of Mountain Ash. This received a thirty-nine-seat body by Northern Counties. South Wales Transport had already taken delivery of chassis 0762042 in November 1934 and this was followed by an order for a further four, which were built in September 1935. These were numbered 0762160–163 inclusive and, with thirty-nine-seat Brush bodies, went in to service in the following month. Also built in September 1935 was 0762165, built for Imperial Motors of Abercynon. This carried a thirty-nine-seat body by Berw of Pontypridd. Dundee Corporation, seemingly impressed by the Weymann-bodied demonstrator 0762039, had 0762176 and 177, built in October 1935, also Weymann-bodied. They were registered YJ 2803, YJ 2800 and YJ 2801 respectively.

A second London order

As deliveries of the 100 4Q4 class chassis neared completion, the LPTB placed a second order with AEC for eighty chassis. Park Royal was awarded the body contract and the type was identified as the 5Q5. These thirty-seven-seat buses were intended for suburban operation and featured an entrance forward of the front axle, much in the manner of the double-decked Q. In order to accommodate the new layout, the front axle was moved rearward by just over 2 feet, the resulting wheelbase being 16 feet 5 inches. The first chassis, 0762182, was built on 18 December 1935. Deliveries continued through to June 1936, the last of the order being 0762261. These received fleet numbers Q106–185.

Exports

Export orders for the Q-type in 1935 came from the Griffin Engineering Company in Johannesburg and from the Christchurch Tramway Board in New Zealand. Chassis 0762171, noted as being of 18-foot 7-inch wheelbase, was built in October and supplied through Griffin Engineering to the Johnston Bus Service in Germiston. Its body was built locally in South Africa. The four Christchurch chassis, 0762172–175, built in November, had a wheelbase of 16 feet 6 inches. With a front overhang similar to that of the LPTB's 5Q5 and the rear overhang lengthened and lowered, they were fitted with front entrance, rear exit transit type bodies. The bodies were constructed in the Christchurch Tramway Board's own garages and a Pay as you Enter fare collection system was employed.

The last Q-type to be built in 1935 was 0762180, on 31 December. Its sister chassis, 0762181, followed on 3 January. This pair had been built for A. Toone & Son of Billesden in Leicestershire. Duple built the thirty-nine-seat bodies to a new 1936 design. Still retaining a distinct and attractive family resemblance to the earlier low pattern body, the new body had five windows rearward of the entrance door instead of the former four and a slightly stepped waist-rail.

Interest in the Q-type in South Wales continued into 1936. Chassis 0762262 was built on 2 January 1936 and sold to Davies of Neath (operating under the fleet name Osbornes). Its thirty-nine-seat body was built by Duple and was contemporary with the pair built for Toone & Son. Chassis 0762018 and 019 had been allocated to Gough of Mountain Ash but following the takeover of the business, they were delivered direct to Red & White Services and entered service with that company in April 1936. Imperial Motors took delivery of 0762166, 167, 168 and 169 in February, April, August and December respectively. All seated thirty-nine passengers; one had bodywork by Norman and three by Berw. By this time, the company had built up the largest Q-type fleet in South Wales. Chassis 0762170 had been built for the Gellygaer Urban District Council on 8 June 1936. Bodied by Strachan, it entered service in January 1937.

Meanwhile, in March 1936, the LPTB had placed an order for a further fifty oil-engined Q-type chassis. These were again to be bodied by Park Royal and identified as the 6Q6. These would be employed on Green Line coach services with seating for a very modest thirty-two passengers. Delivery of this last London Transport batch commenced in May 1936 with chassis 0762287 and was completed in October with 0762336. They carried fleet numbers Q189–238.

On the export front, chassis 0762263, 264 and 265 had been built in July and September for the Johnston Bus Service in Germiston.

The last home market Q-type chassis was built in January 1937. 0762266 was built for Imperial Motor Services and, like the other Q types supplied to that company, the body was built by Berw of Pontypridd. Between order and delivery, Imperial had been absorbed by Red & White and the vehicle went into service with Red & White in July 1937.

In August 1937, AEC received its last two orders for the Q-type chassis, both for export. A single chassis had been ordered by the Johnston Bus Service in Germiston, and two by the Christchurch Tramway Board, but the order for Johnston appears not to have been fulfilled. 0762267 is a mystery chassis, for which there is no record card. It is reported to have been built as, or converted to, a mobile crane in Wellington, New Zealand. The last two chassis, 0762268 and 269, were built for the Christchurch Tramway Board in December 1937. These were again bodied locally and featured bodies of the type built on 0762172–175.

The Three-axled type 763

Expanding the Q-type concept further, a single three-axled Q-type, 763001, was built for the London Passenger Transport Board in 1936 and 1937. Gavin Martin, in his treatise London Buses 1929–1939, reports that the chassis was received at Chiswick on 19 May 1936.

Such evidence as exists suggests that the chassis had an overall length of 28 feet, a wheelbase (measured from the centreline of the front axle to the centreline of the bogie) of 17 feet, bogie centres of 4 feet, and front and rear overhang dimensions of 4 feet and 5 feet respectively. The engine was the now-familiar A170 oil engine and transmission was through a standard fluid flywheel (J137) and an electrically operated D133 epicyclic gearbox. The bogie axles were of the fully floating type and it is logical to suggest that the spring arrangement would have been similar to that of the Type 663 Renown, with a single centre pivoted cantilever spring on each side. AEC records show the tyres to have been 9.75-20s.

Completed, the vehicle returned from Park Royal on 1 February 1937. The proportions of the body forward of the front axle were similar to that of the 4Q4, with a rear hinged door for the driver's cabin. The body, with its flowing lines and radiused window corners, was typical of the late 1930s Chiswick designs while the steeply curved front panel had echoes of the experimental body carried by STL857 (STF1). The central entrance doorway led directly to the stairway to the upper deck. Seating was provided for twenty-four passengers on the lower deck and for thirty-one upstairs. It had an unladen weight of 9 tons.

Q188, as it became known, was licensed on 1 June 1938, carrying the registration number DGO 500. Though intended for operation on the Green Line services covering Aldgate–Romford–Brentwood and Grays, trade union opposition ensured that it never worked as envisaged. After a period in storage, it worked country area bus services from Hatfield Garage on the 340, and from Hertford on the 310/310A. It was de-licensed in July 1940 and placed in store together with double-decked Qs 2,3,4 and 5 at Grays. In May 1942 it was noted as being in store at Romford garage and was sold out of stock in March 1946. It was purchased by H. Brown of Garelochhead and believed scrapped in 1953.

It can now be seen that the six-wheeled Q-type was little more than a design exercise. Many of the mechanical units were, in one form or another, already in service but the compressed air brakes were still at the development stage. The solenoid gear selection, developed for multiple application by AEC on the GWR railcars, perhaps in this instance offered no advantage over the manual arrangement, but the thought processes behind it clearly led to the development of the direct selection epicyclic gearbox twenty years later.

In respect of the body, while retaining the substance of the Q-types, the longer window glasses pointed the direction that future design would take. The steeply sloping front, perhaps exaggerated, nevertheless produced a harmonious effect overall and the central entrance, clearly not suitable for intensive city work, was well suited to coach operation.

Costing

At the time of its official launch in July 1933, the single-decked Q chassis carried a list price of £1,200 and the double-decker £1,225. Comparative figures for the petrol-engined Regal and Regent were £1,050 and £1,125 respectively, though it has to be recorded that in this instance we are not comparing like with like. The prices quoted for the Regal and Regent refer to the standard chassis with the four-speed D124 gearbox, while the Q-type boasted the Daimler patented fluid transmission as standard; on the Regal and Regent it was an extra at a cost of £100. When it became available in 1934, the oil-engined Q-type carried a premium of £300.

Leyland's data sheet for June 1934 showed the petrol-engined Tiger and Titan chassis priced at £1,075 and £1,100 and the oil-engined chassis at £1,325 and £1,350 respectively. By November of that year the price of the petrol-engined Tiger chassis had been reduced to £750 and the Titan to £850 and the oil-engined chassis to £900 and £1,000.

In November 1934, at the Scottish Show, the single-deck oil-engined Q-type chassis was priced at £1,500 and complete with thirty-five-seat Weymann body, £2,298. The Regal for Sutherland's of Peterhead, with a 7.7 litre oil engine and four-speed crash gearbox, had a bare chassis price of £1,350 and complete with thirty-two-seat Duple body, £2,145.

The Q-type in retrospect

An analysis of Q-type production from its inception in 1932 through to December 1937 shows that only twenty-three of the two-axled, double-decked version were built and the single-deckers totalled 319. Of the single-deckers, the LGOC and the LPTB together took 233.

Its unconventional layout placed the Q-type outside the main stream of motorbus operation. Further, it ensured that there was only minimal commonality of parts between the Q and the established Regal and Regent chassis. On the credit side, the positioning of the engine and gearbox on the outside of the chassis frame allowed easy and unrestricted access to all of the auxiliaries and it was claimed that the engine could be removed by two men in 25 minutes. The adoption in single formation of the large section tyres at both front and rear was perhaps controversial. Due to their greater deflection they provided an improved quality of ride, but in slippery conditions it was said that grip at the rear was marginal. This was not necessarily a huge problem with the single-deckers but could be rather more serious if control of the back end was lost on the double-decker.

Though the single-decked Q in bus form could sensibly accommodate thirty-nine passengers, this demanded longitudinal seating where the engine cover intruded into the body-space. Of itself this was not a huge problem on short-duration stage carriage work but was not acceptable for coaches on long-distance touring duties. Neither was the alternative arrangement of a single forward-facing seat beside the engine cover particularly attractive, though Harrington, in angling the seat slightly outward, did present an interesting variation. The high-floor bodies built by Duple and Willowbrook overcame the difficulty but neither matched the elegance of line of the lower built Q-type coaches.

Initial reaction to the double-decked chassis was one of cautious interest but the hoped-for breakthrough in the Metropolitan and Municipal fleets never came. Why, we ask, did the Q-type fail to attract?

One has to suggest that the principal reason for its rejection was that it failed to provide any significant operational advantage over the conventional front-engined bus. In terms of accommodation, the double-decked Q provided physical space for sixty-two passengers but the 10 tons limit of gross weight reduced the practical loading to sixty. The LPTB had shown this number to be attainable on the newly emerging STL Regent. Neither was the front entrance received with universal acclaim. Loading times were significantly slower than with the then-conventional rear platform and it was not until one-man operation became legal (and acceptable to the unions) in the 1960s that the front entrance came into its own. A quarter of a century was to pass before the industry was ready to consider an alternative position for the engine other than at the front and even then the transition was slow.

Despite the forgoing, one has to suggest that had the double-decked Q been accepted by the LPTB, with all the impetus that that would have provided, the story may well have been very different.

A last word

Perhaps we should let John Rackham himself bring the chapter to a close. In the AEC Gazette of November 1935, in reviewing the 1935 Olympia show models, he wrote:

> Lastly, there is the "Q" – still the most advanced type of passenger chassis in Great Britain.

He was right, but in the middle 1930s, it was a bridge too far.

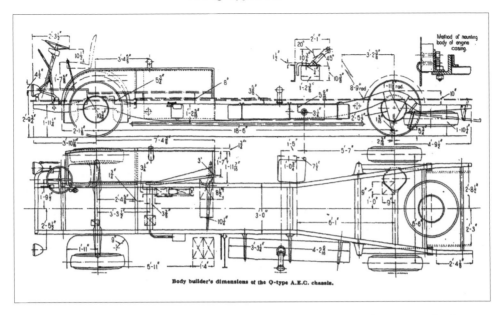

Body builder's dimensions of the Q-type A.E.C. chassis.

The coachbuilder's drawing of the 18-foot 6-inch wheelbase single-deck Type 762 displays quite graphically the long, low look of the chassis. (*Drawing: Origin unknown, Bob Kell collection*)

At first view, this Q-type chassis appears quite standard and unidentifiable. The short front overhang and long wheelbase identify it as a Type 762 and the CAV fuel filter just forward of the fuel tank tells us that it is oil-engined. The gearbox is an AEC-built D133. The organ-type throttle pedal enables us to identify it as one of 100 4Q4 chassis, 0762057–156, supplied to the LPTB for its country services, built between December 1934 and September 1935. (*Photographs: AEC 3707 and 3710, Author's collection*)

Park Royal brought a new shape to the Q-type with US 6895, one of two identical vehicles built for David MacBrayne in Glasgow. The chassis was 0762024 and the engine A170/6, one of the new 106 mm bore, 115 hp '7.7' litre oil engines. Perhaps rather square to some eyes, particularly with the roof-mounted luggage rack, it nevertheless displays an elegance well fitted to touring in the Scottish Highlands. (*Photograph: AEC 0028, Alan Townsin collection*)

BXD 528 was 0762059, one of the 100 BRCW (Birmingham Railway Carriage & Wagon Company) bodied 4Q4s. Two pilot chassis, 0762057 and 058, had been built in December 1934 and the first of the production models, 059, was built on 5 February 1935. The engine was A170/21. The BRCW bodies were rugged, having run throughout the wartime years and into the 1950s. Attractive when viewed from the nearside, the window treatment on the offside was a disaster. (*Photograph: London Transport Museum U17698*)

In a bid to secure a continuing share of the market, Duple offered both high and low floor bodies for the Q-type chassis. The high floor body avoided the seating compromise over the engine but lost out on looks. By the spring of 1934, the low floor body based on the 'Elliott' design had been further developed, examples of which were built for Bracewell of Colne, Sutton's of Clacton and, in 1935, for Corona Coaches of Sudbury and Keith Coaches in Aylesbury. Seen here is Keith Coaches' BPP 137, 762043, the peak of styling expertise. (*Photograph: AEC L1889, Alan Townsin collection*)

It was in 1935 that the first U-number drawings were made for the six-wheeled Q-type and, additional to the standard Q-type specification, the rear bogie and the compressed air braking system were developments of those found on the 664T trolleybus. The preselective gearbox, with its solenoid gear selection, was similar to the system adopted for the Great Western Railway's railcars. Thoroughly modern in appearance, the six-wheeled Q foreshadowed some of the styling trends that future LPTB design would take. (*Photographs: London Transport Museum U26303 and 26310*)

23

The Great Western Railcars Numbers 1 to 17

Hardy Rail Motors Ltd had been set up in November 1925 for the purpose of marketing shunting locomotives and light rail-borne passenger-carrying vehicles constructed by the Four Wheel Drive Lorry Company. These early vehicles were based on the mechanicals of the American 3-ton B-type FWD, but it was not until January 1931 that serious thought was given by the re-formed Hardy Motors board (reformed as a result of the absorption of the Four Wheel Drive Lorry Company into the Underground Group) to the possible design and manufacture of passenger-carrying vehicles for the established British main-line railway companies. The design of a twin-axled, four-wheel drive passenger coach for the Argentine Transandine Railway powered by the AEC six-cylinder petrol engine was already in hand and it was decided that the main line railway companies be approached and their opinions sought as to its suitability for domestic operations.

Outline drawings had been prepared for the London North Eastern Railway in March 1931 but nothing came of this submission as it was considered that the carrying capacity of the proposed vehicle was too small. By July 1931, the Transandine chassis had been completed and was demonstrated at Slough on the 30th of that month before a gathering of British and foreign railway representatives.

In a different approach, a near-standard AEC Regal coach chassis had been converted for rail operation, ostensibly for use by the United Havana Railways Company. After testing on both Great Western and the London North Eastern Railway lines, this converted Regal also went to the Transandine Railway Company. In the event, difficulties were encountered with both vehicles when attempts were made to run them on the rack section of the railway – duties for which neither vehicle was intended. Their eventual fate is unknown.

Railcar No. 1

Work had started on the design of a full-sized mid-engined, rear-drive railcar in October 1931. The work was halted in December 1931 on account of the uncertain future of the FWD and Hardy companies but in due time, following the closure of the FWD's Slough works and the transfer of operations to Southall, the project was revived by the AEC under programme EM, dated 10 September 1932. A full description of this experimental chassis appeared in the Railway Gazette of 14 July 1933 and representatives of that journal were afforded the opportunity of a brief ride on the bare chassis on the Brentford–Southall branch line on some date previous to 11 August. On 19 August the chassis was delivered overnight on a low-loading trailer to Park Royal Coachworks and, with its timber-framed body, was exhibited amid great publicity on the Hardy Motors stand at Olympia from 2–11 November. It was purchased by the Great Western Railway in the sum of £3,000 and its inaugural run from London (Paddington) to Reading took place on Friday 1 December 1933. It entered experimental service on the following Monday.

Chassis details

While the design of the frame and bogies followed normal railway practice in terms of its mechanical specification, considerable reliance had been placed on the use of standard or near-standard AEC automotive units. It was so arranged that the railcar could be driven from either end. Only one bogie was driven and convention suggested that the driven bogie was at the rear end of the vehicle (though both ends of the vehicle were identical). It was built to suit the standard British rail gauge of 4 feet 8½ inches.

The chassis frame was 60 feet long overall and 3 feet 2 inches wide and was carried on two four-wheeled bogies, the centres of which were 40 feet apart. The longitudinal members were 10 inch by 3½ inch pressed steel channels arranged with the flanges outward and the top of the frame was 3 feet 9 inches above rail level. In order to resist bending, each longitudinal was reinforced by a 4 inch by 4 inch x ½ inch angle iron truss which extended from bogie centre to bogie centre and, over a length of some 8 feet, to within 10 inches of rail level. The end cross-members were crescent shaped and the fourteen intermediate cross-members were attached to the longitudinals by heavy angle plates riveted in position. The frame was cross-braced immediately in front of and behind the bogie attachment points.

The weight of the main frame (and body) was transferred to the bogies through four out-rigged brackets and two transverse bolsters. Each bolster was caged within the central section of the bogie and carried on substantial coil springs. The bogies had a wheelbase of 7 feet and measured 8 feet 1 inch in width over the axle ends. The axles, of 5-inch diameter, were carried on roller bearings and the axle boxes were retained in vertical guides in typical railway fashion. Leaf springs 3 feet long, in conjunction with rubber suspension blocks, provided the primary suspension medium between the axles and the bogie frame. The wheels were 3 feet 1 inch in diameter.

In order to provide maximum accessibility, the mechanical units were out-rigged from the main frame on the left-hand side of the vehicle (the left as seen by the passenger looking forward with the driven bogie at the rear). The engine, A165C/203, was a near-standard A165 unit set, it was said, to deliver 130 bhp at 2,000 rpm. The fuel injection pump was a standard CAV-Bosch unit with integral governor and a 24-volt, 1,200 watt dynamo was driven by a short propeller shaft from the engine's timing case. Electric starting was provided by a 24-volt axial starter. The engine differed from the standard automotive type in that the sump casting was flat throughout its length. This allowed for the necessary clearance above the rails. It was also finned to promote the cooling of the oil. At this time, the engine was noted as having an electron crankcase and aluminium alloy cylinder heads. The radiator was of the still tube type and forward facing, having the air drawn through it by a cowled, six-bladed fan. The top tank protruded well above frame level and accommodation had to be made for it under one of the passenger's seats. Cool air was ducted from beneath the car to the radiator and the hot air expelled through vents in the side of the body.

The drive was taken through a fluid flywheel to a four-speed pre-selective epicyclic gearbox, both units being of Daimler manufacture. A separate reversing gearbox with a fixed ratio of 1:1 was employed so that the railcar could be driven in either direction with equal facility. The gearbox had the following forward ratios: 1st, 4.15:1; 2nd, 2.36:1; 3rd, 1.49:1; and 4th, 1:1. The normal reverse gear was retained in the gearbox but was only used for convenience when shunting. The drive to the axles was by underneath worm gear with a ratio of 4.16:1. A differential was fitted on the worm shaft of the first of the driven axles, which allowed for any slight mismatch in the wheel diameters. The worm gear cases were built integral with the axle boxes and torque reaction was absorbed by tubular ball-jointed arms anchored at one end on the gear case and at the other to the bogie's frame. The various transmission units were connected by tubular propeller shafts with sliding splined couplings and fully enclosed Spicer-type universal joints.

The brake assemblies, one to each axle and four in total, were of the automotive internal expanding type. In the case of the driven bogie, these were fitted at the opposite end of the axle to the driving gear. The cast-steel brake drums were of 20-inch diameter, cast in halves, an arrangement which allowed their assembly or removal without the need to press the wheels off the axles. With the halves united and secured by three bolts at each side, the drums were then bolted directly on to the inside face of the wheels.

The brakes were cam-operated and the shoes were 5 inches wide with ¾-inch-thick woven brake linings. Each brake unit was operated by a single vacuum servo, control being by means of a vacuum valve coupled to a hand lever in the driver's cabin. Vacuum was generated by two rotary exhausters, one engine mounted, the second driven from the reversing gearbox. The brake assemblies were carried on roller bearings on the rotating axle shafts and held in position by collars. By slackening the collars, the whole of the brake assembly could be withdrawn from the brake drum for maintenance. Rotation of the brake gear was prevented by ball-jointed torque arms attached at one end to the brake's foundation casting and at the other to the bogie's frame.

The four batteries, with a total capacity of 220 amp hours, were carried on the right-hand chassis frame member just opposite the engine and the 45-gallon fuel tank was carried on the same member opposite the gearboxes. Three pairs of sanding boxes were fitted, one pair at the front and one pair at the rear of the driven bogie and another pair in front of the non-driven bogie.

In many respects, though lacking a steering wheel, the driver's controls resembled those of a bus or commercial vehicle. The gear selector operated in the same manner as that in a London STL and the change speed pedal was equally familiar. The accelerator pedal connected with the fuel injection pump in the usual manner and this was supplemented by a hand-controlled lever which performed the same function. It could be set in any desired position but was immediately over-ridden by operation of the accelerator pedal. There were two further hand-control levers; one operated the service brakes and the other the control valves for the sanding boxes. A second gear lever selected forward or reverse in the reversing gearbox and a multi-pull hand brake lever of the same pattern as was fitted to the heavy-duty commercial chassis connected with the bogie brakes.

The chassis had a dry weight of 13 tons 10 cwts, the leading bogie carrying 6 tons 10 cwts 2 qrs and the driving bogie 6 tons 19 cwts 2 qrs.

The design of the body came about as a result of wind tunnel tests carried out in the laboratory of the LPTB at Chiswick. With only 130 bhp available, reducing wind resistance was clearly an important factor. The design which evolved was a fine compromise between efficiency and attractive appearance. The complete vehicle was 62 feet long and 9 feet wide, the floor height was 4 feet 3 inches and the body was 11 feet 4 inches high at mid-wheelbase. Buffers (added after the vehicle was first shown at Olympia) increased the overall length to 63 feet 7 inches. Entrance was through double doors in the centre of the car and these opened into a vestibule 5 feet wide. Seating was provided for sixty-nine passengers, thirty-nine seats in the forward compartment and thirty at the rear, with a small luggage compartment adjoining. The seats were arranged with three seats at one side of the gangway and two at the other. (AEC's original arrangement drawing, U63203, had provided for two equal-sized compartments, each with thirty-nine seats.) Complete, the vehicle had a tare weight of 24 tons and with a full complement of passengers the weight would have been in the order of 28 tons 10 cwts.

An extract from the AEC Gazette of January 1934, reporting on its inaugural run, reads:

Nothing caused more comment from the press men on board than the silence and smoothness with which the railcar glided from the platform, and the effortless ease with which it picked up speed – so fine, indeed, was the acceleration, that before it reached Slough the car was gaining on the "Limited" with its five minutes' start. [The Limited was a steam hauled train which had left Paddington some minutes earlier.]

Acton was passed in just over eight minutes at a speed of 49 m.p.h., and 2½ minutes later the car was rushing past its birthplace – the A.E.C. Factory at Southall, where crowds of employees had foregathered in the forecourt to cheer it on its inaugural run – at 55 m.p.h. Within the next three minutes speed had risen to 57, then 59 m.p.h., and at 10.56 a.m. it swept through Slough at 61 m.p.h.

A 50-minute schedule had been allowed by the G.W.R. for the 36 miles to Reading, but so quickly did the car gain on this, that many people, who set out with the purpose of seeing it pass through the station, arrived three or four minutes before its advertised time only to find that it had already gone!

Through Burnham, Taplow, Maidenhead, the same high speed was maintained "with a complete absence of vibration", to quote The Times correspondent, and about this point the maximum speed of the trip was reached – 63 m.p.h.! At 11.14 a.m. the railcar drew noiselessly into Reading "down main", having covered the 36 miles from London in 39 mins. 52 secs., at an average speed of 54.2 m.p.h., and having knocked some 14 minutes off the official schedule.

The car was geared to 26.5 mph per 1,000 engine rpm on the direct drive top gear and the 61 mph recorded represents 2,305 rpm. Because this speed was maintained 'through Burnham, Taplow and Maidenhead', it strongly suggests that the engine was governed to a speed somewhat higher than the quoted 2,000 rpm. The return journey, into a head wind, was accomplished at an average speed of 50.94 mph, some 3¼ mph slower than on the outward run.

Railcar No. 1 was allocated to the Southall shed and entered experimental service on 4 December 1933. Working to Slough, Windsor, Henley-on-Thames, Reading and Didcot, it covered 218 miles in the course of the 12-hour working day. It was withdrawn later in that month for modification to the braking system and for the fitting of Automatic Train Control apparatus. It re-entered service on 5 February 1934 and by the end of its first year's working had covered some 60,000 miles and carried 136,000 passengers. It was withdrawn from service in August 1955.

Railcars 2, 3 and 4

The early promise shown by Railcar No.1 prompted the GWR to order six more railcars in February 1934. The chassis were a development of that of Railcar No. 1. The basic dimensions were similar but they differed in that a second 130 bhp engine (the engines now identified as the A165K) had been mounted on the opposite frame longitudinal. The arrangements of the transmission on the first engine were as on Railcar No. 1 except that the pre-selective gearbox was now AEC's recently introduced D132. This had forward ratios of: 1st, 4.5:1; 2nd, 2.53:1; 3rd, 1.64:1; and 4th, 1:1. The worm driven axles had a ratio of 3.12:1, which, on top gear, provided 35.28 mph per 1,000 engine rpm. In service, the cars were governed to about 73 mph, which equates to 2,069 rpm.

On the second engine the drive was taken through a fluid flywheel directly to the reversing gearbox, thence to the first of the bogie axles. This simple but unusual direct drive arrangement required some compromise in respect of the management of the two engines. Because the additional power was required primarily to overcome wind resistance in the higher speed ranges, it was arranged that full power was not available from the second engine until top gear (i.e. direct drive) had been engaged on the primary transmission set.

The two engines necessarily required two radiators and whereas on Railcar No. 1 the radiator had been forward facing, in order to reduce the intrusion into the passenger accommodation and yet maintain the same effective area, the radiators were now wider and shorter than the original. This demanded that they were carried at an angle of 45° to the chassis longitudinals. The engine-driven fan was retained and a specially shaped fan cowl was designed to compensate. Air was drawn through the radiator from a deflector box which, from the outside of the body, had two panels with louvres pointing in opposite directions. Inside the box was a deflector plate which, according to the direction of travel and the air pressure acting on it, automatically took up position to deflect the incoming air into the radiator from one or other of the sets of louvres.

A problem which had become evident on Railcar No. 1 was brake chatter. On Railcar No. 1 the torque reaction was controlled by a single ball-jointed tubular arm, an arrangement which was not wholly effective. The problem was overcome in a new design where a pressed steel arm was rigidly attached to the brake carrier and shackled where it was attached to the bogie's frame. Reaction in the arm now tended to be of a rotary nature rather than the push and pull reaction generated in the earlier design. A similar arrangement was adopted for the control of the worm gear casings on the opposite side of the bogie. While the diameter of brake drums remained at 20 inches and the width of the brake linings at 5 inches, in common with AEC's now-standard automotive practice, their means of actuation was now via a vacuum servo-assisted hydraulic system. A single Dewandre servo unit was mounted within each bogie and the self-adjusting Lockheed cylinders were carried on the brake reaction arms. Vacuum was now generated by three rotary exhausters and storage was provided in four separate tanks.

In order to improve the quality of the ride, the length of the bogie springs had been increased from 3 feet to 4 feet. The bare chassis weight had now risen to 16 tons 9 cwts and the tare weight of the complete vehicle was 26 tons 4 cwts.

A Great Western Railway memorandum, written on 3 August 1934, reads:

GWR Order.
Lot 1522   No of vehicles 6

Description.

To record the purchase from the Associated Equipment Co Ltd., Southall of six 60ft Diesel Mechanical Rail Cars, each fitted with two 130 bhp Engines.
Seats:- Buffet Compartment 4, Saloon 40.

Chassis £3,500 each. Bodies £2,791 each. (Firm will give the company benefit of any reduction in the cost of body and interior fittings.) The cost of Automatic Train Control to be charged to this order.

The Associated Equipment Co will maintain the cars in service, (except tyres and body) for which the GWR Co will pay 1¾d per mile. (Minimum 40,000 miles per annum.) This arrangement operates for one year, the company to have the option to extend it for a further period, limited to five years.

Whereas Railcar No. 1 had been developed primarily for suburban and branch line duties, the first three cars of the new order were intended for the express buffet-car service between Birmingham and Cardiff. Park Royal Coachworks Ltd was again commissioned to construct the bodies, the interior of which had been designed by Heal & Son Ltd of Tottenham Court Road, London, W. Seating was to be provided for forty-four passengers, 'in comfort and luxury of appointment superior to anything so far seen on British railways', as it was described in the AEC Gazette of July 1934. As previously, the body was divided, but by a now much smaller entrance vestibule, the two sections now being identified as No. 1 end saloon and No. 2 end saloon. The No. 1 end saloon accommodated twenty-four passengers, Pullman fashion, in sections of four seats each side of the central gangway. Forward of this was the luggage compartment, with a tip-up seat for the guard, and the driver's cabin. The No. 2 end was rather different. The saloon accommodated sixteen passengers in four sections of four; adjoining it were two toilet compartments and further to the rear was the buffet compartment, which provided seating for a further four passengers. Beyond the buffet was the driver's second cabin.

Car No. 2 was the first of the buffet cars to be completed and a number of trial runs were conducted before it entered regular service (based at Tyseley) on 9 July 1934. On 3 July, on a return journey from Paddington to Oxford, a speed of 70–72 mph was maintained over a distance of 8 miles and 44 miles were run in 40 minutes. On the next day, on a run from Paddington to Birmingham, a maximum speed of 77 mph was recorded. On 6 July a special run was made between Birmingham and Cardiff. On this occasion the party included top management from the GWR and the AEC together with the Lords Mayor of Birmingham and Cardiff, and the Mayors of Gloucester and Newport together with their Ladies. A maximum speed of 72.3 mph was recorded and the 117½ miles between the two destinations was completed in 130½ minutes. When the regular service was started, the scheduled time for the journey was 142 minutes with stops at Gloucester and Newport.

Car No. 3, based at Cardiff, entered service on 17 July 1934 and No. 4, based at Tyseley, on 22 September 1934. With three cars available, two cars ran an out and return service each day, one starting at Birmingham and the other at Cardiff, with the third car held in reserve.

Railcars 5, 6 and 7

Cars numbered 5 and 6 were mechanically similar to the previous twin-engined cars, where the second engine was driven through a fluid flywheel directly to the reversing gearbox and thence to the first of the bogie axles. Car No. 7 was different. Both engine and transmission sets were identical and such was the improvement in acceleration with the inclusion of the second gearbox and the driven fourth axle that all subsequent railcars were similarly specified.

Cars 5, 6 and 7 were the first to carry bodies built by the Gloucester Railway Carriage and Wagon Company Ltd. Dimensionally, they were the same as the Park Royal-bodied cars and because it was intended that these cars should be run on local and branch line services, they were not fitted with either buffet or toilet facilities. Seating was provided for seventy passengers in an arrangement very similar to that of car No. 1. The forward saloon had seating for forty passengers and the rearward saloon seated thirty. Rearward of the rear saloon was a luggage compartment, 6 feet in length, accessed through double doors. The main passenger access was mid-way down the car, with a single door at each side leading into a central vestibule. Visually, the Gloucester-built cars were notable in having more fluid contours and deeper windows than those built by Park Royal.

It was intended that the cars should be ready for the start of the 1935 summer timetable. AEC records show that No. 7 was delivered on 7 July, No. 5 on 21 July and No. 6 on 28 August. J. H. Russell, in his volume Great Western Diesel Railcars, Wild Swan Publications, 1985, virtually corroborates this with the following dates into stock: No. 7 on 8 July, No. 5 on 22 July and No. 6 on 30 August.

Typical of the new services which the cars would provide was that which connected at Oxford with the 8.40 a.m. main line train from Paddington. Leaving Oxford, it then arrived at Worcester at 11.36 a.m., Malvern at 11.52 a.m. and Hereford at

12.27 p.m. A return journey left Hereford at 2.05 p.m., connecting at Oxford with the 4.30 p.m. for Paddington. Another car provided a morning service from Malvern to Birmingham, leaving Malvern at 8.54 a.m. and Worcester at 9.10 a.m. It then ran non-stop to Birmingham, arriving at 9.54 a.m., covering the 36¾ miles in 44 minutes at an average speed of 50 mph.

Railcars 8–17

At the Annual General Meeting of the GWR in February 1935, the chairman announced that an order had been placed with the AEC for a further ten railcars, one of which was to be employed on a new express parcels service. AEC announced the receipt of the order in the July 1935 issue of the AEC Gazette.

Engine developments on railcars 8–17 included the abandonment of light alloys in the construction of both the crankcase and the cylinder heads and their substitution by cast iron. Equally significant was the new gear drive for the camshaft and the belt drive for the fan. In their new guise, the engines were identified as the A165T and were set to develop 121 bhp (thought to be at 2,000 rpm). The twin engines each drove through a fluid flywheel to a D132 four-speed preselective gearbox, thence to the reversing gearbox and on to both of the bogie axles. The braking system made a reversion to straight vacuum operation with the vacuum cylinders mounted on the torque reaction arms. The first of this batch of chassis to be built was 0852009, completed on 7 October 1935, and the last was 0852017, on 20 December 1935. These railcar chassis, incidentally, were the first to be constructed in AEC's new 100-foot-long, 60-foot-wide railcar shop.

The Gloucester Carriage & Wagon Company Ltd was again entrusted with the construction of the bodies. Cars 8 and 9 and 13–16 were to have seating for sixty-nine passengers, arranged in a manner similar to cars 5, 6 and 7 (save that one seat had been lost in the forward saloon to allow for the opening of the vestibule door). Cars 10, 11 and 12 were to be fitted with toilet compartments, which reduced the seating accommodation in the rearward saloon by six to twenty-four and the total to sixty-three. The first complete vehicle, car No. 10, was delivered to the GWR on 20 January 1936 and the last, car No. 17, on the following 7 April.

Distribution and schedules

With sixteen passenger cars now available, twelve cars were placed in regular service. The Cardiff, Birmingham, Weymouth, Pontypool Road, Landore and Southall sheds were each allocated one car while the Worcester, Oxford and Bristol sheds each had two. The four spare cars were nominally held at Worcester, Bristol and Newport with the spare buffet car held at Birmingham and these doubled for any of the aforementioned twelve cars when withdrawn for maintenance. Car No. 17, employed on the express parcels service, was based at Southall.

An extract from the Railway Gazette of 2 October 1936 provides some detail as to the running schedules of the railcars:

The busiest railcar centre is Oxford (summer timetables). Cars work from that city in five different directions, namely to Banbury, Hereford, Witney, Princes Risborough and Didcot and there are 13 railcar departures and 12 arrivals daily, the difference being due to an empty run from Didcot last thing at night. During the 1936 summer timetables the fleet of cars was running over approximately 767 route miles and serving 217 stations and halts; a table showing an analysis of each car's Monday to Friday working during the summer is appended.

It will be seen that the highest mileage is run by the Bristol car which covers 355½ miles per day; at the bottom of this scale the Swansea car is running only 229 miles. An examination of the figures shows clearly the effect upon the average speed of the number of stops made during the day; thus the Cardiff car, which stops only 14 times and has an average distance between stops of 20.39 miles, maintains an average start-to-stop speed of 48.1 m.p.h. On the other hand, the Pontypool Road and Swansea cars average only 29.55 m.p.h.; the Pontypool car makes 135 stops daily with an average distance between stops of only 1.78 miles.

The longest working day according to the timetable is that of the Birmingham car which is in service for 15 hr. 8 min., and the shortest time is for the Cardiff car with a 9-hr. day, but these figures do not include empty running from shed, etc.

The express parcels car was placed in service on 4 May 1936. It had been found that the increase in parcels traffic and the time taken in loading was having an adverse effect on the maintenance of timetable schedules on the regular passenger services and the express parcels car was introduced to overcome this difficulty. Except for the lack of passenger accommodation, the specification of the parcels car was identical to that of cars 8–16. It had a tare weight of 28 tons 17 cwts and the maximum load was set at 10 tons. Its normal weekday schedule started from Southall at 3.30 a.m., proceeding first to Kensington to pick up confectionery from the Cadby Hall bakery of J. Lyons & Co. Ltd. From there it travelled to Oxford via Reading, returning to Paddington at 11.05 a.m. having made some twenty-five station stops en route. A second run departed Paddington at 1.03 p.m. destined for Reading, returning to Paddington at 7.45 p.m. having made a further thirty scheduled stops. The daily load was in the order of 1,100 parcels and the mileage covered was 222. This reduced to 150 miles on Saturday and 132 on Sunday.

In service

Perhaps unexpectedly, the long-distance express services run by cars 2, 3 and 4 proved rather more testing than had been the case with car No. 1. Engine temperatures occasioned by the sustained high-speed running were generally higher than those experienced on the multi-stop suburban operations and oil temperatures in the order of 95° C were regularly recorded. This feature, coupled with the light alloy crankcase, was blamed for big end and main bearing failures.

Cars 5–17 (and possibly cars 1–4 retrospectively) were fitted with an oil cooler where the hot oil was sprayed over a water-cooled gilled tube matrix in the engine's sump. In this arrangement a small quantity of water was tapped off the pressure side of the water pump and passed through an auxiliary radiator which comprised a single continuous snake-like gilled tube some 30 feet in length carried in front of the main radiator. In this manner the water was cooled to a lower temperature than that of the normal cooling system. Having passed through the cooling matrix in the sump, the water was returned to the main cooling system on the suction side of the water pump. This seemingly over-complex arrangement avoided the problem of passing hot oil under pressure through an external radiator and the possibility of the loss of oil from a burst pipe. The temperature of the oil, so cooled, has not been recorded.

A problem associated with the installation of the engine in railcars 2–17 was the lack of head between the top of the engine and the radiator top tank. This resulted in poor water circulation, over-heating and, in some instances, piston seizure. This was overcome by fitting supplementary header tanks underneath convenient seats in the passenger saloon. Experience also showed that larger piston clearances were required on the railcar engines than was usual in road vehicles.

The normal railway pattern clasp brakes, which operated directly on the wheel rims, required more vacuum than was available from the oil engine and for that reason automotive-pattern drum brakes, with their closer running clearances, were adopted on the AEC-built railcars. Cast-iron drums were adopted on car No. 1 and were found completely satisfactory but cracking ensued when high-speed operations were introduced on cars 2, 3 and 4. Cast-steel drums resisted cracking but scored badly and were ultimately replaced by carbon steel forgings. Brake lining life could vary from one car to another, varying from as little as 6,400 miles to as much as 33,100, clearly dependent on operating conditions. The heavy maintenance requirements led to the adoption of clasp brakes on the later Swindon-built railcars.

Bob Fryars writes:

> For a while as Experimental Engineer, I was in charge of the Railcar Shop at AEC but with an excellent experienced foreman in Sid Miller. There were complaints about the quality of day to day servicing given to Railcars by GWR personnel – low oil levels, low water levels, leaking hoses etc. but all that cannot disguise the problem that these 8.8 engines were operating at too high a load factor on the long high-speed routes.
>
> Another aspect that Charles Cleaver failed to appreciate was the kinetic energy level in a 30/40 ton railcar at 60 mph plus – amplified when long down gradients were the approach to the next stop. The automotive type brake drums must have run cherry red at times. No wonder clasp brakes had to be fitted. Railway wheels are an excellent heat sink.

Cars 1 and 17 were based at Southall and were maintained by AEC works staff. Day-to-day servicing of the other fifteen cars was undertaken at local level by six AEC service representatives. Two were based at Birmingham, two at Bristol, one at Newport and one at Oxford. Intermediate and major overhauls were carried out in the Southall railcar shop, at 35,000 miles and 70,000 miles respectively. Some idea of the additional servicing undertaken may be gained from the following extract from the Railway Gazette dated 7 June 1940, relative to cars numbered 1, 11 and 17 for the 12 months' period ending August 1939:

> Car No.1. Overhauled 25.8.1938 to 15.9.1938 after 72,000 miles. Engine changed, gearbox and reverse box overhauled, brakes relined, and tyres turned. Failed 17.9.1938

with loose fuel pipe connection, causing shortage of fuel. 12,000 miles later reverse box was changed because of worn races, and self-starter was replaced as the fields were shorting. Propeller shaft between axles removed for overhaul. On 16.1.1939 the car was withdrawn by driver who suspected strange noise; tappets were found to be slightly out of adjustment but car could have continued running. Oil leak developed at crankshaft filler block after 28,000 miles from overhaul, and engine was changed. Car failed 24.7.1939 with broken reverse control lever. Taken out of service at 42,000 miles for factory overhaul (29.4.1939 to 13.5.1939). Engine overhauled in position, gearbox and reverse box changed, and two pairs of brake shoes relined. Total mileage at end of period 310,805.

Car No.11. Engine changed at 5,000 miles due to noisy timing gears on one engine, and fuel pump changed on other engine. Car failed 23.12.1938 as two pistons were blowing, and car was withdrawn by driver. Two cylinder heads were changed at 24,000 and 25,000 miles respectively. Returned to factory for overhaul 14.2.1939 to 17.3.1939 after 40,000 miles. Engines and reverse boxes changed, but no attention necessary to gearboxes. New brake drums fitted and wheels re-tyred. Car failed 4.5.1939 with broken gear-selector rod, and on 10.7.1939 with seized fuel pump coupling. After 68.000 miles one gearbox was changed owing to a tendency to stick in top gear. Total mileage at end of period 218,463.

Car No.17. Withdrawn after 15,000 miles as one engine developed a slack main bearing, engine changed. Later a self-starter was changed as contact switch was burnt. On 28.11.1938 the car was withdrawn for three days, and two new direct-injection engines were fitted experimentally. A defective water pump was replaced after 23,000 miles. A fused self-starter contact caused a failure on 25.1.1939. Car taken out of service 18.5.1939 to 20.6.1939 for examination of new engines and as tyres needed attention complete chassis overhaul was made (56,000 miles since last one). Engines, gearboxes and reverse boxes were stripped down for examination but were not changed. Three new brake drums were fitted, three pairs of shoes relined, and tyres were turned. On completion car was sent to Swindon for body repairs and repainting, and resumed service 23.8.1939. Total mileage at end of period, 183,158.

On the operational side, complaints had been received from the permanent way gangs that the silent approach of the railcars left them open to danger, particularly in the tunnels. In the case of the steam locomotive, its approach was heralded from afar by the vibrations and noises transmitted through the rails, accompanied in the tunnels by the forward draught it created. The streamlined railcars produced little of these early warnings and the normal automotive-type horns first fitted, one at each end, were totally ineffective. These were replaced by compressed air horns, two at each end, tuned an octave apart and sounded alternately, which, it was said, could be heard 3½ miles distant. These four horns were backed up by four further horns powered independently from electrically driven compressors.

Development of the railcar was ongoing. Whereas railcars 1–17 were designed purely for solo operation, by 1935 thoughts were being directed toward the use of trailers. Car No. 18 was just such a vehicle, designed to haul a tail load of up to 60 tons. This, together with cars 19 to 38, will be examined in a future chapter.

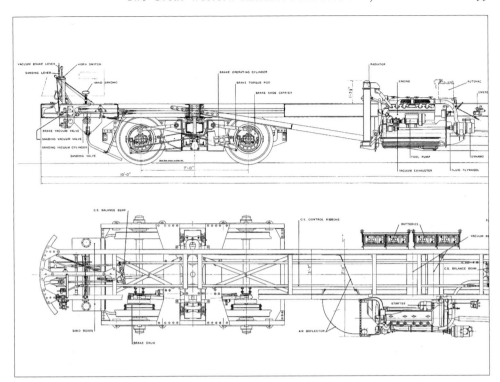

Above and below: Chassis arrangement drawing of Hardy Railcar No. 1. As with the other Railcars, No. 1 could be driven from either end. It differed from the others in that it had only a single engine driving through a Daimler-built fluid flywheel and pre-selective gearbox. (*Drawings: AEC Brochure 145, dated November 1933. Author's collection*)

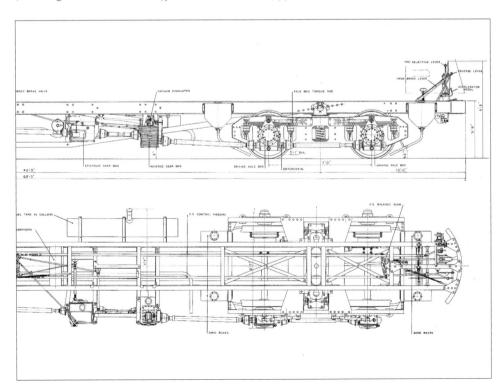

The completed chassis was delivered to Park Royal Coachworks on 19 August 1933 and, complete with body, was exhibited at Olympia at the Commercial Vehicle Exhibition between 2 and 11 November. It is seen here posed for the official photographer at Didcot on 25 November, in advance of its inaugural run from Paddington to Reading on 1 December. (*Photograph: British Rail*)

This superb head-on photograph was taken on the same occasion. While proudly bearing the Great Western Railway's dual coats of arms, the familiar triangle set in the V at the top of the central windscreen pillar clearly gives due recognition of the railcar's design origin. Fast-forward thirty years and the shape of the windscreen as a whole bears an uncanny resemblance to the final version of the Routemaster's iconic radiator grille. (*Photograph: British Rail*)

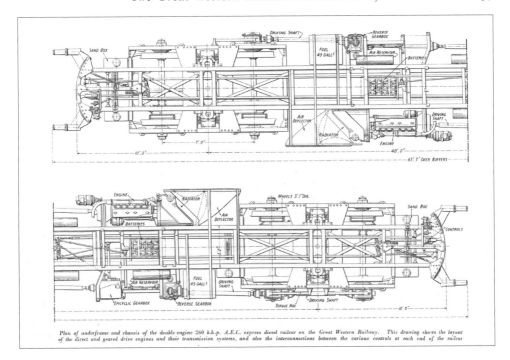

Plan of underframe and chassis of the double-engine 260 b.h.p. A.E.C. express diesel railcar on the Great Western Railway. This drawing shows the layout of the direct and geared drive engines and their transmission systems, and also the interconnections between the various controls at each end of the railcar

Railcars 2, 3 and 4 were built for long-distance express work and at the higher speeds, greater power was required to overcome wind resistance. The addition of a second engine was virtually a duplication of the first save that, avoiding cost and complication, a direct drive transmission was adopted on the second set and the drive taken through the reversing gearbox to the first of the bogie axles. Only a limited throttle opening was applied to the second engine until top gear had been engaged on the primary set. (*Drawing: Reprinted from* The Railway Gazette, *13 July 1934*)

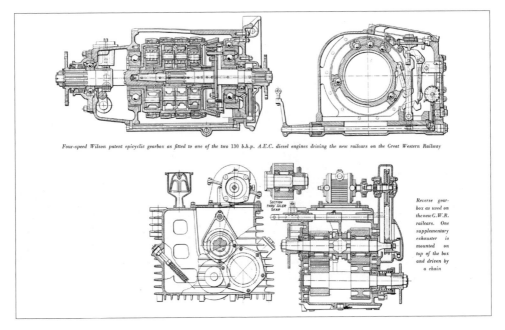

Four-speed Wilson patent epicyclic gearbox as fitted to one of the two 130 b.h.p. A.E.C. diesel engines driving the new railcars on the Great Western Railway

Reverse gear-box as used on the new G.W.R. railcars. One supplementary exhauster is mounted on top of the box and driven by a chain

Railcars 2–17 all featured the AEC-built D132 pre-selective gearbox. The Daimler-built version on Railcar No. 1 was similar in principle but different in detail. (*Drawing: Reprinted from* The Railway Gazette, *13 July 1934*)

Railcars 5, 6 and 7, the remaining half of the six ordered in February 1934, were the first to be bodied by the Gloucester Railway Carriage & Wagon Company. It had been intended that their mechanical specification would be the same as railcars 2, 3 and 4 but in a late change, both transmission sets on railcar No 7 were fully geared. Such was the success of this arrangement that all subsequent railcars were similarly equipped. (*Photograph: British Rail*)

Comfortable accommodation was provided in the first Gloucester cars for seventy passengers in a three and two seating arrangement. Forty seats were provided in one saloon and thirty in the other, the remaining space being set aside for luggage. Above the engine bays, clearance requirements demanded that the floor level, and therefore the seats, be raised by about six inches. (*Photograph: British Rail*)

In February 1935, at the Annual General Meeting of the GWR, the Chairman announced that a further ten railcars had been ordered. Similar in most respects to Railcars 5, 6 and 7, they were again to be bodied by the Gloucester Railway Carriage & Wagon Company. Seating 63 passengers, No. 11, like numbers 10 and 12, sacrificed four seats for the luxury of a toilet compartment. No. 11 is seen here outside the Railcar shop at Southall prior to its delivery to Weymouth on 29 January 1936. (*Photograph: British Rail*)

No. 17 was the last of the GWR railcars designed purely for solo operation. It was mechanically similar to the previous nine but intended solely for the carriage of parcels and other lightweight goods. Based at the Southall shed, it served stations in the Thames Valley and in a normal weekday it was scheduled to cover 222 miles. (*Photograph: British Rail*)

24

The Monarch Types
647/0647 and 648/0648

The Type 647/0647 and 648/0648 Monarch chassis, introduced at Olympia in November 1933, were substantially larger than the original Type 641 of 1930. They were built in both forward control and bonneted configurations to a maximum width of 7 feet 6 inches. The bare petrol-engined chassis had a dry weight in the order of 3 tons 4 cwts and the oil-engined chassis 3 tons 10 cwts. In comparison, the original petrol-engined Monarch (now re-named Mercury, and which remained in production) had a dry weight of 2 tons 18 cwts.

The forward control 647/0647 and the bonneted 648/0648 chassis were designed for a net payload of 5 tons and a gross weight in the order of 9 tons 10 cwts. AEC described them as having a gross load capacity, i.e. body and payload, of 6 tons 5 cwts. The Railway Gazette of 28 September 1934 described the Monarch as 'being in the class to carry the greatest total load allowed by law on two axles'. This, if accurate, suggests that AEC was prepared to supply the chassis suitably specified for operation at a gross weight of 12 tons.

The 647/0647 had a 14-foot wheelbase chassis which provided for a body length of 16 feet but chassis of a shorter wheelbase were built to special order. The Type 648/0648 was built with alternative wheelbases of 14 feet and 16 feet but again there were individual variations. The chassis frame, of nickel steel, had a width of 3 feet and the side-members were 9 inches deep, 5/16 inches thick with 3-inch flanges. The frame height unladen was 3 feet 5 inches. The standard wheel and tyre equipment was 36 inches by 8 inches, singles at the front and twin rears. The front track measured 5 feet 10 inches, the rear track 5 feet 7½ inches and the overall width (over the front wings) was 7 feet 5½ inches. The width over the rear tyres was 7 feet 3 inches.

The standard engine was the four-cylinder 75 bhp A166 oiler introduced in March 1933, with the 65 bhp A139 petrol engine as the alternative. In practice, the higher powered four-cylinder 85 bhp A168 oil engine and the 80 bhp A163 petrol engine were the more frequent choice. The drive was taken through AEC's standard 16-inch diameter single plate clutch to the four-speed D124 gearbox (the bonneted chassis had the D126 gearbox, where the gear lever was in unit with the gear selector cover). The gearbox had the following ratios: 1st, 4.38:1; 2nd, 2.69:1; 3rd, 1.59:1; and 4th, 1:1. Reverse was 5.33:1.

The overhead worm driven rear axle had a standard ratio of 6½:1 (7¼:1 with the petrol engine) and was identified as the F164. Alternative ratios of 5 1/5:1, 8¼:1, 9 1/3:1 and 10 2/3:1 were available. What set the axle apart is that it was the first commercial vehicle axle (and the only one of the Mark I commercial types) to be fitted with the new, lightweight fully floating hubs, first seen on the F156 passenger chassis axle. With the 6½:1 rear axle ratio the relative road speeds at 2,000 rpm were: 1st, 8.5 mph; 2nd, 13.8 mph; 3rd, 23.4 mph; and 4th, 36.2 mph. Reverse gear provided 6.9 mph and the maximum gradient climbable in 1st gear with its rated load was 1 in 8. The petrol-engined chassis with the 7¼:1 rear axle had a gradient ability of 1 in 6.6.

The steering gear was the familiar Marles type and the four-wheel brakes (now standard) were simple, cam-operated with vacuum servo assistance. The brake drums were 17-inch diameter and the shoes were 3 inches wide on the front axle and 6 inches wide at the rear. Whereas in previous practice twin sets of brake shoes had been employed in the rear hubs, in this arrangement, single shoes were employed, operated through both foot and handbrake linkages.

One hundred chassis, forty-five Type 647/0647 and fifty-five Type 648/0648, had been sanctioned for production on programme FX, dated 7 July 1933. A second sanction, programme HD, dated 22 February 1934, provided for the production of twenty-five sets of material to convert type 0648 to 0647 and programme HE of the same date provided for the building of a further fifty 0647 chassis. Programme JB, dated 8 June 1934, provided for the building of a further fifty chassis. Ultimately, 166 of Type 647/0647 and thirty-four of Type 648/0648 were constructed, 200 in total, which matched exactly the quantity programmed.

Of the forward control types, the first chassis, 0647001, with oil engine A166/133, was constructed on 6 November 1933 and the last, 647166 with petrol engine A163/280, on 3 April 1935. An analysis of the deliveries shows that of the ninety operators of this type, sixty-three had only a single vehicle and sixteen operators had two.

Of the larger operators, Orrell & Brewster in Newcastle had three, 001, 002 and 022, and Swindon Transport also had three, with 031, 032 and 078. Three more passed through the Suffolk Motor Mart, 013, 014 and 081. The National Benzole Co. had four in a single run, chassis 053–056, and PLP Motors in Warrington also had four, 045, 046, 047 and 079. Also with four was A. & F. Smith of Mayfield with chassis 061, 062, 083 and 084.

H. A. Newport of Fordham had six, 011, 012, 071, 072, 090 and 122 and W. Dyson in Bradford had seven, 023–026, 075, 076 and 082. The Cement Marketing Company had eight in a single run, 139–146 and the Co-operative Society had nine, numbered 018, 063, 069, 086, 094, 118, 151, 152 and 153.

The largest operator of the type was the Great Western Railway, which took twenty in a single run, chassis 095–114, built in September and October 1934.

An analysis of engine types fitted to the 647/0647 chassis reveals that twelve were powered by the A139 engine, forty by the A163, thirty-four by the A166 and eighty by the A168.

Of the two chassis types, it was in fact the bonneted Type 648/0648 which was first into production. The first, 648001 with petrol engine A163/92, was built on 18 September 1933 and the last, 648034 with petrol engine A163/282, on 22 March 1935.

Single deliveries were made to nine operators. Dugdale Bros had the ex-demonstrator 014, G. F. Jones had 017 and A. H. Gibbons in Ipswich had 018. Curtis & Sons, the London hauliers, had 019. W. Butler, the tar manufacturer in Bristol, had 020 and the Griffin Engineering Company, AEC's agent in Johannesburg, had 027. The Stone Valley Motor Company had 028 and H. Sutton in Yarmouth had 029, a chassis of 10-foot wheelbase. Agar Cross, AEC's agent in Buenos Aires, took 015 and 016, Sellars Bros took 021 and 022, the latter being exported to Mauritius for work in the sugar plantations. Birmingham Garages took 024 and 034 and the Co-operative Wholesale Society had 025 and 026. Shell Mex had eighteen, 001–013, 023 and 030–033.

An analysis of engine types fitted to the 648/0648 chassis shows that one chassis had the A139 engine, seventeen had the A163, seven had the A166 and nine had the A168.

Cardiff-registered Monarch KG 3755, 0647021, with Park Royal cab, was new in March 1934 and is seen here in a busy dockyard scene attending on the SS *Orkney Coast*. Coast Lines, as its name suggests, was a shipping company. Its headquarters was in Liverpool but it was established in all the major ports in the British Isles. The company operated a large fleet of coastal vessels and its motor transport fleet was ancillary to it. (*Photograph: AEC, Author's collection*)

The Great Western Railway ordered twenty Type 647 Monarchs, sixteen of 14-foot wheelbase with 16-foot bodies and four of 12-foot wheelbase with 12-foot bodies. All were fitted with the 80 bhp A163, the more powerful version of the four-cylinder petrol engine. The unusual sliding door cabs were built by Park Royal. Also of interest is the unladen weight of 4 tons 7 cwts. (*Photograph: Author's collection*)

Built on 18 August 1934, with oil engine A168/275, chassis 0647117 is seen close by the Burnley works of Oswald Tillotson, which company built the cab and body. It was delivered to the operator on the last day of January 1935. Typical of the Mark I chassis were the buffer bar in front of the radiator and the rectangular fuel tank. Both features disappeared with the arrival of the Mark II range of chassis in 1935. (*Photograph: AEC L1732, BCVM*)

The two Monarchs seen here, part of an order of eight, were delivered to the Cement Marketing Company in January 1935; the nearest, No. 168, was 0647140. On a wheelbase of 12 feet 6 inches, the body, with its short overhang, would have been of similar dimension. While these were the sole examples of the Type 647 which the company operated, the Cement Marketing Company went on to acquire a further sixty mechanically similar Monarch Mark IIs in the period to September 1939. (*Photograph: AEC, Author's collection*)

This ACLO-badged Type 648 Monarch was one of only thirty-four built and one of only two exported to Argentina. Non standard features were its 16-foot, 9-inch wheelbase and the 38 by 8 1/4 inch low-pressure tyres, Dunlops in this instance. The chassis was either 648014 or 015 and the engine was the smaller 112 mm bore version of the recently introduced four-cylinder oiler. Dressed in chauffeur's uniform, the smiling driver appears happy to let others do the work. (*Photograph: AEC L1692, BCVM*)

Appendix I

The Leyland Merger Negotiations 1929–1933

In 1929, though the staff did not know it, AEC faced an uncertain future. AEC, in its alliance with Daimler, had failed to provide the London General Omnibus Company with the modern passenger-carrying vehicle it desperately needed to replace the obsolescent NS. The Associated Daimler Company had, in all but name, ceased to exist and Lord Ashfield, the prime mover in the setting up of the Associated Daimler Company and the moving spirit behind all branches of the Underground Electric Railway Company, had clearly become disillusioned. AEC was up for sale. John Rackham had been appointed chief engineer in August 1928 and had yet to prove himself capable of pulling AEC out of its 1920s mindset. Charles Reeve, appointed AEC's managing director in October 1929 and, previous to that, assistant to Lord Ashfield, was at the sharp end of the negotiations.

Leyland Motors board documents held at the British Commercial Vehicle Museum reveal that amid great secrecy, exploratory talks had already taken place with both Tillings and Guy Motors and that one party (not stipulated) had offered 32s, £1.60 in today's money, for each AEC £10 share. The offer had been turned down as it was felt that the amount of cash which the 110,000 AEC shares would generate would not provide the UERL with an equivalent return to the £150,000 it made annually from AEC. Clearly, outside of the confines of the London market, AEC was seen to be of little worth. (It is perhaps worthy of note that that there is no record whatsoever of these negotiations in the AEC board minutes.)

It was against this background that, on 2 October 1929, Charles Reeve had met with a representative of George A. Touche & Co., Leyland Motors' intermediary, to discuss details which could pave the way for future direct talks with Leyland. Particular details revolved around the LGOC's future vehicular requirement, which was said to be 6,000 vehicles over the next five years. Charles Reeve asked if he could have sight of Leyland's accounts for the last three years and he in turn would provide similar details of AEC's activities. As far as can be ascertained there was little immediate response but it is clear that Leyland had continued to hold a watching brief on the situation, particularly in view of the progress of the London Passenger Transport Bill and its possible implications for AEC.

By 1931, Rackham had indeed transformed AEC's product line-up, the tide had turned and the company's share capital had been increased to £1,500,000. In November of that year, negotiations with Leyland were re-opened. Touche & Co., together with Davies & Crane of Preston, were instructed by Leyland to examine the accounts of AEC and prepare a scheme which could give effect to a fusion of the two companies' interests. Similarly, Messrs Deloitte, Plender, Griffiths & Co. would examine the accounts of Leyland Motors and report to AEC in like manner.

The joint report provided by Touche. & Co and Davies & Crane for Leyland was dated 12 July 1932 and concluded that as at 30 September 1931, the net assets of AEC was

£1,691,904 and those of Leyland £2,944,494. Add to these the value of goodwill (which reflected the prospective profits likely to be generated by each company in the open market) and the individual asset totals became £1,700,969 for AEC and £4,167,024 for Leyland. On a combination of the assets of both companies, the proportions became 29 per cent and 71 per cent and on these findings, it was suggested that the capital of the projected new holding company should be split in the same ratio. Ultimately, the agreed ratio of the split, should the merger prove successful, was 37½ per cent AEC and 62½ per cent Leyland.

An agenda dated 12 October 1932 indicates that there were still concerns in the Leyland camp in respect of the London Passenger Transport Bill, the guarantee of future LGOC orders, and the possibility that Chiswick may increase its capacity in the manufacture of spare parts and even the manufacture of its own chassis. Other items of concern included the position regarding AEC agreements, particularly those relative to the Daimler fluid flywheel, staff pension schemes and Agency arrangements.

We move now to 28 June 1933, when a conference between the legal representatives of AEC and Leyland (at which Lord Ashfield was present) was still trying to formulate the possible means by which a fusion of the interests of both companies could be made. Five possible schemes were suggested, of which three were rejected. Of the two remaining, Lord Ashfield favoured a merger-holding company. The second possibility, favoured by Leyland, was the simple purchase of the shares of AEC by Leyland, thus making AEC a subsidiary of Leyland.

Talks continued through July, August and into September and an acceptable compromise had still had to be found. There was now a degree of urgency in the situation. The Underground Electric Railways Company was in the final stages of liquidation and it was necessary that the shares of the AEC be distributed among the former UERL shareholders.

It was recognised that in any scheme of fusion there would need to be a single unified management and a single trading account. This in turn would require a total fusion of the assets of both companies. The formation of a merger-holding company would require the purchase the assets of both Leyland and AEC by the holding company and the subsequent liquidation of the two existing companies. Difficulties were envisaged by the Leyland board in its ability to persuade its shareholders of the advantage of such an arrangement.

In an alternative proposition, Leyland suggested the setting up of a merger-operating company. Further, if Leyland Motors itself became the merger-operating company with the name of Leyland Motors changed to Leyland – AEC Ltd, considerable expense would be avoided. The constitution of Leyland Motors would remain unchanged, the sanction of the court and the assent of the Leyland shareholders would thus be avoided. In this event, the assets of AEC would be purchased by Leyland and AEC as a company would be liquidated.

This last proposal was dismissed by Ashfield who, in a letter to Toulmin, the Leyland chairman, dated 28 September 1933, wrote:

> We can only repeat the suggestion contained in my letter to you of the 19th instant, namely, that the amalgamation of the interests of our two Companies should be carried through by an exchange of the Underground holding of A.E.C. shares for an appropriate number of shares in a new company entitled "Leyland – A.E.C.". I am afraid we could not continue the negotiations on the basis of your proposal that the matter should be dealt with by the sale of the A.E.C. assets for Leyland shares.

Leyland was now on the back foot and clearly did not like the reference to the 'new' company.

On 5 October Charles Reeve dashed up to Leyland to have audience with the chairman, deputy chairman and secretary of Leyland Motors. As a result of the discussions, Reeve did achieve the looked-for compromise. The name of Leyland Motors Limited would be changed to Leyland - AEC Limited and the merger of the two companies was to be achieved by way of the exchange of AEC shares for Leyland – AEC shares.

The relative interests in the combined undertaking were to be as previously agreed, Leyland 62½ per cent and the Associated Equipment Company, AEC, 37½ per cent. The new board of Leyland A.E.C. Limited would comprise nine directors, of which six would be nominated by Leyland and three by AEC. The first chairman would be a nominee of Leyland and the first vice chairman a nominee of AEC. Fusion would be effective as of 1 October 1933. Contingent on these arrangements was a satisfactory contract being arranged between AEC and the London Passenger Transport Board in respect of future vehicular requirements.

On the following day, 6 October, Reeve wrote to Phillips-Conn, the Leyland secretary, with a resume of the points which had been agreed at the meeting and which would form the basis of an agreement between the two companies. The Leyland board again met on 10 October to consider Reeve's memorandum and the secretary in turn replied to Reeve on the same day. His document, with only minor adjustments, was substantially similar to Reeve's memorandum and was headed 'Points for Agreement'. In addition was a suggested 'Order of Procedure' which would be placed before the AEC board for its consideration.

Under the heading of 'Points for Agreement', of which there were fourteen, while there remained a number of items still to be settled, Leyland had indeed given ground in respect of the manner in which the merger was to be achieved. It is important to note however, that while item 1 had been agreed, item 2 remained as an item for discussion. Items 1 and 2 of the Leyland memorandum read:

1. The merger to be by way of exchange of A.E.C. shares for shares in Leyland Motors Limited; name altered to incorporate A.E.C.

2. Leyland Motors Limited to be re-named 'Leyland A.E.C. Limited'.

NOTE It is considered that a hyphen after the word 'Leyland' as contained in your various letters in respect of the amended title of Leyland Motors Limited is equivalent to the use of the word "and" and gives a disjointed impression. It is suggested that a hyphen should not be incorporated in the name.

The 'Order of Procedure' made the following suggestions:

1. Settle outstanding points until the only items remaining are the provision of a satisfactory contract and the final adjustment of percentages. The whole of the headings agreed to be set out for initialling with the proviso that the headings are not necessarily exclusive of other matters which may arise from time to time.

2. A.E.C. Solicitors to prepare draft provisional agreement.

3. A.E.C. to obtain contract with the London Passenger Transport Board satisfactory to Leyland Motors Ltd., and to fix the number of vehicles representing the standard fleet.

4. The draft agreement between Leyland and A.E.C. to be approved.

5. Show and Sales policy to be both under the control of the Leyland Board.

6. Issue of agreed circulars to Leyland and Underground shareholders.

7. The Liquidator of the Underground Electric Railway to obtain permission to sell the A.E.C. shares to Leyland Motors Ltd. and to issue Leyland shares to the Underground shareholders in lieu of A.E.C. shares.

8. Leyland and A.E.C. Accounts to be completed and audited by November 30th or as near as possible.

9. Alterations in Articles of both Companies and other details of machinery to be agreed.

10. Leyland pay dividends for one quarter to the 30th September 1933 on Leyland 6% and 7½% preference shares.

11. A.E.C. Annual General Meeting to take place; the shares in the hands of the U.E.R. Co., to declare the final dividend to 30th September 1933, if any. This meeting to be followed by a special meeting to alter Articles.

12. Leyland Annual General Meeting to be held and a dividend, if any, to be declared on the Ordinary shares to 30th September 1933; to be followed by Special and Class Meetings of Leyland shareholders to increase capital, alter Articles. etc., etc.

13. Final examination by Auditors and settlement of final percentages, the necessary adjustments being made.

14. Completion of deal by end of January 1934.

15. Issue and distribution of new shares.

16. Payment of dividends by Leyland A.E.C. Ltd. on the 6% and 7½% Preference shares for the whole issues for the quarter ended 31st December 1933.

At this point, all appeared to be in order. Most of the points had been discussed and a general consensus of agreement reached, but at some point between 10 and 20 October 1933 the course of events took a dramatic change and the negotiations came to an immediate halt. On 20 October, Phillips-Conn, in a personal letter to Reeve, wrote:

Dear Mr Reeve,

It is indeed disappointing that all our continuous efforts over so many months have been brought to nothing owing to circumstances which, I appreciate, were outside the control of either party, and in fact not recognised as existing up to a few days ago.

You have had a very great deal of anxiety and trouble in connection with the matter, and just in this private note I would like to say how much I appreciate the constant goodwill which you have shown and the trouble you have taken throughout the negotiations.

Kind regards
Yours sincerely.
T. Phillips-Conn.

Frustratingly, there are a number of imponderables and we are left to draw our own conclusions. Two points in the memorandum, namely items 3 and 7, if not satisfactorily concluded, would have negated the deal.

Item 3 should not have presented any difficulty. Leyland, in its negotiations with AEC, had been keen at ascertain the size of the LGOC's standard fleet and the probable requirements of the Board in terms of vehicles and spares in future time. (At that time AEC had placed the size of the standard fleet at 4,500 vehicles.) Since June 1930, AEC had supplied the LGOC with some 2,700 chassis of modern type, which implied that a further 2,000 or so would be required in the short term to complete the replacement programme for the obsolescent S and NS type vehicles. Reeve, in a letter to Toulmin dated 19 September 1933, had suggested that a new contract would provide for the supply of 90 per cent of the board's future requirements for the next ten years.

In item 7, reference to the selling of AEC shares to Leyland Motors Limited and the issue of Leyland shares to the Underground shareholders leads to the belief that the change of name of Leyland Motors Limited to Leyland AEC Limited had not at that time been agreed by the Leyland board. Nevertheless, AEC had agreed to the setting up of a merger operating company and fusion of the two companies by the exchange of shares. AEC as a company would remain extant, albeit as a subsidiary of Leyland. While this would not have been the fusion of equals that Ashfield had envisaged, it was the best compromise on offer.

Phillips-Conn refers to their efforts being brought to nothing due to circumstances outside the control of either party. Perhaps a clue is to be found in item 7, inasmuch that it was required that:

> The Liquidator of the Underground Electric Railways Company obtain permission to sell the A.E.C. shares to Leyland Motors Ltd and to issue Leyland shares to the Underground shareholders in lieu of A.E.C. shares.

AEC would have had to make application to the court for such an action. It is thought that the monopoly which would have been created by the merger of AEC and Leyland would not have been viewed with favour by the Government and that the deal would have been vetoed by the President of the Board of Trade.

On 1 November 1933, a little over a week from the time that talks with Leyland had ended, at an Extraordinary General Meeting called by the AEC board, it was resolved that the constitution of the AEC be changed such that it now became a fully independent public company. The share capital of £1,500,000, previously held by the Underground Company in shares of £10 each, was converted into shares of £1 each, to be distributed among the 20,000 individual shareholders.

Appendix II

Legislation and Regulation

The Ministry of Transport

During the 1920s there had been widespread recognition in Government circles of a need for up-to-date legislation in respect of road transport law. A new Government department, the Ministry of Transport, had been set up in 1919 under Sir Eric Geddes, his remit being to bring order to public transport generally but more particularly to that in London. Such were the complexities that it was not until 1924 under Ramsay MacDonald's government that the London Traffic Act came into being and a licensing authority was established.

Metropolitan regulations

Where the vehicle was subject to Metropolitan Stage Carriage regulation, size and weight had always been a problem. The Cabs and Omnibuses (Metropolis) Bill of January 1906 decreed that the maximum vehicle length was not to exceed 23 feet nor the breadth 7 feet 2 inches. Revised regulations in 1909 additionally required that the unladen weight did not exceed 3 tons 10 cwts nor the laden weight 6 tons.

With the introduction of the LGOC's K-type bus in 1919, though the required overall dimensions and unladen weight remained the same, in order to allow for the increased seating accommodation, the permitted laden weight was raised to 7 tons. With the introduction of the S-type in 1921 it was required that the limits of length and weight be further increased to 25 feet and 8 tons. By 1924 the permitted laden weight had again been raised to 8 tons 10 cwts. The maximum width remained at 7 feet 2 inches but was increased to 7 feet 6 inches with the introduction of the pneumatic-tyred NS-type bus in July 1928.

The Heavy Motor Car (Amendment) Order, 1927

New legislation, the Heavy Motor Car (Amendment) Order, 1927, required, in the case of a two-axled vehicle, that the maximum length did not exceed 27 feet 6 inches. Further, where the vehicle was employed on stage carriage work, the weight of any axle was not exceed to 5 tons 10 cwts, nor the sum of those weights to exceed 9 tons. (The original Heavy Motor Car Order, 1904, had not made any provision as to maximum length but had fixed the maximum width at 7 feet 6 inches. Individual axle weights were not to exceed 8 tons nor the sum of all the axle weights to exceed 12 tons.)

Though the 1927 Amendment Order had permitted a maximum length of 27 feet 6 inches, local authorities were empowered to impose lesser limits where deemed necessary. London traffic regulation remained vested in the Metropolitan Police Authority and while it did adopt the new weights laid down in this 1927 Heavy Motor Car (Amendment) Order, the maximum length remained at 25 feet. Thus, in terms of London operation in 1930, the Regent was subject to maxima in length and width of 25 feet and 7 feet 6 inches, and of weight to 9 tons.

The same 1927 order had a provided for a maximum length of 30 feet for the three-axled vehicle. Where it was employed on stage carriage work, it had maximum permitted axle weights of 4 tons 10 cwts and a gross weight of 12 tons. Three-axled goods carrying vehicles had permitted axle weights of 7 tons 10 cwts and a maximum gross weight of 19 tons.

From 1 June 1930 the weight limit for the double-decked four-wheeler was increased to 9 tons 10 cwt and the 1931 Condition of Fitness Regulations allowed for an increase in overall length to 26 feet and of weight to 10 tons as of 10 February 1931. Single-decked four-wheeled buses had a permitted overall length of 27 feet 6 inches and a gross weight of 9 tons, axle loading in each case not to exceed two thirds of the total weight.

The Road Traffic Act 1930

Further and more extensive legislation came in August 1930 with the passing of the Road Traffic Act. New regulation was introduced in respect of motor vehicle construction and use, hours of work, the issue of driving licences and the licensing of omnibus and motor coach services. Traffic Areas, thirteen in total, were to be set up each with its own Traffic Commissioner, appointed by the Minister of Transport, who would have power of jurisdiction on all relative matters. Local authorities would arrange for the organisation of mobile police units, which would assist in enforcement.

The speed limit for pneumatic-tyred motor buses and coaches and commercial vehicles having an unladen weight not exceeding 2½ tons was 30 mph. Vehicles exceeding that weight were limited to 20 mph while solid-tyred vehicles and those drawing a trailer were limited to 16 mph. These speed limits were considerably below current practice and the capability of the modern commercial vehicle. The Brooklands trial in May 1929 of the prototype Regent showed it capable of 58 mph and in a 12-hour period, averaged 43 mph over a distance of just over 500 miles. A laden Mammoth 7–8 tonner, tested in June 1930, achieved a speed of 50 mph and a Monarch tested in August managed 60 mph.

Construction and Use Regulations

The Motor Vehicles (Construction & Use) Regulations, 1931, were in essence an expansion and reaffirmation of the previous twenty-six Locomotive, Motor Car and Heavy Motor Car Orders, made between 1903 and 1930 and which the Construction & Use Regulations now replaced.

The Regulations were dated 10 January 1931, effective from 15 January and were in two parts. Part I was directed to the construction of all types of mechanically propelled vehicle motor vehicle (including motor-cycles and invalid carriages). Among the requirements detailed were those in respect of dimension, steering, brakes and tyres (pneumatics now mandatory except in the case of locomotives and motor tractors). Dimensionally, the Heavy Motor Car was not to exceed 7 feet 6 inches in width, while in length, the four-wheeled vehicle was restricted to 27 feet 6 inches, the six and eight-wheelers to 30 feet and the articulated types to 33 feet. The length of a draw-bar trailer, excluding the draw-bar, was restricted to 22 feet.

Part II governed the use of the motor vehicle with particular reference to maintenance and weight. It was directed that the maximum weight of a four-wheeled vehicle may not exceed 12 tons, the six-wheeled vehicle (either rigid or articulated) 19 tons and the eight-wheeled vehicle 22 tons. The lorry and trailer combination had a similar limit of 22 tons.

The Heavy Motor Car Order, 1922, had provided for the operation of the articulated six-wheeler at 18¾ tons and the lorry and trailer combination at 22 tons. Further Amendment Orders in 1927 and 1930 allowed for the operation of the rigid six-wheeler at 19 tons and the rigid eight-wheeler at 22 tons.

Condition of Fitness Regulations

The Public Service Vehicles (Conditions of Fitness) Regulations, 1931, dated 13 March 1931 were supplementary to the 1931 Construction and Use Regulations. Whereas the Construction and Use Regulations detailed the mechanical requirements of the chassis, the Certificate of Fitness Regulations were directed specifically to public service vehicles and those features which provided for the safety and convenience of the passengers. They had their origin in the 1906 regulations drawn up by the Public Carriage Office of the Metropolitan Police and set out such details the minimum dimensions of seats, doors and gangways, the requirements of leg room and head room, the provision of non-slip floors and grab handles and the height of the entrance or platform step.

The Road and Rail Traffic Act 1933

In August 1932 came the report from the grandly titled Conference on Road and Rail Transport, which had been set up by the Minister of Transport under the chairmanship of Sir Arthur Salter, a senior civil servant. The Committee comprised the chairmen of the four major railway companies (the Southern Railway, the GWR, the LMS and the LNER) together with four appointees from the Standing Joint Committee of the Mechanical Road Transport Association. Pointedly, the Long Distance Road Haulage Association (which later changed its title simply to the Road Haulage Association), which claimed to represent the bulk of the hire and reward sector hauliers, had not been invited to take part in the discussions.

Apparently, the Minister had not laid down strict terms of reference but, quoting the words of Charles Dunbar from his book The Rise of Road Transport 1919 – 1939, Ian Allan, 1981:

> The conference was intended to examine the effect of the development of road transport on the economy, and to consider what could be done to improve the organisation of the industry.

Of particular interest were the subjects of motor vehicle taxation relative to the annual road maintenance cost of £60,000,000 and the delicate subject of regulation of the road haulage industry. The railway interests were, of course, principally directed toward the containment of the expanding road haulage industry. Of particular note is the following extract from the report:

> The Conference records its agreement with the Royal Commission on Transport that it is not in the national interest to encourage further diversion of heavy goods traffic from the railways to the roads. It agrees in recommending that the Minister of Transport should obtain powers to prohibit by regulation classes of traffic which are borne by rail and which, having regard to the character of the commodity and the distance to go, are unsuitable for road haulage, from being transferred in future to the road, and recommends that he should examine the question and take the advice of a new Central Advisory Committee.

The Royal Commission on Transport had been set up in 1928 under the Chairmanship of Sir Arthur Griffith Boscowan and the reports from that body formed the basis on which the 1930 Road Traffic Act was framed.

With the publication of the Salter Report, much was made of the increases in motor vehicle taxation. Rather less prominence was given to the recommendation that:

> Some regulation of goods motor vehicles is necessary and that this regulation can be enforced only through a licensing system. All such vehicles should be required to have licences which are conditional upon the observance of proper conditions as to fair wages and conditions of service and the maintenance of the vehicles in a state of fitness.

Historically, motor vehicles over 4 tons in unladen weight had had an annual rate of taxation of £43 4s and those from 5 tons upward had enjoyed a flat rate of £48. The Conference recommended a new graduated scale whereby the vehicle exceeding 4 tons unladen but not exceeding 5 tons would pay £73 per annum, rising by an average of £30 12s for each ton of unladen weight thereafter. The heaviest, with an unladen weight exceeding 9 tons but not exceeding 10 tons would attract an annual licence duty of £226. With the country in the grip of deep economic depression, the effect of the proposed increases was to create widespread panic in the road haulage industry and a stagnation in the sale of heavier commercial vehicles.

Acting on the Conference recommendations, in April 1933, the Government presented the Road and Rail Traffic Bill. This passed into statute and became effective from 1 January 1934.

On the subject of vehicle licensing, Charles Dunbar writes:

> The Road & Rail Traffic Act, 1933 came into force on 1st January 1934 and completely changed the outlook for the road transport of goods. It made the operation of goods vehicles, whether for hire or reward or for ancillary purposes, illegal except under one of three classes of licence. The 'A' licence was for 'public carriers', the 'B' licence for 'limited carriers' and the 'C' licence for 'private carriers'. The 'C' licensee was not allowed to carry any goods for hire or reward; the holder of a 'B' licence might carry either his own or any other person's goods. If he chose to carry for others, the Licensing Authority (who was in fact the Chairman of Traffic Commissioners under the 1930 Act) might attach such conditions as he thought fit in respect of the type of goods to be carried or the customers for whom they might be carried or the places to which they might be carried. Every licence had to specify the registration marks and unladen weights of the authorised vehicles plus

the number and unladen weights of trailers authorised (if any).

Conditional on the granting of licences was the requirement of the licence holder to maintain the vehicles in a roadworthy condition, to comply with the speed and weight limits, to comply with the hours of work regulations and, importantly, to keep records of the journeys made.

Initially, licences were issued on the basis of existing fleet size. Licences for additional vehicles or for new entrants into the industry would only be issued where a need of such vehicles could be shown. Existing operators could (and frequently did) object to the granting of such licences and crucially, so could the railway companies. In truth, though the new licensing requirements were restrictive and the railway companies aggressive, they did provide protection to those companies already in the road haulage industry. (The issue of A, B and C licences continued in force until the introduction of Operator licensing in 1970.)

In respect of taxation, the proposed rates for 1934 were slightly lower than had been recommended by the Salter Committee but remained punitive. The vehicle having an unladen weight exceeding 4 tons but less than 5 tons attracted an annual duty of £70, each one ton of additional unladen weight thereafter carrying a penalty of £20. Vehicles drawing a trailer would attract an additional duty of £20.